DISCRIMINATION AGAINST THE MENTALLY ILL

DISCRIMINATION AGAINST THE MENTALLY ILL

Monica A. Joseph

Health and Medical Issues Today

An Imprint of ABC-CLIO, LLC
Santa Barbara, California • Denver, Colorado

Library of Congress Cataloging-in-Publication Data

Names: Joseph, Monica A.
Title: Discrimination against the mentally ill / Monica A. Joseph.
Description: Santa Barbara : Greenwood, 2016. I Series: Health and medical
   issues today I Includes bibliographical references and index.
Identifiers: LCCN 2015039445 I ISBN 9781610698917 (hardback) I
   9781610698924 (ebook)
Subjects: LCSH: People with mental disabilities. I People with mental
   disabilities—Abuse of. I BISAC: PSYCHOLOGY / Mental Illness.
Classification: LCC HV3004 .J657 2016 I DDC 305.9/084—dc23
LC record available at http://lccn.loc.gov/2015039445

ISBN: 978-1-61069-891-7
EISBN: 978-1-61069-892-4

20 19 18 17 16   1 2 3 4 5

This book is also available on the World Wide Web as an eBook.
Visit www.abc-clio.com for details.

Greenwood
An Imprint of ABC-CLIO, LLC

ABC-CLIO, LLC
130 Cremona Drive, P.O. Box 1911
Santa Barbara, California 93116-1911

This book is printed on acid-free paper ∞

Manufactured in the United States of America

To the many clients with behavioral disorders with whom I have shared much of my professional life and from whom I have learned so much.

Thank you!

Contents

SERIES FOREWORD

Every day, the public is bombarded with information on developments in medicine and health care. Whether it is on the latest techniques in treatment or research, or on concerns over public health threats, this information directly affects the lives of people more than almost any other issue. Although there are many sources for understanding these topics—from websites and blogs to newspapers and magazines—students and ordinary citizens often need one resource that makes sense of the complex health and medical issues affecting their daily lives.

The *Health and Medical Issues Today* series provides just such a one-stop resource for obtaining a solid overview of the most controversial areas of health care in the 21st century. Each volume addresses one topic and provides a balanced summary of what is known. These volumes provide an excellent first step for students and lay people interested in understanding how health care works in our society today.

Each volume is broken into several sections to provide readers and researchers with easy access to the information they need:

Section I provides overview chapters on background information—including chapters on such areas as the historical, scientific, medical, social, and legal issues involved—that a citizen needs to intelligently understand the topic.

Section II provides capsule examinations of the most heated contemporary issues and debates, and analyzes in a balanced manner the viewpoints held by various advocates in the debates.

Section III provides a selection of reference material, such as annotated primary source documents, a timeline of important events, and a directory of organizations that serve as the best next step in learning about the topic at hand.

The *Health and Medical Issues Today* series strives to provide readers with all the information needed to begin making sense of some of the most important debates going on in the world today. The series includes volumes on such topics as stem-cell research, obesity, gene therapy, alternative medicine, organ transplantation, mental health, and more.

PREFACE

This book is about discrimination against persons with mental illness. There is a great deal of awareness within the last few years about the impact discrimination can have on so many aspects of individuals' functioning including their mental health. A scan of the current literature yields numerous research articles, a number of which document connections between poor mental health outcomes and discrimination, across diverse groups. There is thus little argument that there is an association between discrimination and impaired mental health in the general population. However, for those who are already struggling with a mental disorder, does discrimination create an even harsher burden with which they must survive on a daily basis?

This book is important as it takes a look at how discrimination has been pervasive in almost every aspect of the lives of persons with mental illness for more than two centuries. From the private madhouses of the 18th-century British, to the large 20th-century farm colonies in the United States, persons with mental illness have been viewed pejoratively and have encountered discrimination even from those who have been entrusted with their care. And family members have not been exempt from this role. They too have faced stigma and have not always been able to stand up to discriminatory attitudes and practices, including the abridging of the rights of their loved ones. At times, however, they too have been the perpetrators!

So we know that discrimination is still alive and well. But have we made progress in reducing it, and how? And are persons with mental illness faring better post-deinstitutionalization? This book also examines some of the contemporary issues that persons with mental illness are dealing with, including the intersection between comorbidity, the criminal justice system, and diversity. Legislative protections that have become enshrined in the Americans with Disabilities Act of 1990 and its Amendments in 2008, as well as some of those that have emerged from judicial decisions such as the Wyatt Standards and Olmstead are reviewed. How these continue to play a major role in the current environment is also discussed.

The primary goal of looking at where we have come from, and where we currently are, is to help identify how we can more productively move forward to eradicate discrimination against persons with mental illness. To do this, prevention is thus a critical dimension that is discussed in the book. Are there any promising interventions that can help to stem the tide of prisons and jails becoming the 21st-century repository for persons with mental illness? What about health care disparities such as one of the highest rates of smoking being among persons with schizophrenia or one of the higher rates of mortality being associated with homeless persons with mental illness? And how can we better meet the mental health needs of our veterans?

Clearly, as a nation, we need to do as much as we can to decrease the stigma of mental illness, while ensuring that any form of discrimination is promptly addressed. But our work does not end here. As part of the global community, we are also called upon to share policies and best practices that can be replicated to help end discrimination against persons with mental illness wherever it exists. Therefore, this book's intent is also to contribute to an increased awareness and sensitivity of discrimination against persons with mental illness and potential ways in which we can help to address this.

I would like to acknowledge the assistance received from my editor, Maxine Taylor, across the many months that it took to complete the writing of this book. Her encouragement and feedback were invaluable at many junctures. Thank you for keeping me moving forward!

PART I

Overview

CHAPTER 1

Background and Definitions

WHAT IS MENTAL HEALTH, MENTAL ILLNESS, AND DISCRIMINATION?

What Is Mental Health?

Mental health is integral to who we are as individuals and affects every facet of our lives. But what is mental health? In its basic sense, it refers to one's state of mind—how a person is thinking, feeling, and experiencing his or her world at any given point in time. This can range anywhere on a continuum from extremely positive to very negative. Mental health is also referred to as emotional health or psychological health since both our feelings and thoughts are crucial to how we perceive the world around us. As society has come to understand more about how our mental and physical states are interconnected, we have also broadened how we look at health as a whole. From a holistic perspective, health is now considered to be a status in which both a person's body and mind are functioning normally. In order for this to happen, however, an individual also needs to feel that the social setting in which he or she lives, works, and conducts other daily activities offers some kind of support. Thus, when we look at the whole person, his or her overall health status depends on these three basic components—the physical, the mental, and the social.

Since mental health is an integral part of one's health status, it is important to get a better understanding of what constitutes positive versus negative mental health. In arriving at a working definition, we could say that positive mental health refers to a sense of wellness or well-being experienced by an individual who perceives his or her mind and body to be reasonably in balance with the social environment in which he or she must function. Conversely, poor mental health occurs when an individual's sense of well-being is interrupted, as he or she perceives his or her mind and body to be in conflict with the social environment in which he or she must function.

For all of us in the wider population, having positive versus negative mental health contributes to significant differences in our lives. Having a positive state of mind affects how a person feels about himself or herself, how he or she interacts with others in the environment, and how he or she engages in the activities of daily living that must be completed on an ongoing basis.

For example, an individual, Jane, wakes up in a positive frame of mind. She may feel happy, she is full of energy, and she is willing to start her day and work toward accomplishing her goals. Jane is also more likely to believe that she is a person of value. Because she has this positive self-belief, there is a greater likelihood that Jane can engage with family members and others in the community in a way that can make them see her as a positive person. She is thus more likely to get into situations where she can get cooperation and collaboration from the persons around her. This positive social support that Jane receives can encourage and build her confidence even more. Now, she is more likely to think that she has the capacity to complete the tasks she is required to do at home, school, or work. Jane's positive mental health can thus help her to experience her world as a comfortable place in which to live.

Peter, on the other hand, wakes up in a negative frame of mind. He feels very sad and lonely, and does not believe that he has the energy to get out of bed and make it through the day. Due to the way he is thinking, Peter is more likely to feel that he has little self-worth and that nobody cares about him. Thus, he may avoid interacting with others around him as much as he can. Or, if Peter must engage with others, he might do so in a way that is socially awkward, such as having very limited eye contact, or with very brief responses that do not encourage conversation. Because of this behavior, people around Peter, including his family members, may see him as a "loner" and might be less likely to offer him assistance and social support. Thus, due to his behavior, Peter may have more difficulty completing the needed tasks of daily living at home, at school, and at work.

Over time, individuals are often associated with having a predominant frame of mind. Some persons may be perceived for instance as being mainly upbeat and outgoing (having positive mental health), while others may tend to be withdrawn and view their world as a place that is not welcoming the majority of the time (having poor mental health). Individuals' mental health, however, is also determined by what is occurring with them physically and the social situations in which they find themselves. For instance, a person with a very positive mental outlook develops a chronic illness like leukemia. Thus, most of the time now, he is in pain and is feeling sad at one point, angry at other times, or even helpless and hopeless. However, on a few occasions, he may still be able to remember some of the happier events in his life and demonstrate a more positive frame of mind. His overall mental health has now moved from being primarily positive to the range of mainly poor.

Therefore, persons move back and forth on the mental health continuum based on what is going on in their lives and how it is affecting them physically and socially. From a physical perspective, we are usually affected the most by illness, especially chronic or acute conditions that cause serious disability such as losing a body part. Other conditions such as becoming homeless or not having sufficient money for food can also affect our physical well-being and contribute to poor mental health. From a social perspective, there are broad spectra of issues that can include but are not limited to the type of family and community support we have, whether we have suitable housing and employment, how we interact with the legal system or even with our houses of worship. Overall, it is thus normal for the majority of us to experience and move between episodes of positive and negative mental health without any severe detrimental effects. For some individuals, who develop mental illness, however, this presents major problems.

What Is Mental Illness?

Historically, mental illness has been called by a variety of different names—madness, insanity, lunacy (since mental illness was believed to be caused by the phases of the moon), unsoundness of mind, idiocy, and imbecility to name a few. Today, the term "mental illness" is most often used interchangeably with mental disorders. It can be defined as one or more of a variety of conditions that trigger poor mental health or a negative sense of well-being. These conditions or disorders may have a mild impact. For instance, a person may have a depressive disorder and experience a sense of discomfort at times, but he or she may still be able to engage in the usual activities of daily living with minimal disruption. On the other hand, the same disorder could affect another individual so severely that all areas of his or her normal daily functioning—how he or she thinks, feels, and behaves—become interrupted.

Some conditions such as bipolar disorder and schizophrenia are known to have a higher likelihood of causing significant impairments in daily functioning. These can cause a person to experience psychosis—confusion in how an individual thinks, perceives, and interacts in his or her environment. Thus, the individual may be hearing, seeing, or even believing things that are not real, and may be responding to others in his or her environment based on this faulty information.

In fact, when we look at many historical documents that represent people with mental illness, we often see an image of someone who is disheveled, with wild hair, torn or no clothing, and a fierce facial expression that makes him or her seem as if they are about to attack someone. It is highly likely that this classic stereotyped image of madness may have been referring to a person who was experiencing severe symptoms such as psychosis. Sadly, even today, we still see images such as this in the media. These tend to reinforce the stereotypes about mental illness and contribute to persons who are affected being regarded in a negative manner.

Persons with mental illness or mental disorders therefore exhibit a cluster of characteristics or symptoms. These can include abnormal thoughts, behaviors, and problematic relationships. Different types of mental illness can share the same characteristics, but for ease of reference, they are often grouped based on the major features that have been observed over time.

Some of the major groups include psychotic disorders, anxiety disorders, depressive disorders, mood disorders, personality disorders, and substance use disorders. Individuals with schizophrenia and bipolar disorder, for instance, are said to have psychotic disorders. Persons with panic disorders and post-traumatic stress disorders (PTSD) experience a great deal of worry and fear that affects their ability to participate in usual daily situations such as taking public transportation or standing in a crowd. These individuals are said to have anxiety disorders. Others may experience symptoms like sleeping too much or too little, or eating too much or too little, and may lose their interest in engaging in regular daily activities. Such symptoms that may suggest that the person is experiencing a condition such as major depression or bipolar disorder are referred to as depressive disorders. Since depressive disorders affect an individual's mood or whether they feel happy or sad, they are also called mood disorders. Persons with significant drug and alcohol problems are said to have substance use disorders.

Therefore, there is a wide range of mental health conditions that can be placed into various categories. When an individual experiences and is diagnosed with one or more of these conditions, he or she is often referred to as having mental illness or being mentally ill. Today, medical advocates for the mentally ill include psychiatrists and psychiatric nurses who treat persons with mental illness. Others include licensed psychologists, social workers, marriage and family therapists, and mental health counselors. All are expected to have the requisite knowledge, skills, attitudes, and values to identify and treat the symptoms of the broad range of mental health conditions that can arise. However, it should be noted that advocates for the mentally ill prefer that we use the term "persons with mental illness." Emphasizing the person rather than the illness is seen to be one of the steps in addressing stereotypes that have caused persons with mental illness so much discrimination.

What Is Discrimination?

Discrimination can be regarded as the unfair treatment of a person or group. It can occur due to an individual's underlying thought patterns, attitudes, and values that can cause him or her to view that person or group as different. At present, although there are various sources of advocacy and support for persons with mental illness, when we examine how they have been treated over time, we can conclude that there has been a great deal of discrimination against them as individuals and as a group. This has come from various arenas—from institutions affiliated with a variety of religions, from the legal system, from places of employment, from educational and medical establishments, and from others.

Within the institution of the family, there is an expectation that persons should be able to find safety and solace. For many persons with mental illness, however, this is not a reality as they can receive unfair treatment at the hands of their family members. For example, reports indicate that an ongoing practice among communities in China, and in parts of the African continent, is to chain mentally ill persons to various objects and/or to lock them in cages.

Family members may perceive such restrictions as a means to manage the behaviors of the mentally ill person, or sometimes it might be done simply to keep the individual out of the view of the wider public. Unfortunately, family members too reflect the attitudes and values of their society. They can be so ashamed and fearful of how the family is perceived by the community that they may not even consider how the person with mental illness is affected when he or she is denied the basic rights that a human being should be afforded.

Discrimination against persons with mental illness as individuals, as a group, and as subgroups has thus been alive and well for centuries. For instance, individuals with intellectual challenges such as mental retardation are also subsumed as a category—intellectual disability, under mental disorders. These persons have a long history of being treated unfairly because of their intellectual disability, which can also coexist with physical and social challenges. Many have been denied housing, employment, living wages, opportunities for recreation and socialization, accessible transportation, and education. Further, if these individuals have additional mental health diagnoses such as schizophrenia or bipolar disorder, they can be subjected to increased punitive attitudes and actions that increase social isolation and marginalization. Discriminatory treatment has thus been directed at the person with mental illness as an individual, at subgroups such as persons with intellectual disabilities or substance use disorders, and at persons with mental health disorders as a group.

Two aspects that contribute to discrimination involve stereotyping and stigma. With stereotyping, one perceived characteristic, often negative, may be singled out and used to identify a whole group. For example, a statement may be made that a person with schizophrenia is always late for his or her appointments. While this may be describing a specific person or situation, over time, it may become generalized that persons with schizophrenia are always late for their appointments. Broader stereotypes include that mentally ill persons are usually violent or that they are intellectually slow. Such one-dimensional and often distorted images harm persons with mental illness as a whole in many ways. In fact, they have also contributed to discriminatory behaviors such as persons with mental illness being denied employment, housing, or even better educational opportunities.

Stigma can be regarded as negative ways of thinking about a situation, in this case, mental illness. Since our opinions drive our attitudes, looking at mental illness as negative can directly affect how persons with mental illness are treated. Stereotypes play a major role in stigmatizing persons with mental illness. For instance, the stereotype that all mentally ill persons are violent tends to increase the social isolation of many persons with mental disorders, as once it becomes known that a person has a mental health disorder, he or she can be automatically associated with the stigma of violence. Coworkers, peers, and even family members may begin to fear the person due to their misinformation about mental illness.

Unfortunately, given mass media, actual incidents of violence that are conducted by what constitutes a fraction of mentally ill persons can dominate the news cycle. This can add to the discriminatory ways in which persons with mental illness are treated. Avoiding, isolating, and penalizing mentally ill persons, however, might in turn actually serve as precipitating factors that increase the individual's risk of experiencing a relapse or the onset of more severe symptoms.

Additionally, language has played a significant role in the stereotyping and stigmatizing of persons with mental illness. In some places, it is not uncommon to hear coworkers and peers casually describe the behavior of others in pejorative terms such as "He or she is crazy!" "Mad!" "Loco!" "He did not take his medication today!" "She needs some medication!" "He's acting schizophrenic!" or "bipolar!" or "paranoid!" In the United States, the phrase that a person is "going postal" has also become a pejorative way of describing a person who may be acting in an erratic way. This originated from an actual incident in August 1986 during which a postal worker injured or fatally wounded twenty-one of his coworkers, prior to taking his own life. Perhaps, if "Crazy Pat," as he was called, had received the necessary care and support instead of what appears to have been ridicule, this, and similar tragic incidents, could have been avoided.

Across cultures, words like "mad" have thus had a negative connotation for a very long time. Further, when we continue to engage in the practice of using similar terms, or loosely using the diagnoses and symptoms of mental illness to label individuals, the negative opinions and attitudes that are adopted toward persons with mental illness are reinforced.

In one of the few studies that have tried to obtain data regarding how stigma can affect persons with mental illness, the U.S. Centers for Disease Control and Prevention (CDC, 2010) reported that while approximately 90% of individuals surveyed in the United States believed that mental health treatment can work, less than 60% agreed that people demonstrated empathy and caring toward persons with mental illness. To put it simply, there is a higher likelihood that people with mental health concerns would not be treated very nicely by others in the general population.

According to the Canadian Medical Association (CMA [2008]), a sample of Canadians was also surveyed about how they would respond to various mental health–related issues. While approximately 70% of individuals would not hesitate to discuss the medical diagnoses (cancer or diabetes) of a family member with friends or coworkers, only 50% would share a diagnosis of mental illness. Thus, even if others are willing to be supportive of persons with mental illness, the family members' shame of being stigmatized acts as a barrier for everyone concerned.

Additionally, stigma also affects individuals' life chances to establish a marital relationship, as 55% of Canadians indicated that they would not be interested in forming a union with a person with mental illness. In fact, stigma even affects an individual's ability to have platonic relationships, with about 40% of persons being unsure that they would encourage an individual with mental illness to be part of their social network. Lastly, close to 30% of persons in the general Canadian population reported that they would be afraid of being around individuals with mental illness. Ironically, the majority of times, they may not be able to identify that the person has mental illness.

Therefore, stigma and stereotyping contribute to discriminatory practices being used against the mentally ill, even when individuals may not be consciously aware that they are doing so. Whether this occurs in the home, church, school, workplace, or the wider society, discrimination is hurtful and affects the person with mental illness in numerous ways, sometimes on a daily basis. The sources of discrimination thus lie in every facet of daily life for the person with mental illness. Its painful effects for the mentally ill as individuals and groups thus clearly need further discussion.

HOW MANY PEOPLE ARE AFFECTED BY MENTAL ILLNESS AND DISCRIMINATION?

Mental illness affects people in all parts of the world. There is no country or region that can claim to have a society devoid of mental illness. Although this problem is so widespread, it is very difficult to obtain accurate statistics about the number of persons with mental illness. What is even more difficult is to ascertain the extent of discrimination against mentally ill persons.

Early Documentation Efforts

In Europe, by the mid-1800s, attempts had been initiated to begin to catalog the number of persons who were affected by insanity. An English physician, Dr. Daniel Tuke (1827–1895), was one of the forerunners in this process. Writing in one of the early records of the day—the *Journal of Mental Science*, Dr. Tuke acknowledged the difficulty with compiling and comparing data on the number of cases with insanity. Nevertheless, he believed this exercise was important partly to help assess whether there was any validity in one of the proposed causes of mental illness of the day—civilization.

Dr. Tuke thus began to compile information on the incidence of mental illness from as many sources as he could find. This was published in the *Journal of Mental Science* that was founded as the *Asylum Journal* in 1853. Private and public letters, articles, reports, and books written by European missionaries and other expatriates who had traveled to various locales around the world, including Syria, China, Tibet, and Bengal, all constituted sources of data on mental illness. These contained observations from various individuals regarding insane persons whom they had directly encountered or whom they were told about. In some instances, the provisions that were made for persons with mental illness within their societies were also documented.

Dr. Tuke reported on the earlier chronicles of Dr. Benjamin Rush (1746–1813), who was regarded as the leading person on psychiatric medicine in America in his day. Dr. Rush had documented that he found few instances of melancholy and madness among the indigenous citizens in the United States. The French physician, Dr. Jacques-Joseph Moreau (1804–1884), was also cited. He had traveled across the African continent and the Orient in the late 1830s, and had actively sought information on persons with mental illness. His reports indicated that places such as Algiers, Cairo, Alexandria, and the coast of Guinea yielded few or no cases of insanity. The commander of the U.S. Exploring Expedition in the South Sea Islands from 1838 to 1842 was Lieutenant Charles Wilkes. His reports on places such as New Zealand, Hawaii, Tuvalu, and the Cook Islands also highlighted that there was little mental illness to be observed.

Data regarding the Asian and African continents, as well as the United States and Europe therefore began to be cataloged. Consistently, this suggested that few to no cases of insanity were recorded in the places or among the populations being cited. Based partly on this, Dr. Tuke finally concluded that rates of mental illness among persons who lived in civilized nations were far greater than that of persons who lived in a naturalistic state or "barbarism." According to Dr. Tuke's hypothesis, insanity was therefore one of the inherent burdens of civilization, and this was primarily because of the advanced state of awareness of civilized individuals.

Current Challenges in Documenting Mental Illness

Since the 1800s, we have made significant progress in documenting mental illness. However, there are still various challenges to obtaining accurate data. One of these is cultural. Despite all the information that is available on mental disorders and how they might present, there are still cultures, especially in the developing countries, in which it is taboo to be called mentally ill. Persons who are affected may still be regarded, similarly as in ancient times, as being possessed by evil spirits, as having poor morals, or even as being weak minded.

Further, as previously indicated, stigma can surround not only the person with mental illness, but also their family members. In many of these instances, it thus becomes prohibitive for individuals who may need treatment, as well as their families, to come forward to seek assistance. If we cannot identify who has mental illness, then how do we count him or her?

Therefore, inadvertently, cultural stereotypes around mental illness militate against accurate data collection.

International institutions such as the World Health Organization (WHO) have been attempting to collect data on the incidence and prevalence of mental illness across the globe for years and have been urging countries to develop and use integrated data reporting systems. In fact, in May 2012, in their Ninth plenary meeting, the Sixty-Fifth World Health Assembly adopted a resolution to focus on a comprehensive, coordinated international response for the global burden of the disease.

The global burden is a yardstick used to measure various types of diseases by determining the number of years an individual lives with a disability related to a specific disease and the number of years the person loses due to premature death related to the disease. The overall burden of mental disorders has been increasing and is now calculated at approximately 14%. Further, it is estimated that persons with mental disorders who are living in the developing world spend from about a quarter to one-third of their lives, living with and being affected by their disability.

Even in the developed world where there is access to state-of-the-art medical systems, there are concerns with how mental illness is diagnosed, tracked, and reported. Some countries may include persons with substance use disorders in their mental health data, while others may separate or not report substance use disorders. Also, it is believed that many persons with mental illness do not seek treatment during an episode. Thus, many individuals with mental disorders may never come to the attention of formal treatment systems such as emergency rooms and mental health clinics.

Fragmentation among systems is an additional barrier that affects tracking and accuracy. For instance, a person may be receiving treatment at several different venues. But unless there is collaboration, each system may identify the individual as a new or different statistic. Additionally, the severity and chronicity of the person's illness may go unnoticed so that the full impact of the mental disorder is not captured.

At best, then, what we have are estimates of mental illness. In the United States, Canada, Australia, and the European Union, for example, population surveys have been conducted, which give an assessment of the number of cases of mental illness at that point in time. Population surveys, however, may miss critical groups of people such as those who are incarcerated or are in health care institutions and who may actually have higher rates of mental illness than the general population. Survey data are thus used to help estimate the incidence—number of cases of mental illness, and prevalence—how widespread the problem of mental illness is per a specific number of persons in the population.

Discrimination can be overt and covert. For instance, while it might be easier to track how many persons with mental illness were refused housing in a particular community, it is much more difficult to assess the harm that can be caused from multiple covert ways of discriminating against the mentally ill. Thus, although we have estimates of mental illness, we still can only surmise how many persons are being discriminated against. In fact, it may be more appropriate for us to state that if a person has mental illness, he or she is more likely to be discriminated against as compared with a person without mental illness.

Current Data on Mental Illness

But what current data exist on the number of persons with mental illness? As indicated, WHO is the primary body that has been trying to compile international data on mental illness. It estimates that approximately 450 million are affected by mental illness across the globe. Although about half of these persons come from the Asia-Pacific region, individualized data are not readily available for the majority of countries here and in other low- and middle-income areas. The following statistics, however, were reported for countries in the developing world.

Data on Developing Nations

In Bangladesh, approximately 16% of adults are estimated to have mental health disorders. On the African continent, 19% of all disability is related to mental, neurological, and substance abuse issues. In Latin America and the Caribbean basin, prevalence rates for mental disorders range from 18% to 25% in the general population and from 27% to 48% in treatment-related settings. Substance use disorders were estimated to account for more than 20% of the 35 million new cases expected annually in this region.

Data on Developed Nations

Among the developed countries in North America, Europe, and Australia, there is more structured data gathering. Based on a variety of published reports, WHO has determined that mental illness accounts for the highest burden of disability in these countries, even when cardiac diseases and cancer are taken into consideration.

In the United States, the federal agency that takes the lead for research on mental health, the National Institute of Mental Health (NIMH) in its August, 2008, release of its Strategic Plan reports that about 1 in 17 American adults, or an estimated 13 million persons, has a serious mental illness (SMI) in any given year. Additional data from the U.S. Substance Abuse and Mental Health Services Administration (SAMHSA, 2014) found that approximately 25% of adults had one or more mental health disorders in the prior year that may have included a substance use disorder. The CDC, in its Adult Mental Illness Surveillance Report, further indicates that, over the life span, about 50% of individuals are expected to develop mental illness.

The Canadian Mental Health Association (CMHA) reports that nearly 1 million persons, or 3% of the population, have SMI such as schizophrenia. The Public Health Agency of Canada—Health Canada—also indicates that an estimated one in five persons experience a mental health or addiction issue in any one year. Further, 20% of Canadians will develop a mental health disorder over their lifetime.

In the United Kingdom, the Health and Social Care Information Centre identified one in four persons as experiencing a mental health problem in any one year. The UK's Mental Health Network, however, estimates that about 18% of the population have at least one mental health disorder that can include substance use.

Published reports for the countries within the European Union, and for Iceland, Norway, and Switzerland, identify about 38% of the population as having mental disorders. Of these, about 9% and 1% respectively are believed to be alcohol and drug dependency problems. The Australian Institute of Health and Welfare indicates that nearly one in two individuals in Australia, or 45% of persons between 16 and 85 years of age, are expected to experience an episode of mental illness in their lives.

Gender Concerns

Overall, men are overrepresented with conditions such as substance use disorders, but women tend to have higher rates of mental health disorders related to depression. With regard to pregnant and postpartum women, WHO's Maternal and Child Mental Health tracking found that approximately 10% and 13% of these women, respectively, develop mental health conditions. In lower-income countries, this ranges even higher with about 17–20% of women, respectively, experiencing maternal-related mental health disorders.

Since maternal concerns can increase children's vulnerability, WHO has also noted that between 10% and 20% of children and adolescents across the globe develop mental health conditions. Published reports for Latin America and the Caribbean, for instance, found that between 12%

and 29% of children and adolescents have or are at high risk for mental illness. According to SAMHSA, based on research conducted within the United States, half of all persons who develop lifetime mental illnesses do so by the approximate age of 14. Further, 75% of individuals with lifetime mental health disorders develop these by age 24.

Thus, poor maternal mental health that places children at risk is in itself a major concern, especially as it sets these kids up for other negative outcomes. These can include poor socialization, poor educational attainment, and physiological stress–related symptoms such as hypertension. Sadly, however, it can also include suicide since a significant number of persons who attempt and commit this act are young people. For instance, the CDC reports that 20% of deaths among 15- to 24-year-olds in the United States are attributable to suicide. According to Health Canada, this accounts for 24% in that country. Globally, the picture is not significantly better. Poor maternal mental health is therefore inextricably linked to the overall welfare and mental well-being of their children.

The available data thus provide a snapshot of various countries and inform the global picture of mental health. However, there still are many individuals who are experiencing the direct effects of one or more mental disorders and who are not receiving needed services. Based on data obtained from more than 180 countries, WHO estimated that 75% of persons with mental illness in low-income countries are unable to access the care they need. Each and every one of those persons is at a high likelihood of being on the receiving end of discrimination at some point in their lives. In fact, one can argue that not being able to receive necessary mental health care to prevent and ameliorate distress is in itself a form of discrimination.

Several initiatives have been put into place globally to identify and address some of the significant deficits related to the needs of persons with mental health disorders. Among these are systematic baseline assessments of available mental health resources in low- and middle-income countries using the WHO Assessment Instrument for Mental Health Systems. WHO's Mental Health Gap Action Programme has also launched its Comprehensive Mental Health Action Plan for 2013–2020. This aims to scale up mental health resources internationally, especially in the developing world.

Undoubtedly, progress is being made on several fronts with regard to issues that affect persons with mental illness. Despite this, multiple challenges remain. Persons with mental illness continue to be undercounted, underserved, marginalized, misrepresented, and mistreated in many ways. As previously indicated, a central feature underscoring the discriminatory treatment of persons with mental illness is societal attitudes that have encouraged stereotyping and stigmatization. Therefore, to better understand some of the ongoing discriminatory practices toward persons affected by mental illness, it might be helpful to review the historical context of mental illness and how changing beliefs have affected how persons with these disorders have been treated.

CHAPTER 2

Changing Belief Systems and Historical Treatment of the Mentally Ill

From time immemorial, we have been trying to understand and explain mental illness. To this end, various concepts of and causes for mental illness have been proposed. Evidence suggests that our attitudes toward the mentally ill and how we have treated them have been related to our beliefs about the causes of mental illness. Thus, the religious, social, physical, medical, and more recently, behavioral interventions used to treat persons with mental illness have been influenced by our changing beliefs and attitudes.

As previously indicated, the modern concept of health is that it involves the mind–body–soul connection. Thus, we now believe that any facet of life that affects these dimensions of an individual will also affect on his or her mental health—the biological, psychological, emotional, social, spiritual, and even environmental. For centuries, however, this was not necessarily the case, especially with regard to how one thought about an individual's mental or emotional state. Examining the ancient and medieval beliefs about health can help to clarify how our concept of mental well-being has evolved into that we have today.

ANCIENT BELIEFS

First, we should look at the early Egyptians, whose civilization lasted from around 3000 BCE to about 30 BCE. They are believed to have established the scientific foundation of medicine on which many other others, including the Greeks, Romans, and Easterners, have built. Historians note their extensive medical texts that detail interventions ranging from magical incantations and amulets, to medicines that were often concocted from noxious substances, through injury management procedures that still hold validity today. Some of these interventions would have been directed at persons who exhibited mental/emotional illness.

The Egyptians' view of mental illness, however, was colored by religion. Historians indicate that they were initially a polytheistic people among whom religion held a dominant place. Mankind was believed to be at the mercy of their multitude of gods and goddesses such as Isis and Osiris. One of the ways these gods were believed to show favor to a person was by bequeathing good health to him or her. Being afflicted with bodily illness was thus equated with disfavor.

For individuals who demonstrated mental infirmity or madness in this ancient society, the cause could even be more sinister. These persons were seen as not only being punished, but also becoming inhabited by evil spirits, or by souls who could not find their way to their ultimate resting destination. These beliefs were not discouraged by the Egyptian priests, and sometimes priestesses, who also functioned as the physician healers. In fact, part of their preventive treatment was to encourage the wearing of charms and amulets for protection. Along with this, incantations also constituted an integral component of both prevention and treatment for mental and other ailments that arose. Viewing mental illness from a punitive perspective, and especially as being caused by evil spirits, however, set the stage for persons with such conditions to be reviled and isolated by others.

As thought on health evolved, records suggest that the theory of the four humors gained traction. The four humors or fluids that were found in the body—black bile, yellow bile, phlegm, and blood—were seen as the basis of good health. This theory, believed to have originated with the ancient Egyptians, became the bedrock of medicine for a period of time. Some historians suggest that it provided an early foundation for examining the causes and treatment of disease, and was eventually used as a platform by many others. One of these was the Greek physician, Hippocrates, who lived from 450 BCE to 380 BCE and came to be known as the father of Western medicine.

After studying with the Egyptians, Hippocrates is said to have revisited and expanded the theory of the four humors. Specifically, he postulated that for a person to be healthy, all four of the humors needed to be in balance. Hippocrates is also believed to have linked the imbalance or overproduction of black bile to the development of insanity. This suggested that there was a potential biological basis for mental infirmities, which was contrary to how many other thinkers of the day viewed mental illness.

Hippocrates's scientific hypothesis was additionally instrumental in refuting magic and religion as a cause of insanity or other health problems. It was also one of the reasons why he was adamant that the functions of a physician should be separated from that of religion. As reported by the Public Broadcasting System (PBS) Online, Hippocrates's attempts to treat persons with insanity by changing their occupations and/or their environments, as well as administering various tonics, rank among the earliest treatment efforts. He also encouraged that those with insanity should be cared for by the state. The theory of the four humors was instrumental in establishing what later came to be standard medical treatments—bleeding, purging, and blistering, which were used on persons with mental illness as well as others. Hippocrates was thus very instrumental in laying the groundwork for the scientific study of the etiology, progression, and treatment of both physical and mental/emotional impairments.

Hippocrates was ahead of his time. However, many did not agree with or fully use his novel teachings, and with his death, they became dormant. Historical records indicate that it was not until approximately 250 years later, and the rise of another Greek physician, Galen (130 CE–210 CE), that the Hippocratic school of thought was revisited with vigor. Galen expanded Hippocrates's views on the four humors by linking them with the concept of temperament. This suggested that an internal factor, the fluids within the body, was also responsible for the personality that an individual exhibited. The conversation about the potential causes of mental illness was thus expanding as Galen's work grounded a person's disposition and emotional status within a biological context. Additionally, this framework helped to move the concept forward that mental and physical health were interrelated.

But the influence of religion has always been present. And at the dawn of the Roman Empire, approximately 27 BCE, the Roman goddess of the moon, Luna, remained one of the many deities. While it is unclear when the term "lunatics" began to be used, it was believed that persons could become lunatics if they were moonstruck, or their malady could become worse depending on the phases of the moon. By the decline of the Western Roman Empire, around 476 CE, Christianity, which was then primarily represented by the Roman Catholic Church, was consolidating its base. This would largely continue until around the middle of the 11th century, when the church in the West, which remained known as the Roman Catholic Church or Church of Rome, split off from the Orthodox church in the East. As the Church of Rome extended its reach and crusading fervor against polytheistic and any thought system that was considered heretic, the more measured reasoning of Hippocrates, Galen, and others who sought scientific explanations fell out of favor. In Europe especially, there was a return to mysticism, as the Middle Ages advanced.

MEDIEVAL BELIEFS

The period from roughly 500 CE to 1350 CE is called the Middle or Dark Ages. However, what made this era "dark" as compared with other time frames? Historians highlight the many achievements that were made during the long reign of the Roman Empire—advances in engineering and architecture, education, the expansion of literacy, and structured political institutions in Europe, to name a few. Although many abuses also existed including widespread poverty, slavery, and barbaric justice, there appears to be some consensus that many of these abuses were amplified during the Middle Ages, as the wider society rejected science and education, and returned primarily to superstition and magic. This did not bode well for mentally ill persons across the European continent.

By this time in history, there were little formal systems in place for intervening with those with mental illness. Historical records suggest that they were usually cared for by family and friends. In some instances, towers or fools' towers were specifically set aside to house, most likely, those with mental illness who posed some kind of danger to the community. By 651, France had built what is now known as the world's oldest hospital that still remains in operation as a museum. The Hotel-Dieu de Beaune, as it was then called, supported by charitable donations to provide care for the poor and the sick, set aside a few of its rooms for lunatics. In the Islamic world, it has been suggested that there may have been a more benign attitude and approach to dealing with persons with mental illness. Around 872, a specially built hospital in Cairo, Egypt, provided treatment such as music therapy. Whether this was accessible and available to the cross section of individuals who may have needed it, however, remains a matter of conjecture.

Meanwhile, in Europe, with literacy, the arts, sciences, and medicine now concentrated in the hands of the clergy, their role as healers was re-emphasized and possibly strengthened. Those individuals in the society who were experiencing diseases of the body or the mind thus had little options but to look to them for healing. And in some instances, those deemed to have insanity were actually cared for within the monasteries. The still dominant belief that evil spirits were the sources of madness was supported, even among some learned individuals, by biblical teachings such as that which described lunatics as being possessed. It would thus be expected that exorcisms, Christian conversion, and flogging were used as methods of intervention. However, as this ancient thinking crystallized into a medieval way of life among the wider population, many of whom did not embrace reason, there was a significant social change that made it sinister to view mental illness as an outcome of evil spirits.

Specifically, the Church of Rome was at work systematically attempting to shore up its earthly kingdom, beginning in France and spreading across Europe, and even to places such as Malta, Goa in Western India (which was once a Portuguese colony), and Latin America. Somewhat ruthless in its intensity at varying points in time, the Catholic Inquisition—judicial panels made up of members of the clergy—was established as the wide-reaching arm of the church. These lasted for about seven centuries, from approximately 1184 through 1860. Theologians point to the perceived strength and growing wealth of the church during much of that time. They also note that various European rulers such as King Ferdinand and Queen Isabella of Spain, King John III of Portugal, as well as the wider society, often called upon and depended on the Church of Rome to maintain and defend social/cultural and moral cohesion.

Thus, the judicial panels were entrusted with seeking out, trying, and sentencing baptized Catholics who were deemed to be heretic, many of whom had converted, at times forcibly, from other religions including Judaism and Islam. Since the emphasis was on ensuring the faith, individuals who were believed to be engaging in subversive practices such as witchcraft became targets. For example, published reports document that in the late 1400s, one of the Spanish Inquisitors, Friar Tomas Torquemada, particularly disliked deviance, which included behaviors that are likely to be exhibited by a person with mental illness. Thus, he was prolific in seeking out and dealing with these threats to the body politic of the church. But it was not only in Spain that this occurred.

The Portuguese Inquisition deliberately expanded its jurisdiction to investigate persons accused of witchcraft. Sadly, some of these were persons afflicted with mental illness. The age-old theories that they were inhabited by evil spirits, or were deliberately consorting with evil beings to obtain supernatural powers, were used against those with mental illness, with the accusers at times being neighbors, friends, and even family members who feared for their own well-being.

The prevailing attitudes toward persons with mental illness—suspiciousness and fear—left little room for empirical seeking of knowledge and developing a deeper understanding of the individual and his or her pathology. Thus, as part of the procedure for the Inquisition hearings, accused persons were expected to cooperate with the proceedings and to make the effort to defend themselves. For someone who was experiencing mood swings such as with bipolar disorder, or who was exhibiting little to no emotions and was having a difficult time with focus and concentration such as with schizophrenia, would that person have had the capacity to comply with the expectations of the Inquisition tribunals?

Additionally, records also indicate that individuals who were found guilty might be confined while further evidence was being sought. Could this evidence have been the worsening of symptoms for some of these mentally ill persons, such as transitioning from the depressive to the manic phase of bipolar disorder, or demonstrating hallucinatory, delusional, or other odd behaviors as their psychotic symptoms secondary to schizophrenia became more prominent? It should be noted that it was common to regard persons with mental illness who were muttering to themselves as communing with the devil.

Thus, the primary outcome for some persons with mental illness who were accused of witchcraft and heresy was condemnation, imprisonment, and physical punishment, with the goal of saving their immortal souls. Further, those who survived exorcisms or being tortured could still face being burned at the stake for the misfortune of exhibiting signs of madness. For instance, Germany was known to house persons with mental illness in their "fools' towers." A report published by the Vatican in June 2004, however, indicated that the largest number of persons—approximately 25,000 males and females—were put to death in Germany for witchcraft, during the Inquisition. Additionally, about 10% of the population (300 persons) of Lichtenstein, a tiny principality that shares borders with Switzerland and Austria, also were put to death for witchcraft. Given the prevailing views on the causes of insanity, and the lack of understanding of its symptoms, it is not inconceivable that at least some of these persons who were put to death were mentally ill.

And who was there to advocate for persons with mental illness or to offer them protection? Ironically, the church itself was the primary institution that cared for the poor and the sick across Europe, and in some instances, as has been indicated, persons who were deemed to be insane were housed within the monasteries themselves. One of the primary problems, however, was that persons with mental illness were not considered as having a health-related condition for much of the time frame in question. Further, their erratic behaviors may not have helped their cause. Many were not able to obtain protection from their governments—emperors, kings, queens, and others, under whose authority their executions were conducted. Therefore, as fear and superstition festered among the wider mainly illiterate populace, those afflicted with mental illness were powerless in the face of social, political, and legal discrimination.

Over time, therefore, religion has had a major role in shaping the attitudes toward persons with mental illness and how they have been treated. Rather than encouraging benevolence, it has been known to be instrumental in helping to stereotype, marginalize, and, in some instances, victimize persons with mental disorders. While the advent of modern scientific thinking helped to somewhat level the playing field by allowing other ways of conceptualizing mental illness, it should also be noted that scientific inquiry itself was not a panacea.

In fact, it has also been responsible for other pitfalls that have affected mentally ill persons, such as the development and use of physical restraints, mass institutionalization in the asylums, and the denial of basic freedoms, which would be further discussed. At minimum, however, looking at mental illness through a biological/medical prism brought the focus to bear on how persons with mental illness were being viewed and treated. Therefore, this set the stage to address some of the abusive and discriminatory social, legal, and economic practices directed at persons with mental illness.

MODERN BELIEFS

The Renaissance

The advent of two major sociopolitical movements in Europe created the conditions that brought more focus to bear on those who were considered insane. First, the Renaissance—a period of rebirth or renewal in art, science, philosophy, and other learning—occurred from about the 14th through 16th centuries. During this period, a more secular school of thought developed that moved away from the monasteries and the emphasis on religion. Instead, it embraced man and his relationship with the universe as something that was positive. This ushered in a more modern way of thinking. While still somewhat dangerous, as the judicial tribunals of the Inquisition were in effect, the church as a whole supported the growth of the arts and sciences. Thus, it was no longer strictly taboo to consider the individual human being and his or her well-being outside of the boundaries of religion. A person could thus be sick of mind or of body and the cause did not have to be confined to a particular theology.

This humanistic approach as it was called was more in line with that proposed by Hippocrates, Galen, and others. It encouraged scholarly study to explore the connections between the mind and the body, as well as to empirically try to understand insanity. However, it should be noted that this did not mean that ancient beliefs about evil spirits being responsible for insanity disappeared. In fact, it has persisted over time and continues even today to be regarded as one of the fundamental causes of poor physical and emotional health, especially in some low- and middle-income, or developing countries.

With more interest being taken in the welfare of man, however, it seems logical that the Renaissance should usher in more focus being placed, in Europe, on those who were least able to care for themselves—the indigent, the sick, and the insane. Around 1357, the Bethlehem Royal Hospital in London (later referred to as Bedlam), which was initially opened as a priory in the preceding century, began to admit persons who were identified as insane. Spain followed with the establishment of several institutions during the 1400s, in locations such as Barcelona and Toledo. The Netherlands too, by the 1500s, had established a facility that housed persons with mental illness in Haarlem in North Holland. Today, this site serves as a museum that highlights the various types of artifacts and their associated treatment uses that were directed toward persons with mental illness from its inception until the 21st century.

The establishment of these early institutions in diverse locales clearly indicates that insanity has been of concern across time and cultures. While the interventions used were sometimes benign and many times barbaric, they reflected the current learning and shortcomings of their historical time frame and may even have been ahead of their time in recognizing and responding to a dire social need. Bethlehem, for example, became notorious for practices such as the beating and chaining of persons with mental illness, and generally unhygienic conditions. In some instances, however, chaining individuals with severe symptoms might have been a means of protecting others, and perhaps even the persons themselves, from additional harm.

While private benefactors had contributed funds to establish these facilities for persons with mental illness in places such as Cairo and France, widespread poverty was the norm for most of the population. And with poverty, the vulnerabilities of persons with mental illness, their families, and communities were often multiplied. A concerted response was therefore needed from those who held the reins of power. But much prodding was still needed to obtain basic rights and living standards for persons with mental illness. These early institutions, however, laid the groundwork for the large asylums, and the state hospitals, which were eventually set up across Europe, the United States, and other parts of the world.

The Reformation

The second major movement that affected how mentally ill persons were treated was the Protestant Reformation, which lasted from approximately

1517 to 1648. Spurred on by the new learning, many in the general society began to listen to the intellectuals of that time such as Martin Luther, an Augustinian monk, and John Calvin, a writer from France who is credited with establishing the doctrine of predestination. Both of these men challenged what they perceived as a number of abuses in the Church of Rome, including the selling of salvation.

The Germans and the Swiss were among the first to break away from the Catholic Church. By the mid-1530s, England followed. Then, under the rule of Henry VIII, when he was denied an annulment by the church from his wife of almost 24 years, so that he could remarry, he appointed himself the head of the Church of England. Splintering from the Catholic Church brought more than one benefit to the crown. Officially, it allowed Henry the freedom to marry five more wives so that he could produce the much-yearned for son. Additionally, it permitted him to confiscate the extensive lands and wealth of the English monasteries. With the dearth of the church, however, the primary social system that had for centuries taken care of the indigent and the sick, who often included the insane, was now destroyed.

The last half of the 16th century thus saw a pressing need to care for those who were unable to care for themselves. And how was this to be funded? Local laws across England and Wales began to authorize the Justices of the Peace (JP) to collect taxes. There were many concerns, however, that the poor people who were not truly in need would take advantage of this help that could be provided. Thus, two categories of the poor were established— the deserving and the undeserving. The deserving poor were those persons who wanted to work but could not, perhaps because they could not find work, as well as those who were too young, too old, or too sick to work. This last group of persons was also called the impotent poor. The undeserving poor, on the other hand, were those who could but chose not to work.

But who was applying these criteria, and how consistently could they be used to assess the indigent? Since the law mandated that two Overseers of the Poor must be appointed, localities usually involuntarily selected individuals to these positions. Unpaid, and with little or no formal training or guidance, the Overseers of the Poor undertook the responsibility of making what was sometimes life-and-death decisions. Who deserved financial or other help for basic necessities? Who should be given assistance so that they could see a physician? Historical records detail the extensive abuses, for example, with the indigent and insane being denied medical care. Therefore, those who were less functional by virtue of having a mental disorder were often least able to advocate for themselves and to acquire the basic care they needed.

Beliefs in the Age of Reason

The dawn of the 17th through 18th centuries brought with it the Age of Enlightenment across Europe. Scientists such as Galileo Galilei (1564–1642) became well known for multiple discoveries and inventions, including several laws of mathematics and physics, and building telescopes with which he studied the sky. Galileo had suffered the wrath of the Catholic Inquisition for reinforcing an earlier theory that the planet earth orbited the sun, rather than the opposite. For this "heresy," he had paid with his freedom as, in the final eight years of his life, he was confined to house arrest in lieu of life imprisonment. Other scientists such as Isaac Newton (1642–1727) also challenged established belief systems. Eventually, their extensive body of work would contribute to a revolution in physics, mathematics, philosophy, and other areas that embraced the condition of man and, in many ways, reinforced the humanistic thought of the Renaissance period.

This time frame also came to be called the Age of Reason due to its emphasis on empiricism—observing, testing, and verifying, as evidenced by Galileo. And as science and reason came together, prominent individuals began to use one or more of the same methods to question how the poor, sick, and insane were being treated. By the 1800s, physicians such as Drs. William Tuke (1732–1822), in England, and Philippe Pinel (1745–1826), in France, began to question how the mentally ill were being treated. They sought to back up their view of mental illness as having a biological origin and thus being curable.

Both Tuke and Pinel were proponents of treating mental illness without the use of physical restraints and other abusive interventions. Tuke became well known for establishing the first restraint-free facility, the York Retreat, for persons with mental illness, in 1796, with funds contributed by the Society of Friends or Quakers. Pinel was also credited with removing the chains from patients in two hospitals in France—the Bicetre and Salpetrière. Although he was a proponent of using the straitjacket, which he believed was more humane, he was also considered a pioneer in using interventions such as verbally engaging with patients. Such radical thoughts and practices began to be noticed in Europe as well as across the Atlantic in the new American colonies. Overall, it was influential in ushering in a new era, which emphasized that mentally ill persons needed to be treated not in a discriminatory manner, but humanely, compassionately, and thus morally.

Early American Beliefs

The belief systems that affected how persons with mental illness were cared for in the new American colonies had its genesis in the unique relationship that existed between the early settlers and their native country. By the close of the 15th century, the Italian explorer Amerigo Vespucci had realized that the new land he had encountered was not Asia, but what later came to be called America. With the exploration of this new continent by other Europeans, including the Spanish, Dutch, French, and the English, also came those who wished to settle. As previously indicated, Henry VIII, whose rule lasted from 1509 to 1547, severed his relationship with the Catholic Church. And the passage of his British Act of Supremacy in 1534, often regarded as the beginning of the Reformation in England, spurred on this movement.

As the fervor of reformers spread across the British Isles, buoyed by the teachings of John Calvin, and others, there were still those worshippers who believed that the Church of England was too tolerant of the beliefs and practices of the Catholic Church. Published reports indicate that around 1608, groups of Protestants who later came to be called the Pilgrim Fathers, fearing increasing persecution from the British crown, sought safety to worship in the Netherlands. Just over a decade later, by the close of 1620, the ship, *Mayflower*, had arrived on the eastern U.S. seaboard, relocating these individuals from the Netherlands. On their arrival at the Plymouth Colony, as the new settlers called their intended home, they brought not only the desire to worship as they wished, and to maintain their English identity, but also their beliefs and attitudes. Thus, one of the common beliefs that immigrated to America was that there were persons who could be possessed by evil spirits.

The Indigenous Peoples

But the Pilgrim Fathers did not meet an uninhabited land. The indigenous persons such as the Abenakis, the Wampanoags, and the Pequots already had a civilization that centered around their naturalistic beliefs. Seeking to live in harmony with nature, it would be expected that persons who experienced mental illness were not rejected by their tribe. In fact, within a community where interdependence was recognized as critical to survival, it is likely that persons with mental illness would have participated in communal life to the best of their ability, including receiving basic care from the tribe as a whole. Some historical anecdotes suggest that persons with mental illness could also be viewed as having special powers, which were valued by their community. This seems reasonable given that the indigenous peoples did not appear to be as fearful of experiencing visions or associating these with evil spirits as compared with their European counterparts.

Thus, as part of their spiritual and religious practices, several indigenous tribes in the Americas, especially those who resided in Mexico, and in the southern plains in areas such as Texas and Oklahoma, embraced the use of what is considered a sacred herb—the cactus called "peyote." When ingested as tea or through smoking, one of the multiple psychoactive ingredients in peyote, mescaline, is activated. This is known to alter perceptions of what a person sees, hears, tastes, or even touches, and to contribute to hallucinations. But the visions attributed to the use of the peyote were not seen as something negative. Instead, these could be deliberately sought by shamans or medicine men, sometimes to assist in healing the sick and to gain deeper insight to provide the tribe with critical guidance needed, for example, to protect itself.

Based on their reported worldview, it thus is reasonable to believe that the indigenous persons did not ostracize from their society persons who were experiencing mental illness. Rather, it is highly likely that they were absorbed into the general community and culture of the individual tribes. Without doubt, however, by the early 19th century, as the native way of life was affected by the encroachment, in some instances, of the British and other settlers onto their ancestral lands, it would have become more difficult for the indigenous tribes to take care of persons with mental illness who lived among them. Further, with the passage of the Indian Removal Act in 1830, which was vigorously championed and enforced by President Andrew Jackson and his successor, Martin Van Buren, the way of life of the majority of Native American communities, including the Choctaw and Cherokee in the south, and multiple others across the nation, was irrevocably changed. This act authorized the removal of Native American tribes in any state or territory to lands west of the Mississippi River, that is now Oklahoma. The discovery of gold in places like Georgia did not help the plight of the indigenous peoples.

Ignoring the letter of the law, estimates indicate that about 100,000 persons were forcibly relocated, often at gunpoint from the U.S. Army, with about 15% losing their lives. According to the Cherokee Nation Cultural Resource Center, many died from hunger, exposure, and disease along "the trail where they cried." One could only imagine the abject sorrow, subsequent emotional distress, and even the onset of ongoing mental health symptoms of any people, when they are treated in a manner that deprives them of basic human rights and dignity. We can only guess at what might have been the fate of those who were already experiencing mental illness. But perhaps more painfully for those who survived was the struggle to cope with the involuntary loss of their way of life and the extended trauma to which they were subjected.

The Early European Settlers

What about the Pilgrims? Did any of them have mental health issues, and how did this transported community deal with mental illness? While the majority had volunteered to make a new life in the New World, there were still so many intangibles. The fear and anxiety of not knowing what they would encounter, the personal physical hardships, and the loss of their former way of life, these and others would have contributed to significant levels of stress among these new settlers. Additionally, bereavement would have been a major issue. Historical records indicate that by November 1621, within 11 months of their arrival, the Pilgrims had buried 49 individuals. Only 53 members of their original group remained. Yet, others kept coming. And by the 1640s, the Puritans were instrumental in the establishment of at least three more colonies including Massachusetts (1630), Connecticut (1636), and New Hampshire (1638).

As these transported persons strove to build physical, social, and other structures for their lives, the desire to succeed thus had to be tempered by much sorrow and possibly regret. Those who had more difficulty coping and developed the symptoms of mental illness such as major depression or anxiety disorders were likely to remain integrated into their now narrow social world. For persons who developed major mental health conditions, circumstances should have dictated that they received hands-on assistance if they could not manage themselves, similarly to care provided for those with physical illnesses. However, if they presented as a danger to themselves or others, their treatment might have substantially differed. First, the English settlers, even in this new land, would still be prone to view persons with mental illness through a particular prism.

Specifically, especially among the Puritans, who desired to live their lives strictly adhering to the New Testament, there was the belief that individuals could be possessed by the devil and/or could become witches. Despite the passage of the centuries, this made persons who were demonstrating the symptoms of major mental illness vulnerable to being identified as vessels of evil. Such individuals might thus have been subjected to exorcisms, similarly to that which took place in the Church of Rome. In some instances, they may also have been labeled as witches, condemning them to being excluded from their communities. And as time passed and more formal social structures were put into place, even more viciously, those with mental illness could also be sentenced to jail or to death.

Additionally, in the thinking of the time, wives and daughters were often viewed as the property of their male relatives. This was in spite of the invaluable role that women assumed in the opening up and settling of this brave new continent. Females who developed mental illness were thus entirely dependent on the whims and fancies of their menfolk. For the latter who were armed with religious fervor, and buttressed by a number of biblical passages that were interpreted as madness being caused by the possession of evil spirits, their female relatives with mental illness

could be at risk of being rejected, even within their immediate households and families.

By the close of the 17th century, the belief in supernatural possession
was spurred on by learned individuals such as the Puritan preacher, Cotton
Mather (1663–1728). When combined with general intolerance, this played
a major role in the death of many persons, often women, who were deemed
to be witches, including those sentenced to death during the Salem Witch
Trials, which occurred from 1692 to 1693. Current data indicate that women
are at a higher risk for developing some types of mental illness such as depressive and anxiety disorders. At times, this could be related to postpartum
concerns. Apart from veterans, women are also at a higher risk of experiencing PTSD, which are related to physical and sexual violence. If women
currently remain at greater risk for some kind of disorders, even within a
much more gender-friendly and supportive world, one wonders how many
of these founding mothers were affected, and with what severity. Clearly,
conditions seem to suggest that these women would have been at high risk
of experiencing episodes of mental illness, perhaps more so than men.

Indentured Servants and Slaves

In any discussion of mental illness and the early settlers of the United
States, we must include the large numbers of indentured servants and
slaves who were part of the early years of the American nation. The Virginia Colony was established in 1607, as the initial site settled by the English immigrants. Twelve years later, in 1619, historical accounts indicated
that 20 African slaves were brought to Jamestown, Virginia, as indentured
laborers. One year later, there were at least 2 indentured servants among
the 41 males who signed the Mayflower Compact. This was the contract
drawn up among the new émigrés to govern themselves, and that is regarded as the initial document of democratic governance in the Americas.

Africans who were brought to the shores of the Americas after this,
however, and up until the Civil War, which led to the abolition of slavery
in 1865, were usually slaves. In fact, by 1641, Massachusetts became the
first colony to legalize slavery, followed by Connecticut in 1650. In doing
so, they laid the groundwork for the multiple restrictive pieces of legislation that would deny even basic human rights to one in four persons, as
per the 1790 U.S. census, across the length and breadth of this newly striving democracy. In many ways, this attitude to those who were considered
"others" was reflected in the poor treatment of the indigenous persons,
which led to the trauma they experienced even before, after, and during
the Trail of Tears.

All of the transports to the New World faced similar physical hardships and hazardous conditions and were at high risk of developing mental and emotional problems. There were significant differences, however, in the status of the indentured servants versus the slaves, which could have affected their mental health.

As an indentured servant, one could expect to attain freedom after paying one's debt usually over a five- to seven-year period. These debts may have been for the cost of passage to America, may have been for debts that were incurred back at home, or were judicial sanctions for a particular crime. Many indentured servants knew that they could never return to the world that they knew. But similarly to the other European colonists, they could eventually look forward to establishing a life for themselves. Many, however, were mistreated, and promises were broken by their owners. Historical records indicate, for example, that females who became pregnant, at times at the hands of rapists, had additional time tacked on to their indentures. Conditions that reinforced women's powerlessness and placed them in disadvantageous positions were therefore rampant.

As a slave, there was no expectation of freedom. Legal codes such as in Maryland specified that slaves and their descendants would be slaves for life. As the colonies in the Americas matured, and newly minted plantation owners and investors sought to maximize the profits from crops such as tobacco, cotton, rice, sugar, and others, the economy of each colony came to heavily rely on what historians now regard as one of the most brutal forms of slavery. The majority of Africans were captured and subjected to the horrors of the Transatlantic Middle Passage, the trip in overcrowded and insanitary ships, from the African coast to ports in the Caribbean, from where they were reshipped to the Americas. At the end of this journey of death, disease, and starvation, the African slaves were then paraded and sold on the auction block to the highest bidders, with care being taken to deliberately break up any existing families.

There were those who would have developed serious mental health concerns in those circumstances. But plantation society was not known to coddle slaves. It is likely that individuals who were demonstrating symptoms were beaten in an attempt to cure them. However, if such slaves could not stabilize and produce the multiple hours of backbreaking work that was required in the fields, they may have faced further punishment including loss of life and/or limbs. Who was there to defend those with mental illness when slave codes explicitly classified them as property and, as in Virginia, allowed for runaways to be killed and destroyed? Further, with slaves being regarded as subhuman, and with religious interpretation to justify their owners' actions, more than 200 years of officially sanctioned systematic debasement and dehumanization took place. Thus, similarly to the indigenous persons, this created a pathway for the internalization of features of trauma, and perhaps for ongoing struggles with poor mental health within some of these communities.

As indicated, the early female settlers might have been at high risk for poor mental health. This would probably be accurate also with regard to indentured servants and female slaves. For the latter, who could be regular targets of recurring rape at the hands of plantation owners and others with power, many were not allowed to claim or to nurture their children. They were also not afforded time to work through grief and loss. One wonders what the rates of postpartum depression and/or suicide were among these groups of women.

Early American society was therefore ripe with opportunities for poor mental and emotional health. While the resilience of our founding fathers and mothers are legendary, undoubtedly, some percentage of persons succumbed. Since women were often afforded less opportunities to manage their lives, were more at risk of being targets of physical and sexual assault, and were often viewed as the person who was more likely to be the vessel of the devil, it is likely that they were, overall, also at risk of increased episodes of mental illness. Men, however, within this brave new world, also faced multiple threatening and unstable conditions that could have been a challenge to their positive mental health.

Moving toward Scientific Causes of Mental Illness

By the early 1800s, a movement was under way, with the advocacy of physicians such as Tuke and Pinel to implement moral, restraint-free treatment for persons with mental illness. As previously indicated, while they had already embraced the view that mental illness had a biological/scientific base, they were also interested in creating a moral, humane treatment system for persons with mental illness. As other prominent physicians adopted these changing perspectives, they began to suggest that at least some of the individuals with mental illness could be cured, if they were placed within institutions at the early onset of their illness and received what would be considered professional care.

It should be remembered that there was still a great deal of social opposition to looking at mental illness as originating from any other place than that of religion and superstition. Thus, to help make the case that mental illness was biological and thus curable, physicians of the day began to labor over autopsies of persons who were believed to have died of insanity. They began to extensively document the characteristics of each decedent's brain and body, publishing scientific papers that were circulated and debated across Europe.

But not only physical descriptions were provided. Increasingly, theories were presented on the etiology of insanity, its typology and their associated characteristics, and whether it was experienced in the same way in different countries. It was therefore also around this time that efforts were initiated to begin to catalog the numbers of persons who were affected by insanity to compare their presenting features as well as to better determine the scope of the problem.

As reported in the 19th century *Journal of Mental Science*, among the physicians who contributed to a scientific understanding of mental illness, the following were forerunners, and through their written articles, they had significant influence on the medical community. Doctor Arnold conducted and reviewed postmortems of persons who died and were known to have mental illness. He was convinced that insanity was caused by the thickening of fluids in the brain, as well as the parts of the brain that connects the body to the soul. Portal believed that all mental illness was caused by defects in the brain and spinal cord. Bayle determined that insanity was due to inflammation and irritation of the membranes of the brain. Pinel focused on mania and offered his contribution that it resulted from constriction in the stomach and intestines. It should be noted that since the late 1700s, Pinel had written extensively about mental illness. In fact, his *Memoir of Madness* (1794) is now considered to be one of the earliest texts on psychiatry. Another of his publications in 1798 is also credited with laying out the foundation for classifying mental disorders.

In addition, intemperance was believed to be the primary medical condition that caused mental illness. Published reports of the 1840s indicated that approximately 12% to upward of 18% of British cases of mental illness were linked to the abuse of alcohol. Rates in the United States were believed to be much higher. Physicians of the time, however, did recognize that there were complex interrelated factors that played into mental illness and hypothesized that the united action of drinking and studying could be major contributors.

This acceleration in scientific thinking about the causative factors of mental illness was accompanied by a search for improved methods of treating persons with insanity. For instance, one of Pinel's pioneering treatments called for the person with mental illness to be treated as an individual who should be verbally engaged about his or her situation. This intervention, it was felt, could help the physician to develop a relationship in which he learned more about the person. Thus, the individual with mental illness himself or herself could guide the physician in how to best help him or her.

Other physicians also began to compare treatment mechanisms and to advocate for a variety of physical and medical interventions. Given that excessive study and loss of sleep were also believed to be interrelated causes of mental disease, addressing these burdens of civilization, for example, could reduce or ameliorate mental illness. Additionally, dyspepsia—the term that was used for various forms of stomach diseases—was thought to be another highly likely cause of mental disorders. Treating these stomach conditions with the use of therapeutic and dietetic agents was thus hypothesized to be important and efficient in curing insanity.

In the modern era, the work of these early physicians marked the beginning of scientific inquiry as to the role of neurology and other biological factors in mental illness. It also helped to identify symptoms, and by classifying them into groups, it encouraged a framework for assessing and treating persons with mental illness. While in many instances the work of the physicians was rudimentary, the range of activities that were carried out was extensive for their day. This laid the groundwork for an empirical examination of the etiology of mental disorders, their classification, and the need to view mental health disorders through both a person-centered and a more holistic lens.

Perhaps, most importantly, by strengthening the school of thought that mental illness had a biological basis, the early physicians had some success in combating the predominant belief that religious interventions were necessary to intervene with evil spirits. Individuals with mental disorders thus did not need to be shunned or hidden. Instead, family members could seek the medical treatment that was available for their loved ones. As new physicians interned with the old in the United Kingdom and other parts of Europe, many carried back this new approach to thinking about and treating those with mental illness. These early physicians therefore helped to begin the process of changing negative attitudes toward mental disorders and reducing some of the stigma attached to mental illness, and at the same time, they were increasing access to mental health care, as limited as it might have been.

By the mid-1850s, reports in the *Journal of Medical Science* published the conclusion arrived at by Dr. Forbes Winslow, the incoming president of the Association of Medical Officers of Asylums and Hospitals for the Insane. He instructed that insanity, idiocy, and imbecility were body and brain diseases that were curable. Clearly, this scientific thought movement had given birth to the hope that mental illness could be effectively treated and even cured. What was still needed though was how, where, and by whom persons with mental illness could be adequately cared. Some background on the early legal initiatives and how it influenced the overall treatment of persons with mental illness, including where they could live, work, or even participate in their rights as a member of society, can help to clarify this.

CHAPTER 3

Discrimination and the Formation of a Modern System of Care for the Mentally Ill

The overwhelming need for structured and humane treatment for persons afflicted with mental illness was tempered by a great deal of disagreement on what were the effective mechanisms to do this. Who was responsible for persons with insanity? Where should they be treated? What interventions were needed? Who would bear any costs associated with their treatment, and for how long? Both in the United States and on the European continent, society was grappling with similar questions. Europe, prodded by the changed thinking of the enlightenment, began to respond with the passage of several critical pieces of legislation, which came to have a direct impact on how persons with mental illness were treated, including where they lived and what rights they could enjoy as a member of society.

Across the Atlantic, as the early American colonies borrowed from its English motherland to shape its own journey, British legal initiatives also had a great deal of impact on how the mental health concerns of its population were addressed. A review of some of these influential laws that include but are not limited to the Elizabethan Poor Law (1601), the Madhouse Act (1774), the County Asylum Act (1808), the Poor Law Amendment Act (1834), and the County Asylum–Lunacy Act (1845) can help to trace the development of the large institutions that came to embody housing and treatment for those with mental illness, as well as its ongoing relationship with discriminatory practices.

THE MADHOUSES

However, what social structures were in place to provide for persons with mental illness? Within the United Kingdom, there were a few large institutions such as Bethlehem Hospital that housed the insane, prior to the 1600s. The majority of persons who had mental illness remained in an informal setting with families or friends, many of whom could not adequately care for them. Early governmental attempts to address this took the form of payments being made to proprietors of private homes who agreed to house one or more mentally ill person. This practice led to the development of the infamous madhouses. There was no formal oversight, and guarantee that room and board was being paid was not necessarily reflected in adequate or consistent provision of care to those boarders who had mental illness.

Despite this, the madhouses expanded as they brought economic benefits to their owners, some of whom established what would be regarded today as chains of homes, where they managed more than one dwelling facility for persons with mental illness. It is possible that this expansion received an impetus after the successful treatment of a royal British patient—King George III (1782–1820). Historical records indicate that he was known to have experienced several episodes of psychiatric decompensation over his lifetime. In one of the earliest instances, from around 1788 to 1789, he was confined to one of the private madhouses in Lincolnshire, from where he emerged stable enough to resume the duties of his crown. Unfortunately, by 1810, and after several relapses into mental illness, he was forced to forfeit the duties to which he was born.

The madhouses that had sprung up across the British Isles had thus become an invaluable resource for persons with mental illness, especially if they were able to afford the cost. This made a difference as the profit motive at times was stronger than providing sanctuary and adequate care for those with mental illness. Members of the community, however, began to voice concerns regarding the abusive and/or neglectful treatment provided in some of the madhouses, where many mentally ill persons were supposed to be receiving therapeutic treatment including appropriate supervision. Many persons with mental illness thus became victims of economic discrimination and abuse as although they were targeted based on their ability to pay, there was no guarantee of a minimum adequate level of care.

THE ELIZABETHAN POOR LAW OF 1601

By 1601, the Elizabethan Poor Law was passed. Although officially targeting the poor and the sick, it had several implications for the insane. This legislation reinforced the categories of the poor, deserving and undeserving, and clarified whether they were to receive outdoor relief—assistance in their own homes in cash or kind, or indoor relief—sent to a number of institutions. Children who were supposed to be orphaned were to be sent to the orphanage, the sick were to be sent to hospitals, and those too old to work were to be sent to the almshouses for shelter. The undeserving poor, however, were to be assigned to the poorhouses and workhouses, where they were expected to earn their keep. Many of these workhouses were little more than jails.

While there is no way to determine how many persons with mental illness were assigned to either of these categories of the poor, records indicate that even for persons who were owners of property, one or more bouts of mental illness could leave them destitute. Given that the symptoms of mental illness could range from less to very severe and, correspondingly, could affect an individual's functioning in various ways, persons with mental illness were likely to be found across all categories of the poor. Even among children, given the attitudes of the day, some who had already begun to experience mental/emotional difficulties were treated very harshly and were also confined to the workhouses, or at times, they were admitted to the madhouses. Harsh treatment, in turn, may have also set the stage for the later development of mental/emotional issues.

Since the Elizabethan Poor Law authorized the use of the workhouses or jails, published records of the time from advocates who directly observed and documented the state of these facilities suggest that many indigent persons with mental health problems ended up being confined to the workhouses. Unable to take care of themselves effectively, they faced many abuses including insanitary conditions, poor food, medical neglect, and physical abuse. It should be noted that the British society at that time sanctioned the public whipping and humiliation of the undeserving poor, who were believed to be able to and refusing to work. We would never be able to determine how many persons who experienced this abject punishment were individuals who already were affected by mental illness. What we do know is that this law essentially encouraged discrimination with regard to the indigent with mental illness and where and how they could live or work.

Growing numbers of the insane indigent or pauper addicts, however, made the poorhouses and workhouses an ineffective solution. Further, even the persons who were being housed and clothed at the expense of the state, or those whose family members or estates were considered wealthy enough to cover the cost of their care, could still be subjected to intolerable conditions. Reports indicated that many persons with mental illness were manipulated to maximize the income that was received by the operators of the madhouses. This manipulation at times involved family members who colluded with the owners of the madhouses to have persons admitted who did not need services. In fact, the early literature describes multiple instances of persons being committed for years to the madhouses who were not experiencing mental illness, thus denying them one of the basic rights of freedom of movement.

A group of mentally ill persons who were known to possess property were called the chancery lunatics. They were often assigned to the care of a committee, and many lived in single private houses or in a setting with members of the committee. Theoretically, this committee was the legal guardian of the property of the person with mental illness, as they had gone through a court proceeding, where it was determined that the individual with mental illness was not capable of caring for himself or herself, or making adequate decisions related to property he or she owned. Hence, the committee's appointment was supposed to safeguard the estate of the person and to provide adequate care for as long as it was necessary. Unfortunately, persons who were deemed to be chancery lunatics were also vulnerable to economic abuse and receipt of poor care, especially since there was little oversight of the committee members themselves.

Therefore, a more comprehensive social policy was clearly needed to protect those with mental illness from the vagaries of their caretakers. Specifically, this needed to target those with mental illness, and put checks and balances in place to assure adequate care that would constitute more than incarceration, abuse, or neglect.

THE MADHOUSE ACT OF 1774

The Madhouse Act of 1774 was welcomed as a significant piece of legislation to begin to improve the lives of persons with mental illness. Its intent was to address the abuses in the private system for housing the mentally ill. Thus, any site that housed more than one person with mental illness was placed under the jurisdiction of the Royal College of Physicians. It was mandated that a physician must authorize the care of any individual prior to their admission to a madhouse. Additionally, all such houses had to be inspected and licensed on a yearly basis. Fines were threatened for the operators of those facilities that were not in compliance.

Unfortunately, the Madhouse Act did not recognize that chancery lunatics perhaps faced a higher risk of economic abuse as compared with persons without property and other assets. By excluding the facilities that housed the chancery lunatics from its jurisdiction, it continued to leave this group of persons with mental illness vulnerable to the individual decency of their committee members.

However, the passage of the Madhouse Act was an acknowledgment that there were problems within the formal custodial system that had sprung up to house persons with mental illness. Mandating the certification of mental illness from a physician highlighted that political thinking had come full circle. Thus, instead of mental illness being viewed as trickery and witchcraft, it had attained standing in political circles as having a biological origin. Licensing and inspections were also a way to bring oversight to the broad cross section of madhouses that sprung up with primarily a profit motive in mind. Lastly, this was one of the first pieces of legislation to recognize the basic right of persons with mental illness to a fair/objective assessment prior to their confinement in an institution. It offered needed legal protection for not only persons with mental illness who needed care, but also those persons without mental illness who could be subjected to confinement against their will.

THE COUNTY ASYLUM ACT OF 1808

Despite the passage of the Madhouse Act, it was clear that the private madhouses left much to be desired. One might argue that at least they provided some type of shelter and succor to those with mental illness, in a time when many were ignored and lived in subhuman conditions. Further, roughly two centuries since the Elizabethan Poor Law had gone into effect, the population of persons with mental illness within the poorhouses and the workhouses appears to have increased. So too did the abusive behaviors that were meted out to many mentally ill persons, especially the pauper lunatics, who, in many instances, were beaten and chained.

Therefore, neither the private for-profit madhouses nor the public facilities were fully addressing the needs of persons with mental illness. Advocates who visited the workhouses often reported environments that debased everyone who were confined there, including the pauper lunatics. This was particularly true since no special provisions were made to cater for the individualized needs of those with SMI, as compared with those with less severe symptoms or those who were simply old or infirm and without financial resources.

In an attempt to correct some of the abuses within the poorhouses and the workhouses, the County Asylum Act of 1808 was passed. This mandated that each county could collect taxes in order to build an asylum to house the persons with mental illness who lived within that community. But what was an asylum? This was often a large residential institution in which persons with mental illness could live, some for the rest of their lives and others for an indeterminate period of time. In these settings, individuals with mental illness were supposed to receive the basic daily care they needed—food, clothing, shelter, medical care, appropriate socialization, and therapeutic engagement, in an atmosphere that was free of abuse.

Part of the intent of the County Asylum Act appeared to be to promote better assessment of persons applying for admission to the poorhouses and workhouses. If in fact they were mentally ill, they should be referred to an asylum rather than using scarce resources within the poorhouses and workhouses. Establishment of the asylums would also immediately allow those persons with mental disorders who were already in the workhouses to be transferred into an environment in which they were supposed to obtain the needed care to facilitate recovery.

However, passage of a law does not guarantee its implementation. Some of the county administrators, fearing that the costs of funding asylums would be levied against them as property owners, refused or, in some cases, blatantly chose to ignore the tenets of the law. From approximately 1811 through 1827, published reports indicate that only nine asylums were actually opened. As a result, the County Asylum Act did not meet its goal of setting up a facility for the mentally ill in each county, where they could receive treatment that was better suited to lunacy. Although the passage of the act itself was a recognition of the need to improve where persons with mental illness were housed and how they were treated, the discriminatory attitudes of those entrusted with executing the law acted as barriers. Therefore, as a direct consequence, the welfare of persons with mental illness including their access to basic food, clothing, and shelter continued to be compromised.

THE POOR LAW AMENDMENT ACT OF 1834

By the 1830s, it was clear that abuses continued to be rampant in the facilities in which mentally ill persons were being housed—individual dwellings that would take in a few persons for a fee; the more formally structured private largely for-profit madhouses that could house from a few to several hundred persons; and the local poorhouses and workhouses. British historical records indicate that a Royal Commission (1832–1834) that was appointed to examine how the poor laws were being implemented recommended that males and females should be placed in separate facilities with separate management. This was largely ignored as in 1834 the Poor Law Amendment Act was passed.

This act established an oversight entity, the Board of Guardians of the Poor. They reported to a centralized team of three commissioners who were appointed by Parliament. The primary responsibility of the Board of Guardians was to supervise relief to all categories of the poor who applied for services and to implement the earlier Elizabethan Poor Law in a manner that did not add to the rolls of the poor. Specifically, they were to expand the establishment of workhouses, while implementing the principle of "less eligibility." Using this, the basic conditions in the workhouse would be maintained in a manner that would make it more difficult for a poor person to live there than if he or she was collecting the lowest available wage. Presumably, persons who sought entry into the workhouses had passed the less eligibility test as they were willing to accept a more difficult standard of living.

Unfortunately, many of those who entered the workhouses were persons with mental illness, whose lives were deliberately made even more intolerable by virtue of the less eligibility policy. Contributing to this was the lack of understanding about mental illness across the majority of the wider population. In fact, even in those counties that had complied with the 1808 County Asylum Act, and had established facilities to house the mentally ill, mistreatment was common, and the symptoms of persons with mental illness could be easily overlooked.

Further, the operators of the private madhouses as well as those in charge of the asylums were likely to have no medical background. Thus, they depended on restrictive interventions such as isolation, and the use of hand, foot, and other body restraints. In many instances, these restraints were actual chains that could mangle the flesh of shackled persons and create sores and infections. Flogging was also liberally used, and there was no prohibition on attendants who were appointed to supervise and to care for the mentally ill, striking or being abusive to them as they pleased. Therefore, without a better understanding of the etiology of mental illness, it was difficult to institute more humane policies and procedures to care for those with mental illness, despite the negative daily consequences for persons with mental illness.

THE COUNTY ASYLUM ACT OF 1845
AND THE LUNACY ACT OF 1845

The status of persons with mental illness had been somewhat improved by the passage of the earlier County Asylum Act of 1808. The Poor Law Amendment Act of 1834, however, created almost the opposite effect, as persons with mental illness were forced into the poorhouses and workhouses. It should also be remembered that the goals of the earlier County Asylum Act of 1808 were not fully realized, as many localities did not initiate the construction of new asylums, due mainly to their cost. Had these been established, with a corresponding transfer of the mentally ill from the poorhouses and the workhouses to the asylums, their plight should have been better. Therefore, almost a decade after the Poor Law Amendment Act of 1834, advocates for the mentally ill continued to publicize the conditions under which many persons with mental illness were existing. It was clear that abusive practices were still rampant and that many with mental illness were not receiving even the basic services they needed.

By 1845, the County Asylum Act of 1808 had been revisited, and although it was amended on a number of occasions, as indicated, it had not fully served its purpose. There thus continued to be a pressing need for further action to secure housing for persons with mental illness that was not primarily poorhouse, jail based, or unaffordable as that provided in some of the private madhouse settings. The County Asylum Act of 1845 was believed to hold the solution to ensuring that facilities for the mentally ill be constructed in a speedy manner. The passage of this act had several influential individuals as its backers, including the physician, Thomas Wakley, the founder and editor of the *Lancet*, a journal focusing on medical-related issues, who had long campaigned for moral and restraint-free treatment to be provided to persons with mental illness.

Simply put, the 1845 County Asylum Act attempted to enforce the provisions of the 1808 legislation. To address the discriminatory attitudes of the county administrators, it mandated that all counties that did not have an asylum must establish a committee, which would focus on funding and constructing asylums for their "pauper insanes." Counties and boroughs could meet this need in a number of ways. For example, they could join together or could acquire private madhouses and convert them into public asylums. They could temporarily rent space from private facilities. The committee could also seek loans from the central government to assist in new asylums. Since there were so many indigent persons with mental illness in the poorhouses and workhouses, financial resources for the construction of asylums could also be procured from the Poor Law funds in some districts. Counties were given three years to respond to this updated law or face more directive legislation. This mandate thus reflected an understanding that better accommodations and treatment for the mentally ill were urgent needs.

To ensure a greater likelihood of success given the failings of the 1808 County Asylum Act, an additional law was passed at the same time as the County Asylum Act of 1845. It was called the Lunacy Act, and this piece of legislation worked in tandem with the County Asylum Act. Basically, it put into place the framework for monitoring the implementation of the County Asylum Act. Thus, a major feature of the Lunacy Act was the establishment of what might be referred to today as a board of directors, but was then called the Commissioners in Lunacy. This board was made up of 11 commissioners, including its prominent leader, a member of Parliament, and tireless advocate for better conditions for the mentally ill—the Seventh Earl of Shaftesbury, Anthony Ashley Cooper.

British historical records indicate that this Lunacy Commission had extensive powers and reported directly to the central government. Because of its leadership, close monitoring, and ongoing advocacy for moral treatment for persons with mental illness, it made significant strides in the development and expansion of asylums across the United Kingdom. For instance, the Asylum Committees that were formed under the County Asylum Act had to submit their plans for constructing any new asylums, for prior approval, to the Commissioners in Lunacy. The commissioners were additionally assigned visiting schedules as each was required to make periodic on-site assessments, during each year, of the licensed houses, asylums, or poorhouses and workhouses in which any person with mental illness was kept. The Commissioners in Lunacy also ensured that existing and new asylums were registered with the Lunacy Commission, as specified by the law. They additionally reviewed whether minimum standards were being maintained such as having a physician on-site, having written policies and procedures, and having an available floor plan.

Further, commissioners were authorized to check on the condition of mentally ill persons in family care or who were receiving care through the fee-for-service arrangements. They could also initiate the process to have individuals assessed for mental illness and removed to an asylum if the person was not being adequately cared for in a family or private madhouse setting. In addition, the Commissioners in Lunacy became the final arbiters for discharging persons from care, if there were issues related to their mental stability. Earlier, this function was carried out by the courts.

Perhaps one of the main legacies of that time is the detailed reports compiled by the Commissioners in Lunacy, since all of their inspections had to be documented. These reports had to be mandatorily submitted to the central government by June of each year and have become repositories of data that describe what was occurring in the asylums and in the community in that era. For example, they tracked the number of asylums, both public and private, as well as the number of insane individuals who were admitted and the symptoms that they directly observed. They also cataloged the conditions under which persons were being housed, how many were able to be discharged back to their communities, and how many had died and the causes of their demise. The Commissioners in Lunacy also attempted to produce outcome data regarding successful treatment as they tried to quantify, when they had the relevant information, how many persons returned to their communities because they were rehabilitated.

In addition, both the Lunacy Act and the County Asylum Act sought to address abuses of the mentally ill, for example, by calling for separate spaces for persons with chronic aggression. Checks and balances were also written into the act in an attempt to avoid conflicts of interest. Thus, the Commissioners in Lunacy could not perform other paid functions. There was also a waiting period for asylum commissioners who were physicians, after their term of service, before they could authorize the confinement of any person with mental illness into an institution. Physicians were additionally not allowed to refer mentally ill persons to facilities in which they had a vested interest.

Multiple provisions were thus enshrined by law in the Lunacy Act of 1845 and the County Asylum Act of 1845. In fact, these two acts were almost duplicates of each other and are sometimes referred to as the County Asylum Lunacy Acts. Historical records indicate that they formed the backbone of legislation affecting the mentally ill until about 1890. Given that there were integral mechanisms built into both acts to facilitate collaboration and monitoring, they were very significant in effecting the intent and letter of these acts. Despite the focus on less eligibility, reforms made to the Poor Laws were also helpful in improving access to needed health care for the poor and the insane. As previously indicated, they also allowed for the funding of asylums in some communities. Additionally, both the Lunacy Act and the County Asylum Act of 1845, as well as the several amendments that were made to them over the years, were crucial in supporting the growth of the large asylums across the United Kingdom. Both acts thus had lasting consequences in decreasing discrimination and strengthening a system of housing and care for persons with mental illness.

THE LUNATIC AMENDMENT AND COUNTY ASYLUM AMENDMENT ACTS OF 1853 AND 1862

Therefore, by approximately 1853, the asylum movement could be said to have come to fruition in the United Kingdom. Published reports indicate that these institutions could be found in almost every county and borough, except for four. However, as the number of asylums and their inmates grew, so too did some of the abuses.

The public asylum system continued to be supplemented by the private facilities. Undoubtedly, many who founded and managed these private asylums believed that they were called on to do this as a divine service. For others, it was purely a business. Newspapers of the day such as the *Times* carried advertisements that solicited business for the asylum.

Specifically, physicians were encouraged to refer patients to be hospitalized. In turn, they could expect to receive, as compensation, part of the fee paid by the patient or family. In his inaugural address to the annual meeting of the Association of Medical Officers of Asylums and Hospitals for the Insane, the incoming president, Dr. Forbes Benignus Winslow (1810–1874), lamented about the sad state of affairs with the commercializing of care for the mentally ill, such as advertisements that guaranteed a referral fee of 20% annually on the receipts.

Additional legislation that was passed in 1853 updated the 1845 County Asylum Act and the Lunacy Act, consistent with emerging medical and public opinion that those with mental illness needed additional protections. Among the updates, the position of registrar of lunacy was confirmed and was entrusted with maintaining the records on persons who were deemed to be insane, including the annual and ongoing correspondence that was received from facilities that housed or treated the mentally ill. A board of visitors was also confirmed who would serve to visit, document, and submit a number of reports annually, on the condition of each person with mental illness who was housed within a facility.

These legal updates also addressed property of up to a certain value, which was owned by the person with mental illness. Any income from the property could be harnessed, or it could be mortgaged, sold, or such in order to pay for the care of the person. However, for the first time, the person needed to be notified and could object to the disposal of his or her property. In this event, the transaction could not proceed. It should be noted that in a subsequent Lunacy Act Amendment in 1862, more power was given to the Lord Chancellor to dispose of the estate of persons who were mentally ill in order to provide for their care.

Based on the 1853 Lunacy Act Amendments, however, persons who wanted to challenge their confinement could appeal to the Commissioner in Lunatics, who now had the authority to refer the case to a superior court, where a jury could be convened, a legal right that had been formerly removed from the mentally ill. In addition, certain issues that directly affected persons with mental illness were now made misdemeanor crimes. The bill introduced the use of standardized forms to complete admission medical assessments and to capture additional ongoing data. Misdemeanor fines were to be applied for each count of any poor person being admitted to a licensed facility without receiving at least two independent medical assessments. Further, if a physician was found to be falsifying an admission certificate, that would result in a misdemeanor charge.

One of the hallmarks of the 1853 acts was that abuse, mistreatment, or willful neglect of any person deemed to be mentally ill, by those who were providing care including professionals such as physicians, paraprofessional persons such as attendants, and even family members, was deemed to be a crime. This could also result in misdemeanor charges. In addition, the acts prohibited the use of restraining devices such as chains and handcuffs to be used on persons with mental illness, some of whom were the indigent insane and continued to be relegated to the workhouses. In a number of instances, the overseers in the workhouses were slow to respond to using more humane methods. Now faced with this caveat, they increased their efforts to have persons with mental illness removed to the public asylums.

The updated Lunatic Amendment and County Asylum Amendment Acts of 1853, and 1862, consolidated the earlier Lunacy Amendment and County Asylum Acts, thus reinforcing the bedrock of mental health care in the United Kingdom until the late 19th century. Together, these legislative initiatives sought to improve the overall care and maintenance of persons with mental illness. By directly targeting pauper lunatics, and clarifying and enshrining in law, certain minimum standards for their care, this legislation played a major role in decreasing some of the discriminatory practices experienced by persons with mental illness.

Historical records note that while legislation in England and Wales proceeded almost simultaneously, in Scotland and Ireland, there were delays in enacting and establishing some of their asylums due to jurisdictional issues. However, much of their enhancements that were made toward providing care for those with mental illness mirrored that in England and Wales. Further, while these legislative initiatives benefited from the wider advocacy for persons with mental illness that was taking place across Europe, as well as in North America, they also had an impact on places around the world that were under British rule at that time.

METROPOLITAN POOR ACT OF 1867

By the 1860s, there was a thriving public and private asylum system across the United Kingdom. Subsequent legal amendments such as the 1867 Metropolitan Poor Act and the 1889 Lunatics Law Amendment Act continued to address identified issues and enhance standards of care. As can be recalled, there was an intertwined relationship between laws that addressed poverty and those addressing mental illness, which had often led to the mentally ill being treated in a more punitive manner. Thus, the Metropolitan Poor Act, which made London one large area for administering services to those with mental illness, sought to make a more distinct separation.

Historical records highlight that a Metropolitan Asylums Board was established that became responsible for persons who were sick and infirm, and who would undoubtedly include those with mental illness. This board focused on relocating those with chronic mental illness—the incurable lunatics, who were assigned to the workhouses, to more suitable environments, thus separating them from the able-bodied paupers. By focusing only on those individuals with mental illness, the Asylums Board was instrumental, perhaps for the first time since the advent of the Lunacy Acts, in carrying out a pretty comprehensive relocation of those with mental illness.

In fact, the 1867 Metropolitan Poor Act authorized the cost of caring for mentally ill persons in asylums, from a newly established poor fund, rather than from the local taxes that were used to fund the workhouses. Delighted to rid themselves of this cost, those in charge of the workhouses zealously facilitated the medical assessment process to ensure that any and all lunatics were transferred out. Short on asylum space in London, the workhouse operators ignored the emotional and practical hardships that could occur when family members were placed far away from their loved ones. Persons with mental illness were eagerly transferred to the outer boroughs and counties, far away from the London metropolitan area that they called home. This would entail many miles of travel for family and even friends to remain in contact, as well as economic hardships to afford the costs that traveling would incur. Although this was not its intent, the Metropolitan Poor Act thus had a discriminatory impact on indigent persons with mental illness and their families.

This wholesale transfer of the indigent individuals to other localities additionally presented unanticipated administrative challenges for the Metropolitan Asylums Board. How would members be able to effectively carry out their supervisory functions of regularly visiting and monitoring the condition of those with mental illness? And how could they challenge excessive costs of care in localities that were not under their jurisdiction? Even by 1867, then, there was still a pressing need for suitable housing for those with mental illness within several communities. Recognizing this, the Metropolitan Asylums Board authorized and completed the establishment of two additional asylums for this population by 1870. Published reports indicate that within a year of their opening, these two institutions had a combined total of 3,000 persons in residence.

It is ironic that the intent of the Metropolitan Asylums Board to address the inadequate or nonexistent care that was being received by persons with mental illness due to their economic status was subverted. To a certain extent, this was a predictor of what would occur across the Atlantic in the 1950s, with the advent of the deinstitutionalization of persons with mental illness. It was to their credit, however, that the members of the board acted in an expeditious manner and appeared to have made a great deal of effort to correct some of the unintended discriminatory consequences of the law. In retrospect, one could only imagine the relief of family members and friends who, already deprived of the emotional depth of a relationship with their loved ones due to their mental health impairments, could at least have some level of contact and assurance of their well-being. The Metropolitan Poor Act thus did have some success in creating access to and expanding improved housing conditions for poor persons who were affected with mental illness.

THE LUNATICS LAW AMENDMENT ACT OF 1889 AND THE LUNACY ACT OF 1890

By the latter half of the 1800s, other decentralized institutions such as state and private hospitals began to recognize the necessity for ensuring adequate care for persons with mental illness and began to contribute to their care. This growth of the state mental hospitals is discussed in greater detail elsewhere. In addition, how persons with mental illness were viewed was evolving. Previously, we have discussed some of the changed beliefs that emerged as part of scientific thinking including recognizing mental health as having a biological etiology and being affected by environmental stressors. Now, there was more willingness to see mental illness as episodic for some individuals, and perhaps curable for others. Advances were also being made in employing more humane interventions and in addressing some of the more egregious abuse of the mentally ill. With the advent of the 1880s, the heyday of the asylum movement with its fairly rapid construction of new facilities within London itself, and in the boroughs, counties, and other localities across the United Kingdom, had come and gone.

British historical records indicate that two final pieces of legislation marked the transition from the 19th-century care to modern treatment for those with mental illness—the Lunatics Law Amendment Act of 1889 and the Lunacy Act of 1890.

While conditions for housing persons with mental illness had improved, advocates continued to highlight a number of concerns. Included among these was the initial process for determining that a person had mental illness. Specifically, the individual had to be assessed, face-to-face, by two independent medical practitioners, who would then proceed to certify the person's status.

As per advocates, there were many instances of sane persons being certified as insane. Thus, they were wrongfully confined for indeterminate periods of time against their will. Further, they had little recourse as their appeal was to be submitted to the Commissioner in Lunatics, who could be the final arbiter. Advocates recommended, however, that in the interest of fairness, there should be an additional step, which could consist of a public examination that allowed the physician's diagnosis to be questioned and/ or cross-examined as needed.

Over the objections of many physicians, the Lunacy Act Amendment of 1889 was passed. It stipulated several individual rights of persons with mental illness including the right to privacy, to unrestricted written communication, and to make complaints. For instance, the 1889 Lunacy Act Amendment specified that the individual was entitled to communicate with the Commissioners in Lunacy in writing and his or her mail should not be opened. The person could also request a face-to-face meeting with any of the commissioners or members of the Board of Visitors.

In order to address the issue of persons being confined who were not insane, the Lunacy Act Amendment of 1889 incorporated the use of a judicial authority, prior to a person being confined to an institution as being mentally ill. Thus, except in cases of emergency, no person could be detained or admitted as a lunatic into any facility unless an appropriate order had been obtained from a judge, magistrate, or JP in the area where he or she lived. Further, it stipulated that ongoing detention of the person would also need to be reviewed and reauthorized by the specified court official.

Urgency or emergency orders could only go into effect for seven days, and also needed to be obtained from the court. While relatives or friends could make the petition to the court, it had to be accompanied by a medical report from an independent practitioner. The act additionally stressed that all court proceedings were to be remain private and offered legal protection to physicians and operators/owners of asylums and other facilities who acted in good faith.

The letter and intent of the Lunacy Act Amendment of 1889 can be considered a landmark in ensuring both the individual and institutional rights of persons with mental illness. In fact, through its incorporation as part of the British Common Law in the United States, its basic framework is still visible in this nation with regard to how involuntary commitment is exercised. By enshrining privacy and legal protection, it also sought to balance the interest of all parties and reinforce the need for good faith.

With the passage of the Lunacy Act of 1890, the 1889 Lunacy Act Amendments, as well as those from prior laws, were consolidated into one major piece of legislation. This was significant in addressing some of the personal and institutional discrimination against persons with mental illness. In fact, another tenet of the Lunacy Act Amendment of 1889 prohibited the establishment of new private asylums, a tangible indication that the era of the construction and expansion of large asylums, many of which were unwieldy to manage and monitor, was over. A new movement was now in place to address the care of persons with mental illness, one that recognized their basic human rights, assured a minimum level of care, and sought to balance the interest of society with that of the person with mental illness. While by no means the perfect solution, this legislation would remain the backbone of the mental health system in the United Kingdom for close to 70 years, until it was replaced by the Mental Health Act of 1959.

Therefore, during the 18th through 19th centuries, advances in the way persons with mental illness were viewed, and ongoing advocacy, led to multiple pieces of legislation being enacted not only in the United Kingdom, but also across other parts of Europe including France, Germany, Italy, and Norway. As previously stated, since this was also the age of colonization, in some instances, laws that were passed in these countries also affected their outlying dependencies in places such as Australia and Portugal and had significant consequences for where persons with mental illness were housed and treated, and the basic rights they could experience. But what was occurring on the huge North American continent? A closer examination of the advocacy efforts and the trajectory of the movement to better care for those with mental illness is warranted.

CHAPTER 4

Early American Society and Discrimination against the Mentally Ill

To fully understand the seeds of some of the same discriminatory ways in which persons with mental illness were treated in the United States, it is helpful to look at its birth within the British system. We have already addressed some of the beliefs about mental illness, heavily rooted in the interpretation of religion and superstition that was transported to the New World. Additionally, we should recall the long-held beliefs and attitudes toward the poor that were given full legal sanction in the Elizabethan Poor Law of 1601 and its subsequent iterations. This regularized, within the United Kingdom, how the poor was categorized and whether they were eligible for outdoor relief or indoor, in places such as the almshouses, poorhouses, and workhouses, with the latter sometimes doubling as jails.

As colonial America began creating structures meant to foster and support the social, legal, and economic good, the need to care for those who could not do so for themselves emerged. If you were an able-bodied child or adult, there was a high likelihood you could become indentured to a family with the means to support you, or who would receive assistance from the local community to do so. But as those who were in need began to overwhelm the informal systems, the colonial settlers fell back on what they knew from the mother country. Familiar precedents that were imported as the Common Law in the early U.S. colonies were used to formalize a system of care for the indigent, among whom the aged, infirm, and persons with mental illness could be counted.

ALMSHOUSES, POORHOUSES, AND WORKHOUSES IN THE UNITED STATES

Some of the structures created by the British Poor Laws began to be mirrored in the United States. For instance, historical records indicate that in Boston, Massachusetts, by 1660, those who could contributed money and labor to establish what is regarded as the first poorhouse in the United States. In 1665, local laws in the colony of New Netherlands, now the State of New York, made it the collective responsibility of the home and surrounding counties to provide funds to support the care of persons with mental illness. Further, in 1691 and 1697, instructions from the British Monarchy to the respective Governors Fletcher and Bellomont of New York directed that workhouses for the indigent should be established in convenient locations. By 1701, however, historical legislative documents for New York indicate that the care of the indigent was to be provided for by each town or locality. Theoretically, this should have increased access to care for indigent persons with mental illness. On the other hand, it could also have made it more difficult as prevailing attitudes regarding the worthy and unworthy poor, and lack of understanding about mental illness, were likely to influence who received outdoor and indoor relief—assistance within their homes or in the poorhouses. In fact, Overseers of the Poor were appointed, partly to ensure that assistance went only to those who were deemed to be legitimately in need.

As individual cities and towns sprang up across America, expanding the need to set up these facilities, the destinies of those with mental illness were once again aligned with those in poverty. If you were a person with mental illness, and did not have family and friends with the wherewithal to care for you, there was a high likelihood that you could end up in one of the almshouses, poorhouses, or workhouses of the day, such as that privately set up by the Society of Quakers, in Philadelphia, in 1713. By 1732, the Philadelphia Almshouse, regarded as a model facility, was established as the first publicly funded institution of its kind in the country.

By 1736, records indicate that the City of New York had established a public workhouse, which also served as the house of correction. Further, just as some of these institutions in the British Isles had often become repositories of overall substandard treatment—inadequate food, shelter, and clothing; and ongoing physical, psychological, and sexual abuse—similar problems were noted within some of these facilities that provided the primary means of care for the indigent insane within the early American colonies.

Despite these endemic issues, almshouses, poorhouses, and workhouses were expanded across the colonies. Most likely, the need for these would have increased in the last quarter of the 17th century, spurred on by the widespread turmoil created by the American Revolutionary War of Independence, which took place with Great Britain from 1775 to 1783. Undoubtedly, many facing the front lines of battle would have demonstrated the need for mental health services. In some cases, the confiscation and destruction of property would have added individuals to the ranks of the indigent and insane.

By the early 1800s, numerous pieces of local legislation in the new United States of America continued to expand the workhouses. For example, the County Poorhouse Act was passed in New York State in 1824, mandating the establishment of poorhouses, almshouses, or workhouses in each county. Laws were also passed across states levying taxes to build and maintain these facilities. In some cases, the local charities, religious institutions, and other mutual aid societies either contributed to the public poorhouses, or established and maintained their own facilities. It was also not uncommon for the poorhouses/workhouses and jails to be built within close proximity to each other. Sadly, even with public and private cooperation, the conditions of persons with mental illness in these institutions were not always satisfactory.

The need for better treatment of persons with mental illness was thus pressing. However, there was little commitment from central government to ensure an adequate standard of care. Although advocacy efforts in the United States lagged somewhat behind that of England, by the mid-1800s, several individuals and communities began to fill this void advocating for humane treatment of those with mental illness. Not surprisingly, several Quakers including Thomas Scattergood were in the forefront of this movement. What was unusual for this day, however, was for women such as Dorothea Dix to engage in campaigning face-to-face and through letter writing on behalf of persons with mental illness and their need to be treated humanely. Ms. Dix's campaign was especially noteworthy as it culminated in a direct and potentially successful appeal to the U.S. congress to enact legislation that could improve where persons with mental illness were housed and how they were treated across the United States.

DOROTHEA DIX

By the 1840s, the philanthropist and reformer, Dorothea Dix (1802–1887), was traveling around the United States, documenting where the mentally ill were housed and what was their plight. Ms. Dix had previously visited England and had been directly exposed to the philosophy and structure of the Quaker Retreat, York, as well as to the Lunacy Reform Movement. Back in the United States, historical records indicate that while volunteering to teach inmates at the Cambridge Jail in Massachusetts, Ms. Dix observed the dreadful living conditions being experienced by those confined for crimes as well as those with mental illness, and began her letter writing and advocacy campaign on behalf of these individuals.

Systematically, Ms. Dix visited the various poorhouses, almshouses, and workhouses/jails in Boston and throughout Massachusetts. Observing the plight of the individuals across these facilities, she graphically documented the conditions faced by persons with mental illness, as well as those with intellectual challenges. In her *Memorial to the legislature of Massachusetts,* written in January 1843, Ms. Dix highlighted the "state of insane persons confined within . . . cages, cellars, closets, stalls, pens! Chained, naked, beaten with rods, and lashed into obedience."

Ms. Dix's vivid descriptions told of the plight of men and women who were chained together; were housed in crowded, poorly ventilated rooms; were exposed to the freezing elements in winter; faced the unrelenting sun during the summer; or were physically and sexually abused. She also pointed out that even convicted persons had a right to serve their time without being at the mercy of some of the persons with more serious mental illness. Ms. Dix additionally reported on the practice of auctioning the indigent, insane, elderly, and other vulnerable persons to private individuals.

Ms. Dix was engaged in a six-year letter writing campaign that included the legislature in Massachusetts, other states, and the U.S. congress. Her June 1848 letter to Congress documented her findings including how persons were routinely chained, weighted down with heavy iron balls, beaten, and lived in overall subhuman conditions. Ms. Dix proposed that to address these abject circumstances, hospitals and asylums for the insane should be developed, that could be regulated and supervised, and that 5 million acres of land should be set aside on which facilities could be constructed to house and treat persons with mental illness.

Although the then president, Franklin Pierce (1804–1869), vetoed the congressional Bill for the Benefit of the Indigent Insane, which was passed in 1854, Ms. Dix had been successful in communicating the plight of the insane that epitomized the systematic discrimination and marginalization they experienced. Both houses of congress had in fact concurred with Ms. Dix that this was unacceptable, and their bill allocated more than 12 million acres of land, with 10,000 acres across states to erect facilities to house and treat persons with mental illness.

One could only imagine the tremendous disappointment that Ms. Dix must have experienced to hear the person entrusted with the highest office in the land, President Pierce, insisting that providing concrete solutions that would support the basic rights of persons with mental illness to have adequate food, clothing, shelter, and medical care was the responsibility of each state, and not the federal government. It is a matter of conjecture how this legislative initiative, if implemented, would have changed the landscape of care for persons with mental illness and their families, then and now, within the United States. However, in the absence of a federal will, much needed immediate relief to many in dire straits was thus denied.

It is accurate that private philanthropic efforts, often led by people of faith, played a major role in some states in developing resources and establishing needed facilities. From a practical perspective, the federal government's decision now placed increased responsibility on the shoulders of such groups. But the efforts of religious and private organizations were not always enough to address the widespread need being experienced by persons with mental illness and their families. Specifically, the availability of safe, abuse-free therapeutic facilities, especially for persons with SMI, was a priority.

With the veto of the legislation Ms. Dix had championed, a major political statement had been explicitly made that states needed to work on the solutions to dealing with persons with mental illness. Thus, the ad hoc internal state systems that were dependent on the goodwill of persons in individual state legislatures were now even more important. Some states such as New York attempted to be responsive to the needs of persons with mental illness. In others, it remained lacking sometimes due to little political will or due to limited resources. For instance, historical documents highlight that in 1848, the Senate and House of Representatives in Michigan petitioned their congressional representative to obtain a grant of sufficient state lands to build an insane asylum as well as an institution for persons with intellectual and physical disabilities. This request was repeated in 1849. Ten years later, in 1859, the Michigan legislature was still petitioning for funding for these two institutions, despite the existing social need.

But even in the face of this major setback and its associated negative consequences for persons with mental illness, Dorothea Dix's advocacy continued. Additionally to inspecting more than 500 almshouses, numerous jails, and prisons in the United States, Ms. Dix traveled to many parts of England, Europe, and Asia inspecting and documenting the conditions of facilities in those countries. She also turned her attention to reiterating the need for the establishment of hospitals and asylums to serve persons with mental illness and intellectual challenges. In fact, historical records attribute the establishment of more than 30 asylums, hospitals, and other institutions for persons with mental illness and intellectual challenges to Ms. Dix's advocacy. In conjunction with the psychiatrist, Thomas Kirkbride, one of the first hospitals she helped to develop—the State Hospital in Trenton, New Jersey (1844)—later became her home for approximately six years before she met her demise.

A major legislative victory for persons with mental illness had thus been won and lost in the U.S. congress. One could argue that the bill's veto was as a result of fiscal prudence, or a desire to avoid big government, or even ongoing cultural beliefs about the etiology of mental illness. Perhaps the source of discrimination here was the lack of political power of those with mental illness. Thus, if this group was considered to be a more powerful voting bloc, the outcome might have been different. Despite this setback occasioned by the veto of the Bill for the Benefit of the Indigent Insane of 1854, the movement to reform the abuses in the almshouses, poorhouses, and workhouses continued up until approximately the end of the 19th century.

Though other reformers did not obtain the status of Dorothea Dix, the need to address the existing abuses continued in state and local legislatures around the United States. Whatever their human frailties, it should be remembered that in a time when there was no federal government's commitment to ensuring even minimal social supports, the poorhouses, workhouses, and almshouses, despite the existing abuses, were the primary safety nets providing food, clothing, and shelter to indigent persons with mental illness. But the need for a more structured system of care was evident, and this was partly realized with the opening of new hospitals and asylums to house and treat persons with mental illness.

EARLY HOSPITALS AND ASYLUMS IN THE UNITED STATES

Therefore, a glaring consequence of discrimination in the United States was that despite an extensive advocacy movement, comprehensive legislation such as that noted in the United Kingdom, which could help to improve care for persons with mental illness, was not enacted. Instead, a piecemeal patchwork of laws were passed across various states often as a response to a pressing need such as the overflow of individuals in the poorhouses, which had become a catchment for persons with mental illness. On a practical basis, the absence of reliable core services on which persons with mental illness and their families could rely affected daily decisions such as where they could live safely, whether they could obtain medical and psychological care, and whether they could have opportunities for appropriate socialization or to engage in work or productive activities to the best of their ability. However, several developments that were in process for some time eventually expanded the service network and brought some improvements to the care of those with mental illness.

In the vanguard of this movement, as previously indicated, were groups such as the Quakers, well known for fueling a more humane and moral approach to treating persons with mental illness in England. Joined by other enlightened thinkers of the day, many of whom subscribed to a more reasoned and scientific approach to addressing social issues, rather than using a pathway of superstition, individuals such as Francis Fauquier (1703–1768), governor of the then colony of Virginia; Thomas Scattergood (1748–1814), a Quaker minister; Thomas Story Kirkbride (1809–1883), a physician, whose work was supported by Dorothea Dix; and others were instrumental in the movement to develop and expand hospitals and asylums in the United States.

Although these individuals did not articulate it as such, their advocacy also led to the establishment of a formal health care system that better served the needs of persons with mental illness. Additionally, this set the stage for a public health approach to treating mental illness that will be further discussed in a subsequent chapter. It should be stressed that countless others also contributed to the rise of a formal health care system. However, the following persons played strategic roles in confronting and trying to correct various types of discrimination that was directed at persons with mental illness.

Dr. Benjamin Rush and the Pennsylvania Hospital

In 1751, the first general medical hospital in the American colonies—the Pennsylvania Hospital—was founded with approval from the colony's legislature to provide medical care to the indigent sick and the insane. Conceived by Dr. Thomas Bond, a Quaker physician, and with the support and financial contributions from individuals such as Benjamin Franklin, Thomas Stretch, and others, by 1752, a temporary hospital was admitting patients. Published records indicate that four of the six initial persons were mentally ill. By 1756, however, the permanent site of the Pennsylvania Hospital, which is now part of the University of Pennsylvania Health System, became operational.

By default, the Pennsylvania Hospital is therefore the first hospital in the United States to officially treat persons with mental illness. But given their pioneer status, how effective was this facility? Historical records indicate that Dr. Benjamin Rush, now known as the Father of American Psychiatry, joined the staff of the hospital in 1783. By this time, treatment interventions for those with mental illness had not significantly improved over those imported from the mother country, especially for those with more serious illnesses.

Physical punishment and restraints continued to be the norm, while over-crowding led to persons being hospitalized in less than optimal conditions. Dr. Rush, an avid proponent of moral/humane treatment, was perturbed by the status of those with mental illness within the hospital. However, he disagreed with other advocates that these persons could benefit from being treated in dedicated hospitals. Instead, by 1792, Dr. Rush had convinced the Pennsylvania legislature that to improve conditions, a separate ward needed to be constructed, within the hospital, to treat only persons with mental illness. Additionally, believing that the causes of mental illness included poor circulation and sensory overload, and seeking to improve how people were physically restrained, he invented the circular spinning board and tranquilizing chair to respectively address each situation.

By treating persons with mental illness within the same institution that was treating other health conditions, Dr. Rush reinforced the changing thinking of the day that mental illness should be considered another health problem. Thus, instead of locking persons with mental illness away in hospital basements or other places where they could not be seen, a dedicated ward, with appropriate physical accommodation and supervision, would convey that these individuals had a right to effective and humane treatment. To the credit of Dr. Rush, this then relatively novel idea faced discrimination head-on and continues to be implemented in many hospitals today where persons with mental illness could access care on a dedicated ward as needed.

By 1790, Dr. Rush was linking the "excessive use of ardent spirits" to mental illness. On his *Moral and Physical Thermometer*, a scale related to the use of alcohol, he identified madness as one of the negative outcomes. Further, in his seminal text, *Medical Inquiries and Observations*, *Upon the Diseases of the Mind*, published in 1812, he reported that at one juncture, alcoholism was verified by the resident physician at the Pennsylvania Hospital as the etiology of one-third of the cases. Recognizing, however, that alcoholism also needed to be treated, Dr. Rush is credited as being among the first to identify it as a disease in itself and to recommend several treatments including cold baths, converting to Christianity, and substituting wine, beer, and opium instead of strong liquors.

While Dr. Rush's treatment may appear to be questionable, his perspective contributed to the emergence of asylums in the United States for two separate populations—those with mental illness (the insane asylums) and those with intemperance—the inebriate asylums and homes. This distinction, which marked the divergence in thought regarding mental illness versus addiction, has in many ways been retained within the treatment system even today.

As a pioneer of moral treatment for the mentally ill, Dr. Rush thus helped to decrease discrimination and advance more appropriate treatment interventions. Some of his methods such as bleeding, blistering, purging/ administering medications laced with mercury, although common at the time, were undoubtedly of questionable benefit. But by bringing attention to the plight of those with mental illness, by actively working to ameliorate conditions at the Pennsylvania Hospital, by advancing the philosophy that those with mental illness could be treated and in some instances cured, by advocating for the mainstreaming or integration of persons with mental illness as part of the general health care system, by insisting that persons with mental illness should be productively engaged in activities such as gardening that could bring daily structure to their lives, and by teaching and mentoring new physicians, Dr. Rush played an invaluable role in decreasing discriminatory practices, including neglect, against persons with mental illness.

Francis Fauquier and the Eastern State Hospital

Opened in 1773, Eastern State Hospital is credited with being the first hospital in the United States that was established specifically to treat persons with mental illness. Its founding was directly related to the efforts of Francis Fauquier, the governor of Virginia. Reports indicate that in Virginia, persons who were thought to be exhibiting mental illness were subjected to being screened by a panel of 12 citizens. This panel, after determining whether the person was an idiot, a criminal, or a lunatic, would then pass its sentence—usually confinement in the public jail. Persons with no medical background or formal training regarding mental illness thus acted as the gatekeepers to the welfare and freedom of persons with mental illness.

Governor Fauquier, not comfortable with his duly invested authority to permit the jailing of persons with mental illness, is credited with sowing the seeds that grew into the Eastern State Hospital, in Williamsburg, Virginia. During addresses to the town residents, that is, the House of Burgesses, in 1765 and 1767, published reports indicate that Fauquier highlighted the plight of those with mental illness within the county and appealed to the citizens to approve and fund the establishment of a hospital to shelter and treat these individuals. This came to fruition with the opening of the Eastern Hospital.

The governor had effectively used his position to provide a voice for persons with mental illness and to address a clear injustice that was being meted out to them. Moreover, he had helped to introduce a formal system of care that was used by generations of persons with mental illness.

The New York Hospital and the Bloomingdale Asylum

The first general medical hospital that provided services to persons with mental illness in New York State was the New York Hospital. It did not open for patients until 1791, although the royal charter from King George III established that it was granted since 1771. The second general medical hospital after Pennsylvania Hospital in the United States, its charter specified that it would treat maniacs along with providing usual medical and surgical care. Thus, as per historical records, a person with mental illness—bipolar disorder—was among its first admissions. The inclusion of treating persons with mental illness as part of its stated mission undoubtedly emerged as a consequence of the need for psychotherapeutic care identified within the population of New York at that time.

Nearly 20 years later, in 1798, the New York Hospital Board of Governors reaffirmed the treatment of mental illness as part of its mission. By electing to provide services to these individuals from its inception, New York Hospital established a nondiscriminatory precedent regarding access to mental health care being equally valid to that for other health care issues. Although its restatement of its mission prioritized its treatment purposes as medical, surgical, and then mental health care, this appears to have been more closely related to resource considerations than to discrimination. In fact, according to the Cornell University Medical Center Archives, by 1816, the hospital began purchasing land on which the Bloomingdale Asylum was constructed and operated from 1821 through 1894.

A *New York Times* article of March 17, 1889, reported on the decision made by the Board of Directors to move the facility from the grounds of what is today Columbia University and relocate it to White Plains due to zoning and space considerations. The hospital remains functional today as the New York Presbyterian Hospital/Westchester, and through research and educational initiatives, partly funded by a major donation in the late 1920s from Payne Whitney, a wealthy patron, it has retained and expanded its mission to serve persons with mental illness. While there is some criticism that the Bloomingdale Asylum, with its extensive and elegant facilities, adopted a treatment focus that centered primarily on wealthy patients who could afford to pay, advocates connected with the asylum and the New York Hospital also advocated for the expansion of treatment for the indigent. This was instrumental in the construction of a second psychiatric hospital on Roosevelt Island, then called Blackwell's Island, by 1840. The

Bloomingdale's Asylum separation of individuals and the services provided to them based on income, while discriminatory, was a general practice of the time. It cannot be ignored, however, that by integrating persons with mental illness into mainstream medical care, the New York Hospital helped to move this issue in a better direction that overall helped to obtain better medical/mental health care for persons requiring it.

The Public Hospital of Baltimore (Spring Grove)

In 1798, the second institution that is regarded as specifically focusing on treating persons with mental illness—the Public Hospital of Baltimore (now renamed as the Spring Grove Hospital in 1912)—was established. Historical records indicate that by 1794, a sea captain, Jeremiah Yellott, donated land on which he constructed the Retreat or Hospital for Strangers and Mariners. This treated general medical conditions including persons affected by yellow fever and seamen affected by poor mental health.

By 1797, with the yellow fever epidemic spreading, Yellott reportedly petitioned the Maryland General Assembly for assistance with expanding the Retreat. Their act, passed the same year, authorized the expansion of the Retreat into a hospital to serve the indigent sick and to care for persons identified as lunatics. This legislation established the Public Hospital of Baltimore, which was purchased by the city one year later, as a general and public psychiatric facility.

Despite being managed at varying times either by the city, or leased to private individuals, the Public Hospital of Baltimore has always served persons with mental illness. In 1839, an act passed by the Maryland General Assembly restricted the hospital, renamed the Maryland Hospital for the Insane a year earlier, to accepting only psychiatric patients. Due to multiple factors, including space issues, the original hospital site was sold to the John Hopkins Hospital in 1870, and the psychiatric facility was eventually relocated to Catonsville, Baltimore. Nevertheless, this institution remains one of the few that is functioning and has consistently not discriminated against serving those with mental illness.

Thomas Scattergood and the Friends Hospital

In 1817, the psychiatric hospital that is regarded as the first to be privately managed in the United States—the Friends Hospital or the Asylum for Persons Deprived of the Use of Their Reason—was opened in Philadelphia, Pennsylvania. The Quaker minister, Thomas Scattergood, returning to Philadelphia after visiting the York Retreat in England, recognized that he was coming into contact with a number of persons who were afflicted with mental illness. His advocacy efforts among other Quakers culminated in 1811, at the annual meeting of the Friends Society, in Scattergood's request for concrete mechanisms to be put into place to assist those who were experiencing mental illness.

Public records indicate that a Committee of Seven, including Scattergood, was immediately appointed. Using the prototype created by the York Retreat in England, by 1813, the Friends Hospital had been founded and began providing continuous services four years later, up until today. Although originally intended to serve members of the Friends Society, with their moral treatment philosophy that embraced those with mental illness as fellow men who needed gentle care and concern, the Board of Managers of the hospital voted, in 1834, to accept persons of any denomination who needed mental health care. Needless to say, this went a long way to assure that persons who needed care were not discriminated against based on their religious persuasion.

The Quakers, known to be among the forerunners in providing humane care, introduced what came to be called pet therapy, in 1830. Additionally, the expansion of opportunities for productivity with the establishment of a greenhouse in 1879, and an exercise program by 1889, enhanced the services that were being provided.

Further, the Friends Hospital, which was also called the Frankford Asylum for the Insane due to its location near Frankford, Philadelphia, was also one of the first hospitals in the United States, in 1889, to have a female psychiatrist, Dr. Anna Broomall as part of their treatment staff. Undoubtedly, this would have played an invaluable role, especially for female patients, in enhancing the perceived quality of care they were receiving, in an environment that had been male dominated from its inception. This facility thus confronted some of the discriminatory thinking of the time that women were not suited to be physicians, additionally to providing inclusive, nondenominational-based care to persons who needed it.

Reverend Louis Dwight, the Massachusetts General Hospital, and the Worcester Lunatic Asylum

In 1833, the Worcester Lunatic Asylum, the first psychiatric facility in the state of Massachusetts, was opened. This was due to the efforts of the Quaker minister, Rev. Louis Dwight, who founded the Boston Prison Discipline Society in 1825, after his visits to prisons and jails during which he observed the abominable conditions under which persons with mental illness were housed. The Boston Prison Discipline Society, led by Reverend

Wright, initiated and championed a strong advocacy movement for improved conditions for those with mental illness as well as other inmates.

Two years later, in 1827, Reverend Dwight's efforts bore fruit as they were instrumental in the creation of a committee to assess conditions in penal settings across the state. Further, the committee's recommendation that persons with mental illness should be relocated to the Massachusetts General Hospital was an acknowledgment of the debasing manner in which the mentally ill were being treated in prison. But even at this hospital, there were limitations in the number of available beds and services for those with mental illness. Thus, a later court order mandated the construction of a specialty hospital, the Worcester Lunatic Asylum (or Bloomingdale Asylum), to serve persons with mental illness.

Within less than 10 years of its opening, the new 120-bed facility was overcrowded, with reports indicating that 164 persons were admitted in the first year. Despite the advocacy of persons such as Dorothea Dix, it was more than 30 years later before construction on a larger facility—the Worcester Hospital—was completed in 1876. The overwhelming need for a place to service persons with mental illness thus, at times, militated against more humane conditions. While the political will of the legislature was lacking with regard to providing the economic and other material resources that were required to construct the new facility, Reverend Dwight was still able to highlight the dire need for change and to help ameliorate the conditions of persons with mental illness who were housed in jails.

Thomas Story Kirkbride and the Pennsylvania Hospital for the Insane

It should be recalled that since 1752, the Pennsylvania Hospital had started caring for those with mental illness. Although Dr. Benjamin Rush was instrumental in setting up dedicated wards for those with mental illness, by the last two decades of the 17th century, overcrowding was again a major issue as these patients constituted about 50% of the hospitalized population. In fact, reports indicate this had increased to 66% by the early 1800s. Despite Dr. Rush's extensive advocacy, by the 1830s, more than 20 years after his death, the overwhelming need for more treatment space for those with mental illness resulted in the identification and construction of the Pennsylvania Hospital for the Insane.

Historical records indicate that this facility, later called the Institute of the Pennsylvania Hospital, opened under the management of Dr. Thomas Kirkbride in 1841. A staunch supporter of moral treatment who had interned at the Friends Hospital, he visited other facilities, gathering data on best practices. Further, he built on Dr. Rush's legacy, implementing practices such as private rooms, and structured daily indoor and outdoor activities, which included lectures and the use of a library.

But Dr. Kirkbride also believed that the physical environment itself should be architecturally designed in a manner that would offer maximal therapeutic benefits to the persons served. With a focus on the practical needs of patients such as heating and privacy, as well as space and aesthetics, what came to be called the Kirkbride Plan was adopted for implementation by the Association of Medical Superintendents of American Institutions—the predecessor to the American Psychiatric Association (APA). It should also be noted that Dr. Kirkbride was the founder (1844) and the initial president of the Association of Medical Superintendents of American Institutions.

Overcrowding at his own facility, the Institute of the Pennsylvania Hospital, by the 1850s, gave Dr. Kirkbride the opportunity to test his own plan. Specifically, the construction of a new male wing that adhered to the Kirkbride Plan was completed by 1859. From 1844 through 1870, driven partly by the advocacy of Dorothea Dix and other reformers, the Kirkbride Plan prototype was reportedly used to construct approximately 300 hospitals serving persons with mental illness across the United States. In many respects, the design of these facilities helped those whose symptoms would best allow them to stabilize, to move from living in purely a place of asylum—where safety could be found—to that of a sanitarium—a place in which recovery could take place.

There were other advocates of therapeutic environmental designs such as Dr. Jesse Bancroft, who was the superintendent of the New Hampshire Asylum for the Insane from 1857 to 1881. He recommended the inclusion of small cottages, which could afford greater privacy for those persons with mental illness who needed less supervision.

Dr. Kirkbride, however, appeared to have the most widespread impact in the United States in literally helping to build a physical therapeutic system of care for those with mental illness. His basic hospital design took into consideration the needs of persons served for fresh air, sunlight, privacy, and cleanliness, and integrally recognized their worth as individuals to live in an aesthetically pleasing environment. This latter, he believed, was an integral therapeutic component of their care. Dr. Kirkbride's advocacy for funding of asylums and hospitals using his Kirkbride Plan stands as a measure of the nondiscriminatory approach he used and the efforts he made to correct overt abuse and neglect of those with mental illness, especially with regard to where they were housed and how they were treated.

Therefore, by the close of the 19th century, a viable system of care was in place for persons with mental illness in the United Kingdom and in several places on the European continent, as well as in the United States. While treatment interventions were constrained by the knowledge of the time, there was widespread consensus that persons with mental illness could and should be treated, as well as afforded their basic rights. By the early 1900s, as psychiatry, neurology, psychology, and other scientific fields came into their own, there was a corresponding impact on the approaches that were implemented to treat mental illness.

CHAPTER 5

How Treatment Movements Influenced Discrimination against the Mentally Ill

As discussed previously, changing belief systems, the still emerging etiology of the bio-psycho-social basis for mental illness, social attitudes, and values, and legislative guidance all had interrelated impacts on the system of care that was being developed and refined for persons with mental illness. Several movements have significantly influenced how persons with mental illness have been treated then and now. Consequently, they have also been affected by discriminatory attitudes and practices. These include the movement toward physical treatments, the medication management movement, the public health movement, the disability movement, and the behavioral health care movement.

THE MOVEMENT TOWARD PHYSICAL TREATMENTS

By the advent of the 1900s, a great deal of activity was occurring with regard to identifying new treatments for persons with mental illness. Some of this was focused on developing physical treatments that were usually invasive. This was not new. For example, one of the oldest physical treatments was trepanning. This involved drilling a hole in the head, which it is believed may have been done to allow the evil spirits that purportedly caused mental illness to be released. Historical artifacts have helped to clarify that this practice was used across multiple cultures including the ancient Egyptians, Greeks, Romans, the Incas, and others.

We should also recall that bleeding or blood–letting and purging were also physical methods. These were widely practiced by many reputable

physicians of their time including Benjamin Rush. While they did not necessarily target persons with mental illness, the latter may have been more
vulnerable to these procedures especially since inadequate nutrition was
common, and poor sanitary conditions made infections at the incision site
higher.

By the close of the 1800s, trepanning and bloodletting had become ob-
solete. However, there was still considerable focus on physical methods of
dealing with mental illness. One of these that gained considerable public
support was sterilization of both males and females with mental illness, so
that they would not be able to have children. Sterilization owed its origin to
eugenics. Prominent eugenicists such as Dr. Harry Laughlin believed that
only human beings who did not have degenerate or defective hereditary qual-
ities should be allowed to propagate. The 1922 publication of his Model Eu-
genical Sterilization Law ushered in an era in which approximately 33 states
in the United States adopted Eugenics Laws. This reportedly resulted, by the
1970s, in the forcible sterilization of 60,000 or more persons with mental illness and intellectual challenges, who were deemed to be genetically inferior.

It should be noted that it was not only in the United States that Dr. Laughlin had a following. The Eugenics Archive highlights that his model law
was used as the prototype by the German government. Implemented in
1933, it led to the forcible sterilization of more than 350,000 persons who
were considered to be defective. The eugenics movement and its forced
sterilization thus remain one of the more insidious, discriminatory acts
that have been perpetrated against individuals with mental illness.

Sadly, the U.S. Supreme Court remains a culpable participant. In the
test case—*Buck v. Bell* (1927)—it upheld the sterilization of a 17-year-
old Virginia teenager, who gave birth to a child after she was raped. Based
on the learned assessment of multiple witnesses, as the child of a mother
who was hospitalized in an asylum, as a promiscuous person of poor morals, and as a feeble-minded individual, since a B average in school did not
count (and an A for deportment), she was a prime candidate who met the
legal threshold for sterilization. Published reports indicate that *Buck v. Bell*
has not been repealed as of this time!

As modern neurology and the role of the brain became more of a focus
in mental illness, a number of treatments were developed. Unfortunately,
it was easy to apply these indiscriminately to persons with mental illness
who often had no voice of their own. Shock therapy was introduced in the
1930s, first by using the herb camphor, and then the stimulant medication
cardiozol. By the 1940s, electroshock therapy (ECT) began to be applied
using an electric current. It became a widespread means of treatment especially within the state hospitals. Producing a shock or convulsion to the

brain is believed to help decrease the symptoms of major depression. However, it was also responsible for significant memory loss in some patients.

In order to help decrease the side effects of shock treatment, the procedure began to be implemented differently, with physicians opting to use unilateral brain stimulation as compared with the prior bilateral. Further, the patient began to be placed under anesthesia to help alleviate some of the fear and physical impact on the body. British historical records also document the widespread application of insulin to produce shock. It was used across mental hospitals to treat schizophrenia. It should be noted that ECT continues to be used as an acceptable medical intervention for some individuals; however, there are multiple controls in place including informed consent.

Additionally, during the 1940s–1950s, lobotomies were conducted on approximately 50,000 persons in the United States. In this procedure, nerves in the frontal lobe of the brain were severed, as this was believed to help the person become calm and alleviate other mental health symptoms. According to a report from the National Public Radio, the psychiatrist who performed the majority of lobotomies, Dr. Walter Freeman, became well known as a "showman" in wielding one or, at times, two ice picks that were inserted into the brain through the orbital socket.

One of Dr. Freeman's patients was the sister of President John F. Kennedy, who, post-lobotomy, was even less able to adequately care for herself. President Kennedy's personal experience with his sister—a person with mental health concerns, undoubtedly was an impetus in his championing of the Community Mental Health Centers (CMHC) Act in 1963. Lobotomies were used to treat several conditions including schizophrenia, severe anxiety and depression, panic disorders, and chronic pain. They were outlawed in the United States by 1970. It should be noted that lobotomies were also used in Europe.

Clearly, many of these physical treatments were being tested, and persons who were confined to asylums and hospitals constituted a ready supply of research subjects, especially as there were little to no controls around research activities at that time. This population was thus subjected to significant medical/psychiatric abuse and discrimination with the use of physical treatments and medications, as will be next discussed.

THE MEDICATION MANAGEMENT MOVEMENT

The search for medications to alleviate pain and suffering, as well as to improve mood, has been occurring since time immemorial. By the late 1700s, considerable progress had been made. Some of the standard medications in Europe and the United States included calomel or mercury chloride, usually used as a purgative, as well as opium and its derivative—laudanum, a mixture of opium and alcohol. These were widely prescribed for a variety of ailments, and they were also administered to persons with mental illness to effect cures. For instance, during Dr. Benjamin Rush's administration of the Pennsylvania Hospital from 1783, he documented the use of these medications to treat persons with mental illness. Also, in the latter half of the 18th century, the British Association of Medical Officers of Asylums and Hospitals for the Insane regularly reviewed in their annual meetings various ways in which opium and other medications were tried as interventions for persons with mental illness.

By the close of the 1800s, other medications such as chloral hydrate were being reported. Dr. Jesse Bancroft, the superintendent of the New Hampshire Asylum for the Insane indicated that he found this invaluable in addressing insomnia among hospitalized patients. In New York, Dr. William Hammond, the former surgeon general of the U.S. Army, was also experimenting with lithium to treat mania.

Morphine and opium, however, remained the staples in a variety of patented forms and continued to be used to address some of the symptoms of mental illness. Additionally, it was discovered that persons who developed mood and personality changes related to neurosyphilis, a complication of syphilis, could be cured if they were infected with malaria. By 1944, penicillin was noted to be equally effective for this condition.

But the outcomes of these interventions remained variable. And many of the hundreds of persons with mental illness who entered through the gates of the state mental hospitals were known to never leave. It was of little wonder then that physicians were eager for new therapies that could offer better outcomes. By the early 1900s, psychiatry was an established field and had introduced medications and talk therapies as forms of treatment. For example, Sigmund Freud and his followers had pioneered the psychoanalytic framework. Competing schools of thought soon emerged that were heavily influenced by the field of psychology. Individuals such as John Watson stimulated interest in treating persons through trying to modify their behavior or using a behaviorist perspective, while Abraham Maslow, Carl Rogers, and others focused on a positive or humanistic view.

By the 1950s, physicians were thus largely relying on what could be considered the newer interventions for mental illness—physical treatments such as ECT and lobotomies, behavior modification, and medication. Collaborative arrangements began to spring up between the universities and hospitals such as at the Psychiatric Institute in New York and the State Psychopathic Hospital in Michigan. These relationships presented ideal conditions for the trial of a new wave of medications that were about to be released—the antipsychotics.

The NIMH indicates that the typical or conventional antipsychotics have been available since the 1950s. Thorazine was one of the first. Its sedative properties were discovered as an adjunct to anesthesia by a French surgeon in 1952. PBS reports noted that it was also observed to successfully address agitation and improve lucidity and focus in persons with severe symptoms of schizophrenia. The pharmaceutical company, SmithKline, recognizing its potential, marketed the drug to the state governments as a cost-cutting mechanism.

Grappling with overcrowded state hospitals and rising costs, several states agreed to experimental trials. And the use of Thorazine was off to a galloping start! Two years later, it was approved by the Food and Drug Administration (FDA). Other typical antipsychotics including Haldol, which was synthesized around 1958 in Belgium and was approved by the FDA about a decade later, as well as Prolixin were also found to be effective in managing major psychotic symptoms. Lithium, approved in 1970, was also found to be effective for persons with bipolar disorders.

But the availability of these medications also unleashed a wave of discriminatory practices against persons with mental illness. One of the primary concerns was that these medications were being given to persons with mental illness more often than not without their consent. Given that these were new medications, and this was the first time they were first being tried on a wide scale, inexperienced and overly zealous physicians were likely to overprescribe them. Moreover, they were not always sure of what were minimum versus maximum effective dosages. Further, in an attempt to test the efficacy of various dosages, higher levels of medication than what was required were prescribed for some patients. Thus, individuals with mental illness were in essence being used as guinea pigs. This placed them at risk for developing uncomfortable side effects, which could include tardive dyskinesia, loss of balance, stiffness and weakness in the extremities—arms and legs—seizures, and vision problems.

Another insidious discriminatory practice was the deliberate use of medication as a form of control. Given that some patients were seen as difficult to manage, high medication dosages could be prescribed and administered to them as a form of behavior control. Many patients, depending on their functional capacity, were not able to adequately advocate for themselves. And even as the right to refuse medication became more widely accepted as a medical practice, this was still largely ignored for persons diagnosed with mental illness, many of whom did not have relatives or friends who were actively participating in their care. Even for those who did, their collaterals often did not have the information needed to challenge what was, in fact, medical orders. Social attitudes toward the medical establishment and the high esteem in which fellow citizens have held physicians also militated against family members, friends, and other advocates challenging the orders given by medical professionals.

Notwithstanding these discriminatory practices and abuses, medication per se has been very helpful for persons with mental illness and has opened up a new world for many. As a backlash arose against institutionalization and some of the negative practices, this allowed progress to be made with regard to establishing informed consent as a right and in placing additional checks and balances into medication management. Overall, the medication management movement has been very advantageous to help persons with mental illness to stabilize. Additionally, working in conjunction with public health initiatives, the pharmaceutical companies have focused on the research and development of newer atypical antipsychotics. Medications such as Risperdal (risperidone) and Zyprexa (olanzapine) that were introduced in the 1990s, comparatively speaking, carry lower side effects than the older typical antipsychotics. Expanding the available repertoire of medication choices for persons with mental illness, together with adequate controls to prevent abuse, has therefore helped to decrease discrimination against persons with mental illness.

APPROACHING MENTAL ILLNESS AS PUBLIC HEALTH

In Chapters 1 and 2, we respectively examined some of the early efforts that were made to document the scope of mental illness and some of the more enlightened beliefs about mental illness and the focus on empiricism that arose during the Age of Reason. By the second half of the 17th century, private individuals as well as the legislatures of states and towns across the United States had begun to contribute funds toward establishing hospitals and asylums such as the Pennsylvania Hospital, to address the growing concerns of mental illness within the community. This identification of the problem of mental illness, and the development and application of interventions such as physical treatments and medication management to address it on a broad scale, is consistent with a public health approach. These were therefore instrumental in laying the groundwork for the current public health approach to treating mental illness.

What Is the Public Health Approach, and How Does It Relate to the Mentally Ill?

But what is the public health approach? It can be described as a holistic framework for addressing large-scale health problems, which aims to reduce, eliminate, and/or prevent a particular disease or health condition from occurring in the population at large. By the beginning of the 20th century, to effect this, proponents of the public health approach had used an interaction model of disease causation to help understand and address the factors that contribute to health problems. Based on this model, mental illness can be conceptualized, from a basic perspective, as occurring because of the interaction among the agent, the host, and the environment.

The host is the individual who, for instance, might be biologically, psychologically, and socially vulnerable to symptoms of depression. The agent could be any bio-psycho-social factor such as a recent pregnancy, or medical illness, or other life stressor that the person perceives as significant. The environment would be all the other factors that make up the person's world such as their economic and employment status (educational background, type of employment, whether he or she is living in poverty); housing (whether there is homelessness or another inadequate housing situation); social and interpersonal functioning (whether there are supportive family members or friends, or whether there are other individuals that the person has to care for such as children or older relatives).

The presence of depression and the severity of the symptoms that are experienced would therefore be related to the interplay or interaction between and among the vulnerable person or host, the agent or stressors, and the environment or circumstances in which the person finds himself or herself. If we were talking about an infectious disease such as HIV/AIDS, a route of transmission would also be needed. However, in the context of mental health, the individual's emotional and psychological health could be directly affected based on how he or she is experiencing a particular stressor. Stressors, however, do not occur in isolation, so they are related to the person's functioning within his or her environment.

Some of the causal factors of poor versus positive mental health can thus be evaluated from an interactional perspective. With an understanding of the etiology, public health principles can then be applied to reduce, eliminate, or prevent incidences of poor mental health functioning. In its Global Campaign for Violence Prevention, WHO (2015) identifies four application steps—(1) surveillance/data collection to identify the problem, (2) assessing risk and protective factors to identify causes, (3) implementing and evaluating cost-effectiveness of policies/programs to find out what works, and (4) matching and evaluating specific interventions and populations to identify what works and for whom. Tracing the emergence of the public health approach to mental illness in the United States can help to identify how it affected discrimination against persons with mental health disorders.

How the Public Health Approach Affects Discrimination

Dr. Thomas Kirkbride was correct that providing care to those with mental illness would reap benefits to society as a whole. However, despite his successful advocacy for and the construction of several large, well-constructed, and well-appointed facilities to treat persons with mental illness, by the close of the 1800s, the increase in the numbers of persons needing mental health care had again overwhelmed the system. Many of the early hospitals and asylums that were meant to serve about 300 persons were now expected to treat two to three times that amount at any given instant. This encouraged a return to the use of the basic hospital-type architectural style and, in some ways, ushered in the era of the large state mental hospitals that ended up serving thousands of persons at a time.

Less than a half century before, in the 1850s, many had believed that persons with mental illness could not even feel the coldness of winter or did not need shade from the intensity of the sun during summer. Developments in the medical field in psychiatry, neurology, psychology, and others, however, led to a more widespread acceptance of mental illness, by professionals, as having at least a biological and psychological basis. Most importantly, this now widespread view reinforced that persons with mental illness could be treated using science and that some percentage of individuals could return to stable functioning in their communities.

Perhaps the most visible signs of this change in how we viewed those with mental illness were reflected in where they were now being housed and/or treated, and the language used to describe these facilities. Thus, we had gone from consigning them to the almshouses, poorhouses, workhouses, and jails, to what was considered the most effective treatment of the time in the asylums and sanitaria, then to the less pejorative and more health-oriented hospitals. The promulgation of this more medical approach bode well from a public health perspective. It helped to decrease discriminatory attitudes by allowing persons with mental illness to be viewed, from a more balanced position, as individuals needing and being able to benefit from medical treatment.

Historical documents use the terms "asylums," "sanitaria," and "hospitals" interchangeably to describe facilities serving persons with mental illness. However, by the advent of the early 1900s, many former asylums were being deliberately renamed. For example, the New Hampshire Asylum for the Insane that was opened in 1842, and the Topeka Insane Asylum that was opened in Kansas in 1879, became the New Hampshire State Hospital and the Topeka State Hospital respectively in 1901.

But despite the transitioning toward a public health framework, problems remained, and a change in name did not always correlate with better care for persons with mental illness. Private and state funds could not keep abreast of the costs of maintaining many of these facilities, especially as their population grew into thousands. Overcrowding, inadequate mental health care, physical neglect, emotional and sexual abuse, and other abusive situations, which had never been fully eradicated, returned to bedevil the system.

It should be remembered that the federal government, under President Pierce, had declined to assume direct responsibility for funding or providing other resources for the care of those with mental illness across the United States. However, Dorothea Dix's advocacy did result in an asylum—the Government Hospital for the Insane—being established in 1855, with funds appropriated by congress, so that servicemen from the army, navy, and District of Columbia (DC) could be treated. It was renamed St. Elizabeth's Hospital in 1916, and by 1987, administrative oversight was transferred to the District of Columbia's Department of Mental Health.

The only other facility that was federally financed through a congressional bill in 1898 was the Hiawatha Insane Asylum (also called the Canton Asylum for Insane Indians). Opened from 1903 to 1935, in South Dakota, records indicate that there were few instances of mental illness among the more than 350 indigenous persons who were admitted to this institution. Many were literally incarcerated there from all over the country as retribution for defying the mainstream/nonindigenous status quo. Some were as young as six years old. None were provided with adequate medical or humane care. All, however, experienced horrific conditions that reportedly included physical restraints, sleeping in their own body wastes, and verbal/psychological abuse. In fact, it was complaints from the staff that eventually led to external investigations and the closing of this facility. The ugly head of discrimination had again reared its head and affected a group of persons who were already marginalized in the American society. One cannot help but wonder how many persons who needed mental health care could have been better served with these scarce resources.

Meanwhile, states were seeking mechanisms to care for the growing numbers of persons with mental illness, especially as some of the local almshouses and poorhouses that still existed continued to act as receptacles for indigent persons with mental illness. Social conditions that were affected by World Wars I and II (1914–1918 and 1939–1945), including the large numbers of returning veterans who were affected by mental illness; the series of mini-financial crises that led up to the Great Depression, as well as the Great Depression itself in 1929; and the stresses engendered by both voluntary and involuntary immigration undoubtedly played a role in the increased incidence of mental illness in the first half of the 20th century.

Mindful that they could not ignore the growing scope of mental illness, state governments, in some instances, used collaborative agreements with private facilities. These latter often had more experience in addressing social problems and were better able to provide mental health services with the use of private and public funds and some level of public oversight. In others, the states assumed responsibility for expanding the infrastructure and funded the construction of additional large hospitals. In doing so, however, they attempted to adhere to the philosophical and practical approaches learned during the last half of the 1800s, which took into account what was considered to be the public good. This encouraged the siting of institutions, many of which were now built in the cottage-style formation, in rural-type areas that would allow for fresh air, use of the outdoors, and rehabilitative involvement in a variety of activities. Chief among these was farming, which allowed some of the facilities to become self-sufficient in food. Because of this, some of these hospitals were referred to as "colonies" or "farm colonies." Other chores such as laundering and cooking also assured that some of the facilities became fully self-contained.

In Philadelphia, for example, the Byberry City Farms that housed persons with mental illness later became the site of the Philadelphia Hospital for Mental Diseases. New York State also established several large farm colonies, including the Kings Park State Hospital (Kings County Asylum), Creedmor Hospital, the Staten Island Farm Colony, and Pilgrim Hospital in Long Island, which once housed as many as 15,000 persons and was known as the largest institution for those with mental illness in the world. Unfortunately, even with the best rehabilitative intent, the system was ripe for abuses. Many persons with mental illness worked long and hard hours; however, they were not able to enjoy any pecuniary benefits from their labor. In fact, despite their productivity and valuable contributions, the discriminatory practice of wage theft, in this case a total denial of monetary payment, was widely implemented for many years.

One of the fundamental problems that persisted for the state hospitals was what to do with persons with serious and persistent mental illness (SPMI), especially given considerations such as public safety. Despite the establishment of new sites and the expansion of older ones, chronic overcrowding remained an issue. The fortunes of those with intellectual challenges, alcohol and other drug problems, and mental illness were still invariably intertwined. Moreover, as persons became older and more fragile, and/or had stabilized on medications, or had less serious mental health conditions, was it discriminatory to continue to hold them within an inpatient setting for the rest of their lives?

Deinstitutionalization and Community Mental Health Centers

A public health approach had contributed to the expansion of the large institutions to care for persons with mental illness. Now this began to be questioned especially in the light of some of the long-term abuses as well as the growing movement to obtain and ensure that the rights of persons with disabilities were being respected. Deinstitutionalization can be defined as the movement to house and treat persons with mental illness and intellectual disabilities in the community rather than in institutions. Some historians date it from 1955 through the 1970s due to its connection to the changes engendered by newly prescribed medications. Others indicate that it began in 1963 as a consequence of legislation passed by President Kennedy. As early as 1946, however, conscientious objectors of World War II, who were employed as attendants in the psychiatric facilities, established the National Mental Health Foundation. They began exposing abusive conditions and were one of the early groups agitating for persons with mental illness to be removed to more humane settings in the community.

Regardless of the date, several critical pieces of legislation passed by the U.S. congress furthered a public health approach to treating mental illness. First, in 1946, advocacy from veterans and clinicians resulted in the passage of the National Mental Health Act during President Harry S. Truman's administration. This authorized funding for the establishment of the National Institute of Mental Health (NIMH) to coordinate research, training, and funding related to the etiology and treatment of psychiatric disorders across all states. Additionally, it instituted the National Mental Health Advisory Council to provide input into public policy on an ongoing basis. The NIMH was subsumed into the SAMHSA in 1992.

A second piece of legislation that was passed in 1946—the Hospital Survey and Construction Act, which is also known as the Hill–Burton Act—additionally played a major role going forward in both prevention and intervention. Coming out of the advocacy for people with disabilities, the Hill–Burton Act authorized federal funds to help build hospitals, public health centers, and health facilities that would focus on their rehabilitation.

Third, the Mental Health Study Act was passed in 1955. Additionally to "improving and expanding programs of mental health and public health," it also sought to provide for "an objective, thorough, and nationwide analysis and reevaluation of the human and economic problems of mental illness." Its report was published in 1961, from the Joint Commission on Mental Illness and Health, which examined the issues. According to the National Institutes of Health (NIH), it recommended "a national program," including the development of health facilities and expansion of full-time CMHC, with provision for long-term supports that would help meet "the individual needs of the mentally ill people of America."

Fourth, as a response to the committee's findings, President John F. Kennedy's administration, in 1963, passed the Mental Retardation Facilities and Community Mental Health Centers Construction Act, also known as the Community Mental Health Act. Like its predecessor, it supported the federal government's involvement in mental health policy. Further, as reported by the NIH, it authorized funds for construction and staff, and stipulated that CMHC were to provide:

> services for the prevention or diagnosis of mental illness, or care and treatment of mentally ill patients, or rehabilitation of such persons, which services are provided principally for persons residing in a particular community or communities in or near which the facility is situated.
> (Public Law 88–164, Section 401)

As indicated previously, only two asylums were federally funded during the period of rapid growth of these institutions, from the 18th to 19th centuries. These legislative initiatives thus concretized a less discriminatory approach in the provision of both housing and treatment services to those with mental illness. Moreover, dedicating federal funds to establish institutions that were more than research and training, which could house and treat persons with mental illness, reversed more than a century's worth of government's hands-off policy and signaled a national public health approach to dealing with mental illness.

But these pieces of legislation were grounded within a wider social context. Thus, this now decentralized approach to dealing with persons with mental illness was the confluence of several factors that had created a favorable environment. Among these were the persistent overcrowding of the state mental health hospitals; the medication management movement that discovered new psychotropic medications such as Thorazine, which could be used without the invasiveness of physical methods such as shock therapy; the states' desire to reduce the costs of treating mental illness; and the ongoing advocacy that encouraged increased acceptance of the rights of persons with mental illness.

Persistent Overcrowding

As previously indicated, there were many reasons for the chronic overcrowding in the state mental hospitals in the initial half of the 1900s. By the 1950s, despite the expansion of facilities, a solution to this problem had not yet been found. The PBS reported that while 2 Americans per 1,000 were in mental hospitals in 1904, by 1955, this had increased 100% to 4 per 1,000. Congressional records clarify that 557,000 individuals were enrolled in the state mental health hospitals by 1955. The number of institutionalized individuals with mental illness was, however, higher as patients were also being hospitalized in the wards of general hospitals. Some continued to reside in poorhouses, and in the case of children, in orphanages and reform schools.

Therefore, the large numbers of persons within the state institutions contributed to overwhelming conditions for both staff and patients, and the quality of psychiatric care was once more questioned. Advocates for persons with mental illness began agitating about the warehousing of the mentally ill, sometimes in facilities that were far removed from their communities of origin. Concerns were also expressed that some hospitals, especially those that were affiliated with teaching hospitals, were using persons with mental illness as guinea pigs.

The Costs of Treating Mental Illness

By the 1970s, Thorazine (chlorpromazine), Haldol (haloperidol), Prolixin (fluphenazine), and the anticonvulsant drug lithium that was also used to treat bipolar disorder were extensively prescribed for persons with mental illness. Despite major side effects such as tardive dyskinesia—sudden uncontrolled muscular and facial movements—these new drug regimens were lauded as being effective for a wide cross section of persons with mental illness.

Once these medications had demonstrated some level of success, the floodgates were opened. Specifically, by the mid-1950s, efforts to discharge persons who appeared to be stable began across facilities. By 1963, with the CMHC Act, the states embraced the opportunity to relieve themselves of the high cost of care by pushing persons with mental illness back into their communities. From approximately 1969 through 1977, funding for these legislative initiatives was not renewed; however, demonstration projects that were in effect sought to apply evidence-based practices to the community model of mental health care. Unfortunately, it was often easier for these to treat persons with less serious mental illness, or who were already in the community, while persons with chronic issues remained institutionalized.

The National Mental Health Systems Act of 1980, which was meant to re-prioritize funding and the initiatives for persons with SPMI, never came to fruition. Signed by President Jimmy Carter, it was repealed by President Ronald Reagan less than a year later.

PBS reports indicate that deinstitutionalization rates ranged from less than 80% in places such as the District of Columbia and Delaware, to more than 95% in Rhode Island and California. Consistent across states, however, was that little or no follow-up provisions had been made for many individuals who had experienced chronic mental illness for decades. Consequently, the deinstitutionalization process was set for failure from the onset. For a brief time, available funding allowed some innovative community developments. But court decisions such as *Wyatt v. Stickney* (1971) in the state of Alabama influenced policy all over the United States, as the court ruled that residents of institutions needed to be placed in a least restrictive environment—any place other than the state hospital.

Congressional Deinstitutionalization Hearings held in November 1981 concluded that the process had not worked as intended. All across the United States, rates of homelessness had increased. In large states such as New York and California, this was glaring as former institutionalized patients could be observed living on the streets. Meanwhile, admissions to other types of facilities such as public general hospitals, nursing homes, and even prisons had increased. It did not help that some persons had co-occurring disorders and little adaptive daily living skills.

The last straw, perhaps, was the elimination of direct federal funding for the community mental health initiatives during President Reagan's administration, including the dismantling of NIMH's decentralized supervision. This led to widespread fissures in the already fragile infrastructure that had been put into place to provide limited services to persons with mental illness. Almost overnight, some local agencies were affected with diminished resources, lack of staff, and, in many instances, closure.

It was ironic that concerted advocacy of Dorothea Dix and so many others had helped to create a system of institutionalized care to address extensive discrimination in where and how persons with mental illness were housed and to guarantee them the right to get their basic needs met. Now, that same advocacy had in some ways gone awry.

While it was potentially laudable to have persons with mental illness move back into their communities and be in the bosom of families and friends, inadequate resources, poor planning, lack of will from state and local administrators, limited understanding and/or involvement from family members, and the federal government's reneging on fiscal and practical supports did not allow the needed structures to be created. In fact, the political controversy surrounding deinstitutionalization set the stage for it to become a hotbed of discrimination—a tangible indicator of how the welfare and well-being of persons with mental illness has been trampled in the 20th century.

The United Kingdom and Other Developed Nations

In the United Kingdom, one might recall that the passage of the Lunacy Act (1890) had severely restricted the opening of new asylums for persons with mental illness. The Old Age Pensions Act of 1908 for the first time allowed the elderly, 70-year-olds or more, to receive a stipend that could help them have an independent source of income, whether or not they had a history of mental illness. This was clearly a benefit to persons with mental illness whose work life had been affected and who could now depend on this as a means of subsistence.

By 1911, the lessons learned from the ad hoc system of health care occasioned by the British Poor Laws helped to pass the National Insurance Act. This was limited only to those persons who were paying into the plan and were thus insured. For those with mental illness who were incapacitated and unable to work, this was thus discriminatory. By 1919, however, this was corrected in the Ministry of Health Act, which for the first time included prevention and specified that physical and mental defects were to be treated. One year later, there were further enhancements for the care of persons with mental illness as the Ministry of Health assumed all of the prior responsibilities of the Lunacy Acts.

Like the United States, the United Kingdom with their large asylums also moved toward a more health-oriented system. By the passage of the National Health Service Act in 1946, the mental health institutions were integrated under its umbrella, and services for persons with mental health issues became part of the responsibility of the public health service. For example, the Buckinghamshire County Asylum that was established in 1853 was converted to the Bucks Mental Hospital in 1919. Later, in 1948, it was transferred to the jurisdiction of the National Health Service and was renamed the St. John's Hospital. Integrating care for the mentally ill into the regular health care system can thus assist in decreasing stigma and ensuring access.

Therefore, as advocates for those with mental illness continue to work internationally toward improving their care, in the United Kingdom and other more developed nations, they seem to have been spared much of the chaos that have occurred within the U.S. system. But the deinstitutionalization march is not yet fully over. There is still a need to determine what is the right balance of institutional versus community-based care for persons with mental illness, whether it is in the United States, United Kingdom, or other areas around the globe. Tangible evidence of the public health approach can be found in WHO's adoption of its 2013–2020 Comprehensive Mental Health Action Plan, which integrates leadership, responsiveness, and evidence-based promotion and prevention for optimal mental health outcomes internationally, "including a central role for . . . community-based care."

APPROACHING MENTAL ILLNESS AS A DISABILITY
What Is the Disability Movement?

As part of its legal definition of disability, the American with Disabilities Act (ADA) indicates that it is an impairment that substantially limits one or more major life activity. This can be due to any aspect of an individual's physical, intellectual, psychological/emotional, sensory, or social functioning. Today, we take it for granted that mental illness can significantly affect a person's daily functioning, especially as it relates to their behavioral and social status. This was not always the case. A large debt is owed to the disability movement in bringing this to the forefront.

But what is the disability movement? This is regarded as a social movement within the United States, which was led by both persons with disabilities and their advocates—parents, brothers, sisters, friends, attorneys, human services workers. Social scientists are divided on when exactly did the disability movement start and with whom. While some credit Dorothea Dix's unflagging focus and energy, we could look at a broad swath of persons including Benjamin Rush and Thomas Kirkbride and their contributions that laid a solid foundation for the field. Others date the start of the movement with the establishment of the first educational facility in 1817, to cater to people with disabilities—the Connecticut Asylum for the Education and Instruction of Deaf and Dumb Persons. Another suggested starting point for the movement has been when persons with disabilities became the primary advocates for themselves through the formation of a variety of issue groups to address concerns of the visual, hearing, intellectually challenged, and others.

The Connection between the Disability Movement and Mental Health Advocacy

While it is difficult to determine a formal initiation of the disability movement, advocacy for persons with disabilities, be they physical, mental/emotional, or intellectual, has followed similar trajectories. In some cases, they were one and the same. An indication of this is reflected in the written communication of the 18th and 19th centuries that juxtaposed terms such as "idiots and insanes" and "lunatics and imbeciles" to refer to persons with mental illness or who had intellectual challenges. These could even be found in legal language of the time. The U.S. Immigration Act of 1882, for instance, stipulated the exclusion of "lunatic(s), idiot(s), or any person unable to take care of himself or herself without becoming a public charge." Precedents set for the treatment of the worthy versus unworthy poor by the way the early British Poor Laws defined these groups also bound together persons with psychological, physical, and intellectual disabilities.

More recent 20th-century developments have strengthened the connection across groups of persons with different types of disabilities. This was partly occasioned by World Wars I and II, which increased the numbers of individuals in the society experiencing physical difficulties secondary to their service including traumatic brain injury (TBI), as well as psychological problems related to PTSD and other mental health conditions. The intersection of physical and mental disabilities also served to push the movement forward. In conjunction with other interested parties, groups of persons with disabilities formed to publicly advocate for themselves—the Disabled American Vets in 1920, the League of the Physically Handicapped in 1935, the National Federation for the Blind in 1940, the National Mental Health Foundation in 1946, the National Association for Retarded Children/Citizens in 1950, Disabled in Action in 1970, and many others. Thus, the advances made or lessons learned by one contributed to strengthening the movement and carrying it forward for all groups, invariably intertwining the disability movement and mental health advocacy.

How Attitudes toward Disability Affect the Mentally Ill

The 20th century was full of advocacy for disability issues. Advocates and persons with disabilities themselves used multiple tactics to be heard, some of which were borrowed from the Civil Rights and Women's Movements. These included card, letter writing and public speaking campaigns in the media, large-scale protest demonstrations, the occupation of buildings, blocking of traffic, and the now famous or infamous Capitol Crawl. The latter occurred on March 13, 1990, when hundreds of persons with disabilities, many of whom were in wheelchairs, conducted a rally in front of the Capitol building to protest delays in Congress's passing the Americans with Disabilities Act (ADA). At the completion of the rally, members of Congress were taken by surprise when many persons with mobility impairments began to climb, crawl, and ambulate up the 100 steps of the Capitol building to the best of their ability.

As the public at large became familiar with the plight of various groups of individuals with disabilities through these and other strategies, corresponding shifts in thinking and attitudes were inevitable. How could one not empathize with a person who had lost their limbs fighting for his country and was now bedeviled with the flashbacks and trauma of the battlefield? What about persons who were born with intellectual disabilities and/or behavioral disorders who were being denied any chance of education or training to make their lives meaningful? Who would not be affected when they viewed through firsthand accounts and later pictures of the conditions of persons within the large mental health institutions?

By the middle of the 20th century, social attitudes toward persons with disabilities including mental illness had become more favorable, with a corresponding belief that the barriers they faced to daily living needed to be ameliorated if not fully eliminated. The disability movement had clearly made significant gains including in obtaining legislation to address the needs of various groups of persons with disabilities. For example, Vocational Rehabilitation Acts were passed by Congress in 1918 and 1920, to address the needs of disabled veterans and civilians, respectively. The passage of the Social Security Act in 1935, authorized benefits to persons who were blind and children with disabilities, as well as reinforced the Vocational Rehabilitation Acts. By the passage of the Rehabilitation Act of 1973, the precursor to the ADA in 1990, the federal government unequivocally prohibited discrimination based on disability, including mental impairments, in entities run by or contracted by the federal government or receiving federal financial assistance.

President George Herbert Walker Bush's signing into law of the ADA on July 26, 1990, represented how far the United States had come in terms of its attitudes toward persons with disabilities. While this law was opposed by many in the business community and in some evangelical religious circles due to concerns over cost and undue intrusion respectively, according to the U.S. Department of Justice (DOJ) Civil Rights Division, it prohibited "discrimination on the basis of disability in employment, State and local government, public accommodations, commercial facilities, transportation, and telecommunications." The U.S. Equal Employment Opportunity Commission (EEOC) became the designated federal entity to ensure employer compliance with the 1990 ADA law, as well as additional amendments made in 2008. As reported on their website, the ADA Amendments Act of 2008 was signed into law by President George Walker Bush. This extended the definition of what is a disability and further clarified the intent of the law to provide "a clear and comprehensive national mandate for the elimination of discrimination."

As stated in the ADA Amendments Act, a disability can affect major life activities such as " . . . concentrating, thinking, communicating, and working," as well as major bodily neurological and brain functions. Further, this impairment might be "episodic or in remission" but "would substantially limit a major life activity when active." Many persons diagnosed with mental illness can be represented even if we look only at these partial phrases within the legal definition. Thus, approaching mental illness from a disability perspective, and the inclusion of persons diagnosed with mental illness as one of the groups of individuals with disabilities who require protection, has gone a long way in helping to address discrimination.

APPROACHING MENTAL ILLNESS AS A BEHAVIORAL HEALTH ISSUE

In Chapter 2, we reviewed some of the causes of mental illness that had emerged by the 19th century. One might recall that some of the early literature on mental illness referenced alcoholism either as a cause of or as synonymous with mental illness. Dr. Benjamin Rush, for instance, hypothesized that the outcome of chronic untreated alcoholism would be mental illness and reported that about one-third of the cases of mental illness at the Pennsylvania Hospital were due to alcoholism. Historically, then, some percentage of the persons initially with alcohol, then with opium and cocaine habits, were admitted into the insane asylums and other facilities catering to persons with mental illness. It is likely that private paying facilities were more willing to admit persons with alcohol and drug disorders, especially as, similarly as today, helping these individuals to stabilize could be fraught with challenges.

By the 1850s, however, we see competing schools of thought emerging with regard to the etiology of alcohol and other drugs. And morality as a cause was still championed by many versus a more medically oriented paradigm. By the mid-1850s, advocacy for treating those with alcohol and other drug problems resulted in the establishment of what came to be a system of care for addiction. According to White (1998), these included inebriate homes and asylums, as well as proprietary hospitals, sanitaria, and institutes. Further, those seeking to make a profit outside of these facilities concocted various home remedies or mass-produced medications that were widely sold through mail. Unfortunately, there were no controls in place to ensure that medications met any standards or did what they were advertised as doing, until 1906 and the passage of the Pure Food and Drug Act.

Unfortunately, even when administering opiate medications to persons who had developed dependency on opium, morphine, and similar medications made sense, social attitudes of the time militated against serving these individuals. As a result, legislation such as the Harrison Narcotic Tax

Act of 1914, which was meant to tax the buying, selling, and transporting of opium and other narcotics (including cocaine), led to the criminalization of several medical professionals. Some of these prescribed morphine or other opiates to their patients, many of whom were women who had developed what we would now call an opiate use disorder. Under the act, however, addicts were not patients. Thus, several physicians who continued to treat their patients were arrested and incarcerated. Incarceration also became one of the primary mechanisms during the 1900s for dealing with persons with substance use disorders, including with the passage of restrictive legislation such as the California Civil Commitment Act of 1961 (which, in 1962, the Supreme Court found was cruel and unusual punishment to incarcerate or to commit a person solely because of their addiction) and the NYS Rockefeller Drug Laws.

It was not until 1956 that the American Medical Association recognized addiction as a disease. And it was not until the early 1960s that the opioid agonist medication, methadone, was pioneered by Dr. Vincent Dole and his wife, Dr. Marie Nyswander, as a viable treatment for opioid addiction. Consequently, during the administration of President Richard Nixon (1969–1974), federal authorization was provided for the setting up of clinics, especially within the inner cities to address the extensive opioid dependency problem, among whom veterans of both the South East Asia and the Vietnam Wars were overrepresented.

The field of alcohol and drug addiction treatment thus showed tremendous growth from the 19th through the 20th centuries. Failed prohibition laws including for alcohol (1919–1933) and marijuana (1937) highlighted that this was an ineffective solution to prevent individuals from experimenting with and/or using alcohol or drugs recreationally and potentially becoming vulnerable to addiction from one or more drugs. Although alcohol prohibition led to the closing of many of the facilities that had been established to treat alcoholism, a corresponding inpatient (or hospital-based), residential, outpatient, and medication-assisted system of care arose to serve persons with alcohol and other drug disorders.

But this system of care had two primary characteristics. First, it distinguished between persons with alcohol use disorders and those with other drug use disorders. Thus, two separate systems of care emerged to serve individuals with either disorder. What happened to persons who were exhibiting symptoms of both an alcohol use and another substance use disorder? Second, the alcohol and drug use programs were often not equipped to provide effective interventions for persons with mental health issues. Thus, these individuals were often selected out at the point of admission.

It should also be remembered that the system of care for alcohol and drug users was existing in the same environment with the extensive institutional-based system that had developed to treat mental illness. During much of the 19th and early 20th centuries, persons with alcohol and drug disorders had sought care within the asylums. By the mid-1950s, overcrowding and other pressures in the asylums, which were moving toward deinstitution-alization, led to greater discrimination in the criteria for admitting persons into psychiatric care. Further, by the time the CMHC began to be set up in the late 1960s through the 1970s, there was already a great deal of compe-tition for services. Thus, persons who appeared to have primarily alcohol or drug use disorders were routed to those type of programs.

Given that the severity of mental health disorders can vary and that symptoms cannot always be readily discerned, many persons who needed mental health care were redirected. Similarly, persons who needed to be treated for coexisting alcohol and drug use disorders often did not receive appropriate care. By the close of the 20th century, it was clear that there were structural problems within the alcohol, other drugs, and mental health treatment systems. Some clinicians have referred to them as silos that pro-moted little collaborative or holistic care, especially since they were also restricted by funding streams. The result of this divergence was that per-sons with mental illness and substance use disorders were almost guar-anteed to be discriminated against in one or more of the systems. Service gaps, lack of adequately cross-trained clinicians, lack of needed specialists such as psychiatrists within the substance use settings, and addiction spe-cialists within the mental health all contributed to less than optimal care, especially for persons who were diagnosed with more than one disorder.

What Is Behavioral Health?

To address some of the concerns noted in the existing systems of care for persons with mental illness, alcohol use, and/or other substance use disorders, the concept of behavioral health care began to be promulgated. This refers to an integrated system of care in which a person's primary health care needs can be addressed, within the same setting as their men-tal health and/or substance use disorder needs. By combining all aspects of the person's medical needs, the health care provider/s can focus on col-laborating with the individual to help him or her cultivate the health be-haviors that would produce optimal outcomes in all areas of functioning. Behavioral health thus views the person through a holistic prism that can better guide his or her individualized health care needs.

How a Behavioral Health Approach Can Affect
Treatment and Discrimination

Using a behavioral health approach can help to decrease the barriers to accessing treatment for persons with mental illness and other health conditions. Specifically, if an individual can go to one health care provider and can be screened and assessed for his or her medical, mental health, and substance use disorder needs in the same place, it significantly reduces gaps in accessing care. This can be especially helpful to persons who have difficulty with mobility and transportation. Patients should also be able to develop a more trusting therapeutic relationship with qualified providers who are sensitive to their needs. This can be a significant benefit for the person with mental illness who may be experiencing symptoms such as withdrawal and isolative behaviors.

There is also an opportunity for the provider to focus on wellness and prevention, as well as ensuring there are no gaps in service delivery. By managing all aspects of the person's care, behavioral health care also has the potential to reduce costs while improving patient satisfaction and quality of care.

Through the use of electronic health care records (EHR), all aspects of the person's care can be coordinated, including any referrals for specialized treatment. This can significantly reduce wait times for accessing critical data. Most importantly, for persons who may need to receive medication-supported treatment for substance use disorders, along with medication to maintain mental health stability, or to manage chronic health problems, having all their care coordinated especially with the use of an EHR can help to reduce health care errors due to missing information.

The adoption of a behavioral health approach to treat persons with mental illness can thus create several enhancements in their access to and receipt of health care. It can also go a long way to reduce stigma as the person can be seen as simply receiving needed health care.

CHAPTER 6

Forms of Discrimination against the Mentally Ill and the Influence of Diversity

BASIC HUMAN RIGHTS OF THE MENTALLY ILL

The Universal Declaration of Human Rights, which was adopted by the UN General Assembly in December 1948, lists 30 articles that represent the basic human rights due to each and every individual. Thus, when we refer to the rights of persons with mental illness, this provides an excellent comparative starting point. As the historical review has highlighted, for a long time, it was common practice to deny the basic human rights of those with mental disorders.

For example, Articles 3 and 5 assure the right to life, liberty, and security of person, as well as to freedom from torture, cruel, inhuman or degrading treatment, or punishment. The extent of abuses that were found within the facilities in which persons with mental illness have been housed, be it the almshouse, asylum, or state hospital, in the United States, Europe, and other localities, is well documented from the 16th through 20th centuries. There are legitimate reasons at times to temporarily restrict an individual's freedom of movement to protect the person and/or others around them. Indiscriminate application of physical restraints, however, was common. And even while restrained, persons were subjected to physical, sexual, emotional abuse, and other degrading punishments.

According to Articles 6 and 7, everyone has the right to be recognized as a person and to equal protection of the law. Persons with mental illness were treated as subhuman, and some believed they had no capacity for feeling. If you were a female who was affected by mental illness, your situation was even worse. Existing laws that deemed women were the properties of their husbands already provided legitimacy for the discrimination against women and girls. Now that you were experiencing emotional and other difficulties, you were in an even more vulnerable position. In fact, there were documented incidents of women such as Elizabeth Parsons Packard and Sophia Olsen, both of sound mind, being committed by spouses. Reforms implemented by the County Asylum Act and others in the United Kingdom helped to create some checks and balances, but these were not always sufficient to prevent discriminatory practices.

Some of the major violation of the rights of persons with mental illness could be linked to Article 12, which indicates that individuals should be free of arbitrary interference with their privacy, family, home, or correspondence. If you belonged to the category of persons who were identified as the indigent insane, Poor Law Legislation in both the United Kingdom and United States ensured that you had no way to protect yourself from interference with your privacy, family, and home.

If your family was in receipt of outdoor relief, frequent unexpected visits could be anticipated from volunteer visitors. In the early days, the primary goal of these visits was to ensure persons truly deserved to receive poor relief in their homes. Hence, they were meant to be intrusive. After 1869, these visitors were usually members of the Charity Organization Societies, whose goal was to encourage self-sufficiency. In the weekly visits from visitors who could be volunteers or paid staff, their focus was on assisting persons to learn improved life skills. Despite their positive intentions, this oversight was generated by the fact that these individuals were poor. Thus, this constituted, to some degree, arbitrary interference into their lives.

Further, Article 13 refers to the right to freedom of movement and residence. Legal restrictions, however, were placed on the families of, as well as many indigent individuals who were, mentally ill. In fact, moving from one county to another might have meant being excluded from obtaining critical resources that were needed to support themselves. Additionally, the right to freedom of residence was constrained. If you were determined to belong to the category of the unworthy poor, your only chance of receiving indoor relief was to move into a poorhouse or workhouse. The social condition of poverty was thus reason enough to disregard these rights.

Arbitrary interference with one's correspondence was also an issue for those who were institutionalized. They were already at the mercy of the superintendents and staff of the asylums and other facilities. Their rights to freedom of movement or speech were in so many cases already severely limited, and once confined, a significant percentage of persons with mental illness had little to no further contact with the outside world. But what means of communication was there if any person wanted to maintain contact with family or friends when lucid?

Letter writing, the primary means of communication of the day, was actively discouraged in some facilities. This could have been partly due to the fear that confined persons would complain to persons on the outside about the abject conditions. Letters were frequently intercepted and routinely destroyed, with retaliation being taken against some of the writers. In fact, it was only after significant advocacy that legislation was passed mandating that persons confined in these institutions still had the basic right to communicate with others on the outside through the mail.

One of these advocates was Elizabeth Parsons Packard. Denied the right, as per Article 10, to a fair and public hearing by an independent and impartial tribunal, Ms. Packard was committed to the Jacksonville Insane Asylum in Illinois by her spouse. There she spent three years, fighting to prove that she was not insane. Around 1875, a bill to approve the Postal Rights of Inmates of Insane Asylums gained traction. Shortly thereafter, it became illegal to intercept or prevent persons with mental illness from writing to individuals of their choice.

One area in which persons with mental illness have had some protection is with regard to the right to own and not be arbitrarily deprived of property (Article 17). Historical records indicate that early English Law (around 1324) identifies the monarch as the person who has the prerogative for safeguarding the estates of mentally ill persons and ensuring the person received adequate care. Hence, this was called the Statute of the King's Prerogative. As referenced previously, these persons were grouped into a special category called the chancery lunatics. Special courts and committees were appointed to ensure that their properties were appropriately managed and that they were supported from any income that was forthcoming.

Another area in which some persons with mental illness were able to engage was in the right to freedom of religion. Many private institutions were founded and/or managed with religious overtones. The involvement of the Quakers in the moral movement in the United Kingdom and the United States has already been addressed. Additionally, there were other denominations, most of whom followed other offshoots of the Christian sect.

The reformer, Dorothea Dix, was known to distribute reading materials including the Bible when she visited institutions around the country. Volunteers and paid employees from the Charity Organization Societies were encouraged to integrate a religious approach during their weekly community visits. Many of the large institutions, especially those who were self-contained, also had designated houses of worship on-site. Undoubt-edly, this allowed some persons with mental illness to participate and might have been viewed as an integral part of getting them involved in productive activities. However, for the large numbers of people who were continuously restrained in chains, locked cages, and the like, there would have been a total violation of all their basic rights, including that of freedom to worship.

It should be noted that in some localities in Europe, and on the African, Asian, and Latin American continents, published reports have indicated that persons have been committed to insane asylums for political reasons. Thus, their right to freedom of thought, conscience, and religion, including being able to practice, worship, and observe, has been severely comprised, under the guise that the person is mentally ill.

As a general practice, most nations in the developed world now prohibit the use of physical restraints except under very limited conditions. Insti-tutions that treat persons with mental illness are expected to have written protocols that specify when and how restraints or any restriction of rights will be used. Medical professionals, that is, psychiatrists or other physi-cians must be involved in treatment team decisions that anticipate the use of restraints and rights' restrictions, and are the designated persons to pro-vide such authorization.

Other members of the interdisciplinary treatment team also participate to ensure the person's safety and that other less restrictive interventions are being considered. Physical restraints and rights restrictions should only be interventions of last resort! Documentation is an integral component of any episode of use of these interventions, and this must be available to external international certification and accreditation organizations such as the Joint Commission on Accreditation of Healthcare Organizations and the Commission for the Accreditation of Rehabilitation Facilities during inspections.

Therefore, reforms conducted from the 1950s to the present, some as a result of court cases, have sought to correct the gaps in the system that has led to major abuses of the rights of persons with mental illness and to put a variety of accountability processes in place. Part of the impetus for the movement toward deinstitutionalization in the United States, and a more community-based system of care in the United Kingdom, has in fact been to address old wrongs and ensure the current rights of all persons with mental illness, be they adults or children. Any patient now receiving men-tal health treatment in the developed nations must be informed in advance of his or her rights and responsibilities, and must be engaged to the best of their abilities around their plan of care.

For example, a review of a patient informational brochure, for instance, that is produced by New York State—Rights of Inpatients in NYS Office of Mental Health (OMH) Psychiatric Centers—spells out both the civil and personal rights of the patient, and how each and/or their legal representative can seek redress for any violation. Mandatory practices to inform patients of their rights and other measures have thus assured significant progress in addressing discrimination against persons with mental illness.

How Federal and State Laws Affect the Rights of the Mentally Ill

Limits of Confidentiality and Privacy

Confidentiality can be defined as the act of keeping a patient's information secret, while privacy allows it to be kept safe. Both concepts are clearly intertwined and are currently enshrined in law with regard to persons with any type of illness including mental disorders. The practice of medicine has been associated since time immemorial with confidentiality between physician and patient, based on the Hippocratic Oath. By the 1850s, as there was greater recognition that mental illness was a disease, it would be logical to assume that the privilege between physician and patient also included persons with mental illness.

However, that has not always been the case. Perhaps, the public nature of some mental disorders, that is, the symptoms of a condition such as schizophrenia, that can sometimes be readily discerned by anyone contributed to less controls. On the other hand, the belief that persons with mental illness were oddities also influenced how they were treated. In fact, persons with mental illness were often not even offered the opportunity for privacy of their persons.

For instance, Bethlehem Insane Asylum was well known for paying customers who would walk through to gaze at persons with mental illness, many of whom were in chains and cages. Some asylum owners also permitted persons with mental illness to be displayed at fairs and carnivals. As has been previously discussed, in the United States, mentally ill persons were placed on the auction block, where they were sold for the highest bids from the public. Dorothea Dix described in her memorials how men and women were often housed, chained, and so on, together. In several instances, she reported on females who were not even provided with clothing to assure them modesty. Clearly, privacy or confidentiality was not considered a priority to be afforded to persons deemed to be insane, or their families.

It was not until the moral movement had made substantial inroads that more emphasis was placed on basic personal privacy for persons with mental illness. The physicians, Thomas Kirkbride and Jesse Bancroft, were leaders in this respect. Both integrated this into their physical plan designs and advocated for the new facilities that were being constructed to use these models.

But what about the extensive amount of personal information that was being accumulated for individuals with mental illness over the years they remained in institutions? As the courts passed legislation to license and regularize these facilities, documentation requirements increased. Published reports indicate that there was no right of privacy or confidentiality in early English and U.S. law. Thus, it is primarily within the 20th century that legal protections have been implemented to ensure confidentiality and privacy for persons with mental illness.

42 CFR, Part 2, and CFR 45, Sections 160 and 164

Currently, two federal laws provide guidance within the United States. First, the Health Insurance Portability and Accountability Act (HIPAA) was passed by congress in 1996. However, it did not become effective until April 2003 as the Final Privacy Rule (CFR 45, Sections 160 and 164) delineating the provisions that govern health/mental health care. But prior to HIPAA, another federal law has been in existence, the Code of Federal Regulations, Section 42, Part 2 (42 CFR, Part 2), the Confidentiality of Alcohol and Drug Abuse Patient Records. This law first emerged as the Narcotic Rehabilitation Act of 1966 and went through several permutations before it was finalized in its current form. Given the coexisting relationship between alcohol and drug use and other mental health disorders, 42 CFR, Part 2, has applied to persons with mental disorders within chemical dependency settings for a long time. In some respects, this law is stricter than the recent HIPAA legislation and behavioral health care facilities that serve persons with co-occurring disorders adhere to the more stringent standards.

Additionally to these two comprehensive federal laws, there is also a patchwork of mental hygiene legislation across states that can vary. In New York State, for instance, the OMH documents on its website that psychiatric care is governed by the Mental Hygiene Law. However, for persons with mental illness who have coexisting forensic issues, the Criminal Procedure Law, Penal Law, and Correction Law also apply. Generally, where state law is stricter, this standard will be used for mental hygiene services. However, if a conflict arises between state and federal laws, federal law will take precedence. Also, in conflicts between the two federal laws, the more recent will apply.

CFR 42, Part 2, protects patient identifying information (PII). This refers to any information that can identify a person as having applied for services, being in receipt of services, or having received services. The U.S. Department of Health and Human Services website describes the HIPAA Privacy Rule as covering any patient protected health information (PHI) that is generated and transmitted, or maintained in any format, electronic, paper, or oral. This includes "individually identifiable health information . . ., including demographic data, that relates to: the individual's past, present or future physical or mental health or condition, . . . and . . . for which there is a reasonable basis to believe that it can be used to identify the individual."

Basically, both regulations recognize the confidentiality of the patient's relationship with the physician, as well as with various qualified mental health practitioners—licensed psychologists, social workers, marriage and family therapists, mental health counselors, and others. However, confidentiality is not absolute, and certain exclusions or waivers are permitted by federal and state laws. As the basic rule, communication between patients and health care providers should not be disclosed to third parties without the person's informed/written consent.

Generally, however, under certain conditions, limited disclosures can be made to entities as specified by law, without prior patient consent. This includes obtaining emergency health care for a patient who is experiencing a condition that creates an immediate medical threat. Thus, medical/psychiatric emergencies such as that which can be occasioned by a person who decompensates and is at immediate risk of harming himself, herself or others do not require prior patient consent to seek medical care. For persons who are not institutionalized in a medical setting in the United States, 9-1-1 emergency ambulance services are usually used to effect the process of transporting the individual to the nearest emergency room. In many states, it is common for this type of psychiatric medical emergency call to initiate a protocol in which law enforcement personnel also respond, together with the medical emergency staff. The individual with mental illness is also restrained in handcuffs as a protective mechanism, until the person's arrival in the emergency room.

Additionally, disclosures of PII and PHI are authorized for the reporting of child abuse and neglect to the state hotlines, or to emergency 9-1-1 services if the child is believed to be in an immediate threatening situation. In fact, the reporting of victims of abuse, neglect, or domestic violence to law enforcement is a permitted disclosure. Crimes that are being committed on the premises of a facility or against personnel can trigger mandatory reporting. Reporting to law enforcement is also permitted to mitigate a serious and imminent threat that is made against a person or the public, and may also involve notifying any specific person who was identified as the target. This is often referred to as the "duty to warn," which was the outcome in a major California court case—*Tarasoff v. Regents of the University of California* in 1974. The HIPAA Privacy Act's incorporation of reporting serious and imminent threats thus places licensed mental health professionals at the forefront in evaluating the potential behavior of persons with mental illness.

There are other situations in which disclosure may be permitted for legal proceedings such as child custody hearings or criminal prosecution that is already in process. If the person is not willing to provide informed consent for his or her record, the court can institute the use of warrants, subpoenas, and court orders. Civil and criminal court orders can be required, and they may need to meet the "good cause" standard to obtain information about the person with mental illness, especially if he or she is involved in addiction treatment. Good cause means that a judge has conducted a hearing and may have reviewed the person's record privately or "in camera." The judge has then determined that the information may not be available from any other source and that the public's interest and need for the information to be disclosed outweigh any potential injury to the patient or the therapeutic relationship in which he or she is involved.

HIPAA Security Rules

The HIPAA Security Rules are also in effect. With the 21st century's relatively rapid pace of emerging technologies, documentation that is being used for the treatment, payment, and operation of facilities has moved from paper records to electronic systems. This has brought with it increased risks of inadvertent disclosures of patient PHI. Given that having a mental disorder can still be perceived as a stigma, breaches of patient data can be detrimental for persons with mental illness. The Security Rules thus are meant to provide protection for electronic PHI, that is, patient data that are received, maintained, or transmitted in electronic forms.

The confidentiality and privacy of persons with mental illness are thus now assured through multiple laws and statutes, and have gone a long way in alleviating some of the discriminatory practices against them and in offering certain protections for treatment. However, treatment professionals need to ensure that they are knowledgeable about the various facets of the law that apply to the persons with whom they are working, to protect the person, the public, and the professionals themselves. It should be clearly noted that the information discussed here is simply to inform the reader. Treatment professionals should be receiving dedicated ongoing training regarding how confidentiality and privacy apply to persons with mental illness whom they serve.

EDUCATIONAL DISCRIMINATION

Lack of Educational Supports for the Mentally Ill

According to Article 26 of the UDHR, "everyone has the right to education. [It] shall be free . . . in the elementary and fundamental stages . . . [and] compulsory . . . Higher education shall be equally accessible to all on the basis of merit." By the early 1900s, a system of private and public education had been established across the majority of states in the United States. Many institutions were funded by religious orders that have always been in the vanguard of education in Europe, the United States, and other parts of the world. But as a system of primary and secondary education emerged, it was the children of the affluent who were best placed to obtain an education. For others, including those with mental illness, the rigors of daily life precluded their ability to benefit from a formal school system.

To address educational supports for persons with mental illness, however, we must expand our discussion to persons who are diagnosed with mental challenges, many of whom also have other mental disorders. If we can recall, historical records indicate that children with mental illness fared little better than adults during the 16th through 18th centuries. They were also sent to the poorhouses, workhouses, and other institutions of the time. Additionally, children who were orphaned sometimes met this same fate.

The common practice of indenturing poor families and persons with mental illness was likely to be highly discriminatory toward children. In that environment, children may have emerged as desirable indentures for a number of reasons. Besides costing less to support, they could also be trained for placement in various service-type jobs and those that required manual labor. They may also have been easier to manage. To be a poor child thus set the stage for a life of hardship. To be a poor child with mental illness or an intellectual challenge significantly decreased the life options that one had.

By the early 1900s, as the various states took more responsibility for constructing asylums and hospitals for persons with mental illness, the need for separate housing for children with mental illness was clear. In places such as New York, large institutions or residential state schools also began to be built to serve this population. Many of these children not only were affected with emotional disorders, but also had intellectual challenges. According to the thinking of the time, this latter group was not believed to be able to maximally benefit from educational services. Thus, they were largely warehoused with the primary focus being on custodial care.

However, even with regard to custodial care, the system became a failure. By the early 1970s, exposés from media personalities such as Geraldo Riviera documented the abuses that were rife inside facilities housing persons with mental illness and developmental disabilities in states such as California and New York. The Willowbrook Exposé (1972), as it came to be called, highlighted the abject conditions that could once more be observed within institutions housing vulnerable individuals—an institution in which Riviera's brother, like many others, had met their demise. In this instance, children had also been used as guinea pigs, as they had been injected with the hepatitis virus in order to track its natural history.

As concerned members of the public once more began to clamor for changes, the focus was placed on providing both humane conditions, and the educational and other structures that could best benefit persons with mental illness and/or intellectual challenges. By the time the Willowbrook Consent Decree was issued by the court in 1975, the state had already begun its deinstitutionalization process for the large state mental hospitals. Along with persons with SMI, those with mental challenges now joined the process.

Elementary and Secondary Education Act (ESEA)

It was not only at the state level that changes were occurring. By 1965, President Lyndon Johnson had championed the Elementary and Secondary Education Act (ESEA). He saw this legislation as crucial to the future of America as it was meant to address gaps in funding and educational resources targeting poorer families. One year later, this act was updated to better serve students with disabilities as it called for a free and appropriate education for these students at the state level.

In 1975, there was a further amendment to the ESEA under President Gerald Ford. This proved to be the most comprehensive as it outlined the six criteria that needed to be effected, including that every special needs child aged 3 through 21 years was entitled to a free and appropriate public education and that no child should be rejected.

Further amendments to the ESEA in 1986 implemented early intervention services. By 1990, the law that was renamed the Individuals with Disabilities Education Act (IDEA) expanded the definition of persons who could be served including encompassing a growing category of children—those diagnosed with autism.

Ongoing advocacy by parents and persons interested in the welfare of children with mental challenges has helped to consolidate gains made for this population. While there has been concerns such as a lack of qualified professionals, and how resources are assigned, the essential issue of access to education has been largely resolved, and children with special needs cannot be simply kicked out of the classroom. Thus, tremendous progress has been made with regard to eliminating educational discrimination against children with mental illness, especially those with intellectual challenges.

While there has been a much needed focus on children with developmental challenges, there has also been a need to address secondary education services. One group of individuals who were sorely in need of better opportunities were the World War II (1939–1945) veterans. By 1944, many young servicemen were returning to the United States, traumatized by the ravages of war. As the country tried to make sense of the millions of persons who had given their lives, the U.S. government sought to mitigate the social problems that could be occasioned by an influx of unemployed individuals. Thus, the Servicemen's Readjustment Act of 1944, often called the Government Issue (GI) Bill, was passed.

The GI Bill provided tuition grants for secondary and vocational education. Additionally, it allowed for the construction of veterans' hospitals that were desperately needed to treat the large numbers of individuals with physical and mental impairments, such as PTSD. The GI Bill thus helped to increase access to treatment facilities as well as make education accessible for veterans. The VA reports that by the time the initial program ended in 1956, close to 8 million veterans had used tuition benefits.

In an attempt to continue to decrease discrimination against veterans, many of whom are affected by mental illness, the GI Bill has been updated on two occasions, in 1984 and in 2008. Access to education and training opportunities are assured as part of an enhanced package of benefits.

Restrictive Policies Adopted by Educational Institutions

Additionally to the IDEA Law, several pieces of legislation support the provision of educational and other services to persons with mental illness in a nondiscriminatory manner. Specifically, the ADA of 1990, which was updated in 2008, identifies its goals as assuring "equality of opportunity, full participation, independent living, and economic self-sufficiency" for individuals with disabilities. Because persons with mental illness have continued to encounter restrictive policies, for example, with being admitted to certain professional degree programs, the ADA is important to help provide guidance.

The updated act clarifies that "an impairment that is episodic or in re-mission is a disability if it would substantially limit a major life activity when active." Further, it specifies that a "qualified handicapped person" is one "who meets the academic and technical standards requisite to ad-mission or participation" in postsecondary and vocational educational services. Thus, persons with mental illness who experience episodes of decompensation are covered under the act and have legal recourse through the EEOC if they are discriminated against by being hindered from partici-pation in the educational setting or in the workplace.

CULTURAL DISCRIMINATION

Social and Religious Beliefs about the Causes of Mental Illness

The social and religious beliefs regarding the causes of mental illness have been previously discussed. This has ranged from it being caused by the phases of the moon, to being punishment or lack of favor from the gods, to the result of possession by evil spirits. By the 18th century, as the physicians of the day grappled with what mental illness was, causes such as the rigors of civilization were also proffered.

Although medical science has now largely moved us forward in try-ing to understand the etiology of various mental disorders, there are still pockets of thought that still see mental illness from a religious perspec-tive. For instance, it is still not uncommon to hear persons with mental ill-ness being advised to seek treatment through their religious provider than their physician. In some indigenous communities, beliefs about the causes of mental illness also have a more naturalistic spiritual orientation, which highlights the imbalance between various forces of nature that are in the individual's life.

These ways of looking at the causes of mental illness have had signifi-cant impacts on how persons with mental illness are treated. On one hand, it has contributed to extensive discrimination when individuals are seen as being punished and/or being possessed. It has also militated against ef-fective treatment. On the other hand, social belief systems such as that in some Eastern cultures that view the person with mental illness as a gift have promoted a more accepting attitude toward those with mental illness.

How the Mentally Ill Are Portrayed in the Media

As indicated previously, perhaps, the earliest media portrayals of per-sons with mental illness occurred at places such as Bedlam when the wider public paid to enter the asylum to view persons with mental illness, or when persons with mental illness were caged and placed on display at fairs and carnivals. While this no longer occurs in the developed world, media portrayals of persons with mental illness run the gamut from sensitive to inappropriate.

Currently, media refers to a diversity of sources. These include the older print media such as newspapers and magazines, which are now supplemented with an online presence including blogs. Radio communication has been replaced in many instances with interactive television, and social media applications such as Twitter, Instagram, Facebook, and others have replaced the old "snail mail" way of mailing letters. There has never been a prior time in history when images and information can be so promptly transmitted and affect so many people. Thus, how persons are portrayed in the media can have a very significant impact on many other areas of their lives.

To be fair, as more prominent individuals in the society have spoken out about their own struggles or that of family members with mental illness, media portrayals have reflected empathy more, especially when they allow persons to tell their stories in their own words. Unfortunately, however, as media outlets vie for the competitive advantage, sensational cases of persons with mental illness engaged in criminal behavior have often been the images that dominate the six o'clock news.

And the images have been too many! The case of the deliberate downing of a Germantown airliner carrying almost 150 persons, by a pilot who was reported to have a history of depression, understandably caused a great deal of consternation. Additionally, there was the Middletown massacre in which a mentally ill teenager took the life of more than 20 individuals, most of them children. A mentally ill male traveled from his home in Philadelphia to New York City, after injuring his girlfriend, to randomly target two police officers on duty. A young male dressed in a Batman suit opened fire in a crowded movie theater in Aurora, Colorado, leaving behind one of the most heartbreaking live scenes witnessed in such a place of entertainment. A 21-year-old young man sits in a Bible study class in Charleston, South Carolina, then fires on the parishioners around him. And, we can go on.

Due to advocacy from organizations such as National Alliance on Mental Illness (NAMI), media outlets are more apt to try to reflect accurate images of persons with mental illness, partly due to the swift retribution that can occur on sites such as Twitter if offensive images are used. Thus, several television shows and movies have integrated issues related to mental health. There is sometimes exaggeration and misinformation. However, these instances have been decreasing.

Perhaps the major negative outcome of the media's portrayal of mental illness has to do with the emphasis on heinous acts that are committed by a few persons with mental illness, which can exacerbate stigma. Individuals in the wider society may believe that persons with mental illness engage in higher rates of violence. In a Canadian study, for instance, close to 30% of persons in the general population stated they feared being around persons with SMI. Additionally, 46% of respondents thought that the term "mental illness" was often used by individuals to cover up their bad behavior.

An additional concern that has been noted is with regard to benefits that persons with mental illness might seek. For instance, recent newspaper articles in the United Kingdom discussed the number of persons receiving disability income and the percentage of revenue this represented. The majority of commentators who posted responses on the newspaper's website were very scathing. In some cases, vitriolic language was used to describe persons with disabilities. Many felt that the disability was purely being used as an excuse and that persons who were reportedly suffering from conditions such as anxiety and depression were stealing money from the state's coffers.

The media can therefore play a crucial role in perpetuating or helping to alleviate discrimination against persons with mental illness. Producers, actors, news reporters, and other media personnel still need to become more sensitized to the impact negative portrayals of a few persons with mental illness can have on the wider community. For instance, although reporting about a crime that is committed by a person with mental illness is expected, care should also be taken to highlight that this behavior is not representative of the millions of people who experience episodes of poor mental health across the life span.

POLITICAL DISCRIMINATION

Political Attitudes toward the Mentally Ill

Political attitudes can be defined as those that are held by individuals and organizations regarding how access to the state or government should be gained, and how power and resources should be distributed. Political attitudes toward persons with mental illness are driven by how persons in the wider society view this condition. Thus, when persons with mental illness were viewed as subhuman and as objects of derision, we see that there was little political will to afford them even basic human rights. An integral part of politics, however, involves being able to get your point of view heard, and hopefully acted upon. The voices of many early individuals and groups formed a groundswell, which helped to move the issues of persons with mental illness to the political forefront.

For instance, the legal persons in the early English courts who passed the 1800 Act for the Criminally Insane recognized the need to afford some kind of protection to persons with mental illness, regardless of the severity of the crime they had committed. Individuals like the Earl of Shaftesbury became well known for championing the Lunacy Commission. As previously indicated, this used the 11 Commissioners in Lunacy for several decades from the 1840s, to monitor the asylums and to try to ensure compliance with a basic standard of care for persons with mental illness.

In the United States, the Quakers borrowed from their English counterparts, and along with persons such as Dorothea Dix, went directly to the legislature and other political institutions to help build a system of care and housing for persons with mental illness. In fact, some of the strategies that were used extensively throughout history continue to be implemented. These include speaking out in the living rooms of open-minded persons; addressing religious and other institutions; creating smaller then larger groups of like-minded individuals; traveling, documenting, and letter writing; and developing relationships between and among key advocates and politicians. In addition, with the advent of social media applications such as Facebook, Instagram, Messenger, and others, their instantaneous coverage of events across the globe, has been helpful in providing education about mental health conditions as well as in publicizing concerns related to persons with mental illness.

Their Participation in the Political Process

Over time, an extensive amount of political action has therefore taken place in order to address historical wrongs and to ensure persons with mental illness are able to benefit more equitably from the political process. Article 21 of the UDHR states that "Everyone has the right to take part in the government of his country, directly or through freely chosen representatives." This right has not always been guaranteed for persons with mental illness. The fact that many were homeless and marginalized effectively impeded their access to any participation in the political process. The passage of Eugenic Laws that viewed persons with mental illness as defective implicitly suggested that they should not be part of the political process. While many places around the globe have remained silent on whether persons known to have mental illness can take part in the political process, others, especially in the developed countries, have come to recognize that persons with mental illness, their families, and well-wishers constitute a powerful voting bloc.

It is accurate that depending on the type of mental disorder and its severity, a person may not be able to participate in the political process in a meaningful way. However, for many others, mental illness can be episodic, and they do have the cognitive capability. Given the nature of mental illness, it may be that a majority of persons are actively participating in political activities including voting, and especially in the developed world, they may actually be in prominent political positions. Over time, more public officials have been forthcoming about their struggles with depression, alcoholism, and other mental health conditions.

With the current extensive social and other media coverage that is available, these individual stories have brought a more humane face to mental illness and have contributed to less overt political discrimination against persons with mental illness. Advocacy organizations such as NAMI in the United States, the Mental Health Foundation in the United Kingdom, the CMHA, and the Mental Health Foundation of Australia have been involved in working toward destigmatizing mental illness and allowing persons with mental health disorders to participate fully in all aspects of political, social, legal, economic, and other aspects of life.

Thus, today many politicians have recognized the political power of the voting bloc created by persons with mental illness, their families, and advocates. During election campaigns, it is not uncommon for persons who are running for office to meet with, visit, and engage in dialogue about their political and legislative intent toward this community. In fact, during a period of time that this author was administratively responsible for different treatment organizations that served persons with mental illness and co-occurring disorders, clients as a group received invitations to participate in community-based political events. Additionally, politicians were not averse to visiting these facilities on more than one occasion to speak with clients and ask for their vote, or to use the facility itself as a backdrop for their political agendas.

Discrimination against persons with mental illness has thus decreased to a significant degree especially in the developed world. However, there still exist many places around the globe where persons with mental illness, especially those who are more seriously impaired, still do not have basic access to adequate mental health care and have little or no political voice. While advocacy is being conducted by the WHO and other nongovernmental organizations to help address these concerns, there continues to be a need to actively focus on expanding and ensuring full access to participation in the political process, to the best of their ability, for all persons with mental disorders.

How Diversity and Discrimination Affect the Mentally Ill

Within a societal context, diversity refers to the perceived or real characteristics that distinguish one individual from another. According to the

Civil Rights Act of 1964, diversity is protected in the workplace based on race, color, religion, sex, or national origin. This latter act in fact has been very significant in the lives of persons with mental illness. Although it focused on addressing discrimination for persons of color and women, it was the prototype on which the ADA Act of 1990 was based. Further, many of the strategies that were used to help build political pressure to pass the Civil Right Act were also used during the movement for disability rights. While persons with mental illness are those assured their rights in the workplace and in the society due to both acts, they have to be continually vigilant as they may still encounter discrimination related to these areas.

Gender Differences

Our society as a whole has an extensive history of treating individuals differently based on gender. Many times this has been linked to religion and culture. For instance, preferential hiring of males has occurred as men have historically been identified as the breadwinners. Employers have also been concerned that women may become pregnant or might be responsible for caregiving, which could affect their attendance and productivity. The Civil Rights Act explicitly prohibits discrimination against "women affected by pregnancy, childbirth, or related medical conditions." Another major area of gender discrimination has been with regard to pay. According to the U.S. Department of Labor (2015), on average, women still earn 78 cents of every dollar earned by a man. This is true even for women with higher education degrees. Women who experience episodes of mental illness over their lifetime may need to miss work at certain intervals to take care of their mental health needs. This may lead to them earning less and experiencing more difficulty with independently supporting themselves over the life span.

Age Differences

The Civil Rights Act protects persons over age 40 against employment discrimination "including hiring, firing, pay, job assignments, promotions, layoff, training, fringe benefits, and any other term or condition of employment." Persons with SPMI often worked within sheltered workshops due to difficulty tolerating the stressors in the regular work environment. While age discrimination protection covered these worksites, discriminatory pay contributed to the enforcement of the federal Olmstead Act and phasing out of the sheltered work settings.

Differences in Racial/Cultural/Ethnic Identity

The U.S. society is known as one of the most multicultural in the world. However, historical factors related to the indigenous inhabitants, to the legacy of slavery and indentureship, and to multiple waves of immigration have contributed to lingering stresses, especially due to competition for finite economic resources. In recent years, some of these underlying issues have erupted and brought issues related to racial/cultural and ethnic tension to the surface. This has spurred several 21st-century social movements as a response including the Occupy Movement and the Black Lives Matter Movement. Since persons with mental illness reflect the diversity of the United States, they are also affected by conditions that may be inequitable and may in fact be at a higher likelihood of experiencing discriminatory behavior due to their disability.

Researchers highlight that there is a process by which people develop a racial/cultural/ethnic identity and that many individuals are not aware of their own limited, stereotypical or prejudicial, thinking. Others do not believe that diversity is in the interest of the society as a whole or that any effort is required to become more comfortable with diversity. Since persons with mental illness are often misunderstood and are still identified by many in the wider society using stereotypical terms such as "crazy" and "loco," they can face similar discriminatory practices as that which may arise due to racial/cultural/ethnic identity issues. Additionally, some persons with mental illness who identify with racial/cultural/ethnic groups that are already marginalized may experience discrimination based on both this status and having mental illness.

It is thus important for individuals with mental illness themselves to work toward addressing their own person racial/cultural/ethnic biases. Additionally, the need remains for them and their advocates to confront discriminatory attitudes based on these characteristics that can affect their ability to live, work, and socialize in their communities.

Sexual Identity Differences

An individual's sexual identity comprises his or her sexual orientation and gender identity. Sexual orientation reflects the person's preference such as for a same-sex relationship. Gender identity on the other hand reflects whether the individual self-identifies as a male, female, transgender, or other identity regardless of his or her sex at birth. Persons with mental health disorders have varied sexual identities similarly to persons without mental health concerns and thus have been caught up in some of the social and legal controversies surrounding those who self-identify as lesbian, gay, bisexual, transgender, or queer (LGBTQ). Overt symptoms of mental illness among persons who self-identify as LGBTQ can place them at higher risk of becoming victims of crimes including assault. As the incidence of violent crimes increased against LGBTQ persons in the United States, several states made targeting individuals based on their sexual identify a hate crime that comes with more severe punishment.

Additionally, over the past two decades especially, the Marriage Equality Movement has been involved in a flurry of legal action in state legislatures due to covert and overt discrimination against individuals, including persons with mental illness, based on their sexual identity. On June 25, 2015, the Supreme Court ruled in favor of Marriage Equality thus ending decades of discrimination against persons who chose to marry within same-sex relationships. These legal protections have been beneficial to persons with mental illness who self-identify as members of the LGBTQ community and can go a long way in helping to decrease violence and discrimination against them because of their sexual identity.

Overall, diversity has had a major impact on the way persons with mental illness have been treated partly due to deep-seated beliefs, attitudes, and values related to issues of gender, race, class, age, sexual identity, and others. Efforts made within the U.S. society and globally to understand how the isms might intersect and impact—racism, sexism, ageism, classism, and so on—have created greater awareness and given many groups a voice. While persons with mental illness have benefited from various movements related to these concerns, given socializing influences, we have not yet arrived at a postracial, post-gender, post-sexual, or other identity. Therefore, continued vigilance and targeted activism is required from persons with mental illness and their advocates, as well as the society-at-large, to ensure that we continue to remove discriminatory barriers related to diversity.

PART II

Controversies

CHAPTER 7

How Comorbidity Affects Discrimination

What is comorbidity? This refers to the presence of two or more medical conditions in an individual. During most of the 1990s, the term was used primarily to refer to persons who had both mental illness and substance use disorders. However, as we have been moving toward viewing health care from a comprehensive behavioral model, comorbidity is being used more frequently in its correct context. While one of the most common comorbid relationships remain mental illness and substance use disorders, the nature of either of these conditions, by itself, can also contribute to comorbidity. Thus, a person with a diagnosis of major depression whose symptoms include overeating and oversleeping may develop or be at high risk for obesity and diabetes. An individual with a cocaine use disorder can also be at risk for or develop cardiovascular conditions. The presence of any two or more medical conditions thus signifies comorbidity.

MENTAL ILLNESS AND SUBSTANCE USE DISORDERS

As stated previously, the extensive incidence of coexisting mental illness and substance use disorders was partly the impetus for the behavioral health care movement. As we discussed earlier, by the late 1850s, the field of mental illness had split so that many persons with substance use disorders began to be treated in different settings from persons with other mental health disorders. Within the substance use disorders field, there was an additional dichotomy, as the predominant belief was that alcohol use was fundamentally different from use of other drugs. Thus, persons who developed disorders related to either could not be treated within the same setting. Just as separating mental illness from use of substances created quandaries for treating persons with both disorders, so too did this artificial separation between alcohol and other drug use disorders. Where was an individual with both an alcohol and another drug use disorder supposed to get treatment? What about those with either an alcohol or another drug use disorder and a mental health disorder? Conceptualization of these disorders thus led to overt discrimination across the treatment system as persons with one or more disorders were denied access to treatment in specific settings.

By the 1980s through the 1990s, advocates from both fields began questioning this system that was discriminatory to persons with one or more conditions. In New York State, which is known to be one of the most progressive in the nation in terms of substance abuse treatment, regulations were not implemented until December 2, 2002, to consolidate outpatient alcohol and drug use facilities into outpatient chemical dependency (or 822) treatment programs. This meant that patients with both alcohol and drug use disorders no longer needed to shop around for programs or try to manipulate their symptoms in order to access treatment. Now, persons could apply to an outpatient chemical dependency treatment facility for a screening/assessment and could be admitted for either an alcohol or substance use disorder.

Nicotine Use Disorder

When discussing substance use disorders, nicotine addiction must be included, especially due to its negative effects on both active smokers and second-hand (passive) smokers. While large-scale public service campaigns have contributed to a declining rate of smoking in the general population, from close to 21% in 2005, to 18% in 2013, as reported by the CDC (2015), these gains do not appear to translate to persons with mental illness. Among persons self-reporting disabilities, 23 out of 100 were smokers, as compared with 17 out of 100 for persons without disabilities. In fact, data reported by the NIH (2015) highlight that while 41% of persons who experienced an episode of mental illness within the prior month were smokers, for those with a diagnosis of schizophrenia, 90% were smokers. Persons with mental illness thus appear to be at higher risk of also having a nicotine use disorder.

In cities such as New York, which placed a great deal of emphasis on smoke-free work environments and public places since the early 2000s, the rights of smokers have become severely restricted. Citizens-at-large are expected to comply with laws that dictate where they could smoke. In settings in which persons with mental illness reside, what has emerged can be described as inconsistent application of the law. For example, individuals who are admitted in an institutional setting are usually allowed the opportunity to exercise their choice to smoke. Given that they may already have concerns with impulsivity, anxiety, and other behaviors, smoking may become a means for them to self-medicate. It is thus not uncommon to observe persons with mental illness engaged in chain smoking. Unfortunately, this unhealthy behavior might be characterized as reverse discrimination, since constraints are placed on well-adjusted individuals to refrain from smoking. However, there appears to be emphasis on the rights of persons with mental illness to engage in smoking as compared with their rights to participate in healthier behaviors. Thus, persons with mental illness are often given much more latitude to smoke as much and as often as they want.

Medication-Assisted Treatment

It should be noted that methadone maintenance treatment programs (MMTs or MMTPs) are also incorporated under outpatient chemical dependency treatment programs. These serve persons who are diagnosed with opioid use disorders related to drugs such as heroin, morphine, and OxyContin. These individuals receive replacement therapy using medications such as methadone, buprenorphine (Suboxone or Subutex), or naltrexone. But these latter are not the only medications that are available for treatment.

Today, an individual can enter a treatment program and receive medications such as Chantix (naltrexone) to help reduce the craving for nicotine, or Chantix in conjunction with Zyban (bupropion or wellbutrin), which has shown greater efficacy. For alcohol use disorders, disulfiram or Antabuse has existed for many years. ReVia (naltrexone) can also be used, as well as gabapentin or Neurontin, and acamprosate or Campral.

Several research trials are also in process to obtain more effective treatment for drugs of abuse including cannabis (the transdermal tetrahydrocannabinol patch), and cocaine (topiramate or Topamax, the TA-CD vaccine), to name a few. Many of these medications are also being used in trials and, like Zyban and Chantix, in conjunction with others to determine whether they may also assist in decreasing the withdrawal, craving, and side effects of other chemicals of addiction, or whether they can improve the efficacy of treatment. Thus, methadone is being tried for cocaine, or potentially other stimulants such as methamphetamine. Naltrexone is also being prescribed with other medications to determine whether its demonstrated treatment effectiveness can be enhanced.

Medications are therefore widely used in the treatment of substance use disorders as well as mental health disorders for the same persons. To more fully recognize this fact, and to decrease stigma, we have moved away from referencing the programs that primarily provide opioid dependency treatment as methadone programs, to the more inclusive medication-assisted treatment (MAT) programs. Additionally, the concept of medication-supported recovery has been promulgated by the New York State Office of Alcoholism and Substance Abuse Services, partly to recognize that many persons may need to remain on medications for the rest of their lives to help prevent relapse and/or decompensation and to support their long-term recovery.

Unfortunately, active use of chemicals of addiction can contribute to psychiatric decompensation, while psychiatric decompensation can contribute to active use of chemicals of addiction. Among some medical professionals, this issue becomes a barrier to effective treatment. Specifically, some physicians are at times hesitant to treat a client's psychiatric symptoms when he or she is under the influence of or continues to actively use a chemical of addiction. This can present concerns with accurate diagnosing and thereby prescribing of medications, and can also place clients at a greater risk of experiencing harmful outcomes such as overdose. However, if left untreated for mental health issues, it is less likely that the client would adequately stabilize. Since so many persons with psychiatric diagnoses continue to use substances even when in chemical dependency treatment, not providing needed mental health care in conjunction with substance use care might represent a discriminatory approach to intervening with this population.

Other Issues and Controversies

Despite the extensive body of data that documents the efficacy of treatment medications, especially those that are prescribed as opioid replacement therapy, they remain a potent source of controversy. Persons who disagree and often misunderstand how medication management works, especially with the population with co-occurring disorders, often ask why addicts should be given other drugs to get high? The pharmacological properties of the treatment medications such as their longer half-life, or their affinity with certain neurotransmitter systems in the human brain, which are necessary to help support treatment success, are viewed as negatives by some persons.

Many also question the ethics of treating one drug with another drug. Anecdotally, persons on MAT programs are often viewed as being prone to engage in illicit sales of their medication or as manipulative, so that they could obtain higher medication dosages than what they actually need. Data trends for the first decade of the twenty-first century have shown an increase in the illicit sales and use of psychotherapeutic medications. These include benzodiazepines such as Klonopin, opiates such as Percocet, and stimulants such as Ritalin and Adderall. In fact, national surveys indicate that deaths due to prescription drug abuse and overdose now outnumber that due to the use of illicit drugs including heroin and cocaine.

Given that these psychotherapeutic medications are prescribed, the question that arises is: How do these get into the hands of unauthorized individuals? What responsibility do prescribing professionals have to ensure better controls including more thorough evaluations of persons who present for treatment? Initiatives promulgated by the federal government have encouraged states to establish Prescription Drug Monitoring Programs (PDMPs). According to the U.S. DOJ's Office of Diversion Control, the PDMP refers to an electronic database that is established within a particular state to track the prescriptions that are issued. More than 40 states including California, Arizona, New York, and Rhode Island have already established PDMPs. These can be used by prescribing professionals to check on the medications that a patient is actively receiving and thus serves as a mechanism to deter the receipt of multiple similar prescriptions, as well as to identify potential medication interactions and side effects.

Additionally, the PDMPs have helped to weed out some of the prescribing professionals who appeared to be somewhat indiscriminately writing prescriptions. This, in conjunction with aggressive law enforcement, is also being used to address prescription drug abuse. However, the role of law enforcement itself has been questioned. Are arrests for prescription drug abuse the best use of law enforcement time? And should persons who are identified as abusing or misusing prescription medications that they acquired legally or illicitly be redirected to treatment or punishment?

As indicated, while deaths due to overdoses have emerged as a major concern, those due to opioids are being examined even more closely. This is partly because methadone is the primary opioid analgesic medication that is prescribed in the pain management clinics. In a number of states, incidences of mortality associated with opioid overdose have been inaccurately attributed to the MAT programs, while the role of the pain management clinics has often received less attention. Ironically, within the United States, the federal, state, and local regulatory guidelines regarding MAT are much more onerous for those settings than that pertaining to other medical facilities. As a result, there is a higher likelihood that more controls are in place within methadone treatment programs as compared with other settings that prescribe similar medications.

Other detractors of MAT refuse to recognize replacement therapy as a valid treatment and stress that it should be used purely as harm reduction. But what is harm reduction? This refers to a disease management approach in which the primary focus is not on immediately eliminating the disease or problem. Instead, emphasis is placed on the adoption of less harmful behaviors that can ameliorate the most damaging effects of the disease, until the person becomes more motivated for change. For example, instead of a person continuing to smoke cigarettes (due to the disease of nicotine addiction), he or she may be encouraged to use the patch (nicotine replacement therapy). Thus, for a period of time, nicotine replacement is provided to help alleviate the major withdrawal symptoms, while the person's dosage is decreased. Hopefully, the person can become nicotine free by the end of his or her treatment.

Another harm reduction practice that has triggered a great deal of social disapproval is the implementation of needle and syringe exchanges. Injection drug users are at one of the highest risk of mortality due to drug overdose, infectious diseases, and related complications. From a public health perspective, the risk of disease contraction can be reduced by encouraging the individual to use safer practices such as not sharing needles and syringes. Thus, providing this in a neutral setting, often in conjunction with outreach and education, aims to fully engage the person in treatment and eliminate the injection drug use behaviors.

Evidence suggests that this intervention does provide a pathway to formal treatment. Communities have rejected the placement of needle and syringe exchanges. From a moral perspective, some believe that this is giving a green light to negative behaviors and should not be tolerated, especially as these settings also encourage the use of barrier protection as a means of reducing unwanted pregnancies and diseases. Others highlight that this strategy has been successful in decreasing the economic impacts associated with communicable disease infection and the costs in areas such as health care that must be borne by society after the person has contracted an illness.

But what should occur for patients who are unable to or have substantial difficulty remaining abstinent from chemicals of addiction without the use of medications? While methadone and buprenorphine can be prescribed with decreasing dosages, there is a subset of persons with chronic opioid addiction, many of whom continually relapse when they are detoxified off of these medications. Among this group of persons are veterans who may have developed both addiction and other mental health disorders during their active service. To help eliminate the cycle of active use of harmful substances as well as the associated risky behaviors that have contributed to higher rates of HIV/AIDS, hepatitis C, and other infectious diseases, research has substantiated that maintaining such persons on a stable medication dosage allows them an opportunity to stabilize and benefit from comprehensive care to address needed life issues. In fact, work done by researchers such as Don DesJarlais in New York City has highlighted the cost–benefit of MMT including the significant effect it has had on reducing transmission of communicable diseases. Yet, critics question: Why would anyone need to be on medication management for a substance use disorder for the rest of their lives?

Professionals in the field also point to the impact of these opioid-based medications on the mental health of clients. The question that often arises is: Which comes first—the chicken or the egg? Thus, persons who are experiencing symptoms such as anxiety and agitation that might have preceded their onset of drug use may benefit from the sedative effect of methadone and buprenorphine as it can help them to feel calm. Similarly, an individual with preexisting depressive symptoms who might favor the use of nicotine to help stimulate a more positive mood could benefit from being treated with the antidepressant Zyban to help improve his or her functioning. Is it that persons with mental illness gravitated toward substance use to feel better? Or is it the opposite? According to the NIH (2015), ongoing research suggests both pathways—that substance use can cause mental health symptoms, while symptoms related to "overt, mild, or even subclinical mental disorders" can cause self-medication (para 2).

The research in fields such as neuroscience (the study of the brain and nervous system) and epigenetics (the study of changes that can occur in the non-DNA part of the genes due to environmental factors) is helping us to better understand the pathways that can be shared by both mental health disorders and other substance use disorders. As indicated by NIH (2015), one of the early causative pathways between mental illness and substance use disorders involves "overlapping factors such as underlying brain deficits, genetic vulnerabilities, and/or early exposure to stress or trauma" (para 3). The National Institute on Drug Abuse also recognizes addiction as a chronic relapsing brain disease. Despite this clinical determination, critics still question whether substance use is a disease. After all, don't addicts cause their own problems? Aren't their decline and inability to stop ingesting the substance related to their moral weakness rather than to any disease? What are the reasons we are coddling people in treatment programs rather than taking a more hard-line approach?

Some of the ongoing controversies have ensured that discrimination remains endemic toward persons with substance use disorders. It is valid that the behaviors associated with this condition cause a great deal of family chaos, trauma, and heartache, and can spill over into the community. This has contributed to the marginalization of this group of individuals as a whole. However, persons on opioid maintenance therapy face higher levels of stigma, as compared with other substance users. This is especially so if they are on methadone. Since treatment with buprenorphine has been marketed as office/physician based, and can be more discreetly prescribed, there is more acceptance of its use among some segments of the wider population.

Substance users, however, remain one of the groups that continue to experience discrimination in where they live, work, or even receive medical treatment, especially if they are on older medications such as methadone. If these individuals are also diagnosed with mental illness, they can face even more stereotyping and bias. One of the ongoing controversies has centered around where to locate facilities to treat and/or house persons with substance use and mental health disorders. Many communities have protested the establishment of opioid treatment or any kind of treatment program close to or within their environs. Additionally, homeless shelters, supported living, and transitional apartments, which are often used by persons who are trying to stabilize from substance use and mental health disorders, have also faced hostility and community rejection. In fact, in many parts of the U.S. society, NIMBY—not in my backyard—continues to be alive and well, thus highlighting the attitudes and responses of many in the wider society toward persons with mental illness and substance use disorders.

MENTAL ILLNESS AND OTHER CHRONIC HEALTH DISORDERS

Research has been trying to clarify the relationship between mental illness including alcohol and other drug use disorders and other chronic health disorders. These latter cover a wide range of medical conditions such as diabetes, respiratory concerns such as asthma and chronic obstructive pulmonary disease, and cardiovascular-related problems such as hypertension and congestive heart failure. In fact, WHO (2011), in its Global Status Report on Alcohol and Health, indicates that:

Alcohol is a causal factor in 60 types of diseases and injuries and a component cause in 200 others. Almost 4% of all deaths worldwide are attributed to alcohol, greater than deaths caused by HIV/AIDS, violence or tuberculosis. Alcohol is also associated with many serious social issues, including violence, child neglect and abuse, and absenteeism in the workplace. (p.10)

Injection drug use of both opioids such as heroin and amphetamine-type stimulants, including cocaine and methamphetamine, is also one of the primary sources of HIV/AIDS and other communicable disease infections.

Medications that are prescribed or the nonprescribed use of legal drugs are also sources of chronic health problems for persons with mental illness. All medications can have side effects. However, some may be more debilitating than others and can compromise various organ systems including the gastrointestinal tract, the liver, and the kidneys. If the person is already genetically, medically, or environmentally vulnerable, he or she can be at a higher risk of developing an associated medical illness. For example, studies have shown that medications such as olanzapine, which is used to treat persons diagnosed with psychosis, and lithium, which is used to treat bipolar disorder, have been linked to the development of diabetes. Prolixin, which is administered as an intramuscular medication especially as it can aid medication management compliance over the long term, is also associated with the development of cerebral atherosclerosis or hardening or building up of plaque in the arteries of the brain. This latter can contribute to stroke and an increased risk of death.

Since persons with mental illness may be on long-term medication management regimens, or may be mandated at times to take prescribed medications due to serious psychiatric decompensation, care has to be taken to ensure that they are not victimized. For those with severe behavioral concerns, for example, there have been historical precedents with high dosages of medication being used as a form of restraint. While persons with developmental or intellectual challenges often have advocates such as consistent treatment team members and human rights committees to ensure that they receive the least restrictive dose of any psychotropic medication, other persons with mental health issues are at a disadvantage. They may receive treatment in a haphazard and disjointed manner if they have frequent emergency room episodes or are not linked to designated mental health providers with whom they have developed a therapeutic treatment relationship. Therefore, it is imperative that prescribing professionals, together with persons with mental illness and their family members or other advocates, work toward optimizing both their mental and medical health.

MENTAL ILLNESS AND GAMBLING

Another mental health disorder that has emerged as significant is gambling disorders. A U.S. congressional commission (1997–1999) that examined the impact of casinos concluded in its National Gambling Impact Study that approximately 1% of persons in the U.S. population have gambling disorders. Further research has been trying to better understand the difficulty these persons have in refraining from playing games of chance for monetary or similar wagers.

All things being equal, the average person should be able to play one or more games and walk away from a gaming table at any point. For persons with a gambling disorder, however, this is easier said than done. Like the person with the alcohol use disorder who cannot easily stop drinking once he starts, the gambler also cannot readily stop placing bets. Thus, this individual may remain at a gaming table chasing his losses and trying to win back or get ahead of them. Unfortunately, the outcome is usually that the person ends up accumulating serious financial debt. He may exhaust all his savings, may borrow sums he is unable to pay back, and may even get involved in embezzling and other illegal activities in order to continue to fund his gambling activity.

As a result of the symptoms exhibited by persons who engage in consistent problematic gambling, they are considered to be experiencing an addiction. While many have highlighted that they are not ingesting a drug or a drink, research has found that the neurological responses the individual is experiencing is similar to that of a person who is affected by a substance use disorder. Gambling disorders can probably be better understood from the perspective of a process addiction. Thus, the person who is gambling becomes addicted to the entire process that leads up to and includes the gambling behaviors. He may experience the anticipatory thoughts that help stimulate the overwhelming urge to gamble. His thoughts may trigger elevated cardiovascular responses such as rapid breathing and pulse/heart rate, and even sweating. He may then feel compelled to find an outlet to gamble, whether it is on the Internet, or a casino, or even at the local corner store where he can purchase a variety of lottery tickets. He can then continue to engage in this activity for an extensive period of time, until he has exhausted all his funds, and may even try to borrow or obtain additional funds on the spur of the moment.

The person who has a gambling disorder thus can contribute to major familial and personal dislocation. This can include families becoming bankrupt and homeless, children being neglected, and responsibilities overall being abandoned. Yet, the person's distorted thinking may continue to suggest that he can make it right once he gets a big win. Despite the evidence to the contrary, the person may not recognize that he has a serious disorder and can remain trapped in the cycle of gambling addiction until some external event such as a medical crisis or an arrest precipitates him into treatment.

Persons who are vulnerable to gambling disorders are at a severe disadvantage when we consider the widespread availability of gambling opportunities in our society. In fact, published data indicate that gambling is a $240 billion industry, which employs thousands of people. An individual no longer needs to travel to a designated racetrack or casino. Anywhere a person is, he can have access to gaming activities on an electronic device, whether a smartphone, tablet, laptop, or similar device. For some persons, even Internet games such as Candy Crush and Minecraft can prove addicting. In fact, this can become a serious issue for youth and young adults who may still be working on developing better self-regulation mechanisms.

Persons with gambling disorders are often looked at in an unsympathetic manner. Some of the religious stereotypes that have been assigned to substance use and other mental health disorders are also used to label them—sinful, immoral, weak, doing the devil's work. Consistent with this, persons with gambling disorders have been treated in a discriminatory manner by not even having access to treatment. For instance, while the problem of pathological gambling has existed for centuries, it is not until the 1990s that we have slowly started to systematically address this issue. To date, facilities and qualified professionals who can treat this disorder are still not readily available in many high need areas.

Despite this, public policies continue to encourage gambling behaviors. Perhaps one of the most visible examples is the widely advertised state lotteries that have contributed to the proliferation of gambling opportunities. Since these are often used to fund education initiatives, any attempt to reduce or constrain their scope tends to be fiercely resisted by lawmakers. Another instance of insensitivity toward persons who are vulnerable to gambling disorders can be seen in the siting of casinos and other approved gambling institutions closer to residential areas. While some locals disagree, the data indicate that this does not lead to increased rates of gambling disorders in the surrounding communities.

Therefore, there has been a push in a number of states including New York to obtain more revenue with decentralized gambling. Thus, New York

City residents no longer need to travel out of the city to the large casinos in places like New Jersey, Connecticut, or Delaware. Instead, individuals can travel within the city limits to places such as the Resorts Casino in the borough of Queens. Based on local sentiments, do such facilities truly contribute to the greater welfare of persons in the neighboring communities?

Another concern regarding the siting of gambling facilities and the availability of gambling activities is related to persons with bipolar disorders. Persons who are experiencing an episode of this disorder may engage in symptoms that include frenetic gambling activity. For this subset of persons with mental health disorders, increased opportunities for gambling work against their stability and recovery. Additionally, casinos and other gambling institutions are well known for their other entertainments, which include bars that serve alcoholic beverages around the clock. In some, persons are also allowed smoking privileges. This presents as a risk factor for many individuals. Thus, one of the more common patterns is that a person with a gambling disorder also has a coexisting alcohol use disorder and a nicotine use disorder.

Persons with gambling disorders are also likely to present with coexisting mood disorders. Sometimes, these are triggered by the situations in which the individual finds himself secondary to his gambling behaviors. They additionally have one of the highest rates of suicide and attempted suicide among persons with addictive disorders. The National Council on Problem Gambling indicated that approximately 20% of all gamblers try to commit suicide at some point. Researchers have highlighted that this seems to be underreported since few places around the world have developed standardized indicators for tracking mortality related to gambling disorders. One of the few countries that has been attempting to do this is Canada. The Canada Safety Council's assessment is that around 200 persons with gambling disorders commit suicide annually. Since 2003, if a risk factor such as a gambling debt is known, a suicide could be classified as gambling related. Similarly to substance use disorders, gambling disorders thus need to be addressed more proactively with monitoring and awareness of suicide risk indicators to help prevent this occurrence.

In order to address some of the concerns and criticisms regarding the detrimental aspects of gambling, the gaming industry has attempted to be more responsive to the risks posed by casinos for some individuals. Thus, several initiatives have been implemented including education and the availability of self-help referrals and advocates in some settings. More recently, self-exclusion agreements have become legal in several states in the United States and Canada. This allows persons with known gambling disorders to voluntarily sign/agree to a self-exclusion agreement.

With the self-exclusion agreement, if the person violates the agreement and gambles, even if he wins, he would not be entitled to receive the earnings. To a certain extent, this agreement may be somewhat discriminatory especially as a person may be forfeiting money that he desperately needs. However, given the process aspect of a gambling addiction, this is meant to dampen the satisfaction or euphoria that accrues with winning. Persons with gambling disorders thus are also represented among persons with mental health disorders and often require special interventions to help address this condition. More attention needs to be focused on this group to ensure that they receive adequate treatment as well as protections.

MENTAL ILLNESS AND NEURO-DEVELOPMENTAL DISORDERS

Defining Neuro-Developmental Disorders

What is a neuro-developmental disorder? The European Environment and Health Strategy Draft Report (2003) defines neuro-developmental disorders as "disabilities in the functioning of the brain that affect a child's behaviour, memory or ability to learn, e.g mental retardation, dyslexia, attention deficit hyperactivity disorder (ADHD), learning deficits and autism." The WHO clarifies that a unified definition of neuro-developmental disorders has not been determined. As a result, the same conditions may be labeled differently in many places around the world. Despite this, a basic definition of neuro-developmental disorders should refer to conditions that occur in the individual that are related to impaired growth and maturation of the nervous system, which can affect the usual developmental processes. Persons with neuro-developmental disorders can thus demonstrate problems with the usual developmental milestones such as onset of walking, speech, and the ability to focus on a task. They can also experience behavioral and intellectual challenges.

Neuro-developmental disorders are recognized mental health disorders. According to the DSM-V, they can be categorized based on the primary domain in which symptoms fall—intellectual, communication, autism spectrum, attention deficit, specific learning, and motor disorder. Thus, a child may be diagnosed with a disorder in any one or more of these areas, as well as with another mental health disorder such as depression or anxiety. While legislative and social policies in higher-income countries have sought to decrease discriminatory treatment toward these persons in critical areas such as access to education and health care, on a daily basis, these individuals can still be significantly affected by lack of knowledge among individuals with whom they come into contact. For example, children who exhibit symptoms such as deficits in communication or stereotypical behaviors may be more likely to be teased and bullied by others. Within the classroom, they may also be seen as disruptive and may fail to fully have their adaptive behavioral or learning needs met.

How Many Children Are Affected?

Research reported by the WHO (October 2011) indicates that in the industrialized countries, at least one in six children has a neuro-developmental, behavioral, intellectual disorder, which may include cerebral palsy, IQ deficits, learning disabilities such as dyslexia, attention deficit hyperactivity disorder (ADHD), autism spectrum disorders, and developmental delays such as that found in Down's syndrome. In the United States, the CDC (August, 2015) reports that the incidence of autism spectrum disorders appears to have increased as a study found that 1 in 68 children were diagnosed at age eight.

While it is difficult to clearly identify the causes of these disorders, it is believed that they are related to both genetics and environmental insults such as prenatal exposure to alcohol (fetal alcohol syndrome) or postnatal contact with lead, which has been found to be a contributory factor for the development of ADHD and some other conditions in a percentage of children. Despite multiple controls in higher-income countries to limit the ability of hazardous chemicals to enter the food, water, and air supply, there have been increased incidences of neuro-developmental disorders, and the belief is that some subsets of these are linked to environmental concerns. It is thus estimated that there are much higher prevalence and incidence rates of neuro-developmental disorders in lower-income countries due to poorer and in some instances nonexistent environmental controls. Countries such as Australia also report higher rates of neuro-developmental disorders in their indigenous population.

Potential Causes and Outcomes

Toxic Emissions

The international issue of greenhouse gases that have been associated with climate changes such as higher temperatures and severe tornadoes is also linked to increased incidences of neuro-developmental disorders. Power plants, especially the older ones that are fueled by coal, are known to be one of the most significant sources of emissions that contribute to environmental concerns. Gases that are known to be detrimental include carbon dioxide, nitrogen oxide, and sulfur oxide, all of which affect the quality of the air and can contribute to higher rates of respiratory and other diseases. In fact, some environmental activists in the United States have been highlighting the locations of some of these industrial plants and other facilities such as bus depots in or closer to lower-income communities.

It has been suggested that this latter practice is in essence discriminatory, as it contributes to higher rates of emissions of toxic chemicals in these neighborhoods, which directly affects individuals living in the surrounding vicinities. In some instances, data have shown increased rates of asthma, cancer, and developmental disabilities among children in these communities. According to the U.S. Environmental Protection Agency (EPA), Children's Environmental Health Facts (2015):

> Cancer is the second leading cause of death among children 1–14 years of age, with unintentional injuries being the leading cause . . . A number of studies suggest that environmental contaminants, including radiation, secondhand smoke, pesticides and solvents, may play a role in the development of childhood cancers.

Thus, income disparities may leave low-income families with little choice but to seek work in the limited industrial settings that are still available, as well as obtain nearby housing that place them in the vicinity of harmful chemical emissions over time. This therefore has a direct impact on their children and can contribute to mental illness and/or neuro-developmental disorders.

Earning Ability

Even for adults with mental illness, dependence on social insurance programs such as Supplemental Security Income and Social Security Disability Income may constitute their primary means of support. Although persons may desire to relocate to communities that are perceived as healthier, individuals with mental illness and neuro-developmental disorders may have very limited opportunities to seek improved housing in communities that are less affected by environmental concerns, especially since they may be one of the least likely groups who have the capacity to capitalize on their earning ability.

Lead Exposure

Another major contributing factor to neuro-developmental disabilities is exposure to lead. Although its effects on young children has been known since the 1970s—lowered intelligence, learning disorders, hearing impairment, attention deficit disorders, delayed puberty, and reduced postnatal growth—close to 25 million homes are still affected including with the presence of lead-based paint (EPA, 2015). Again, in higher-income countries such as the United States, one might think that the infrastructure is in place to address this health concern. However, discriminatory attitudes and competing values regarding how such initiatives should be funded have militated against its full resolution. Unfortunately, this increases disparities in several areas of functioning that can be observed among poorer children. It thus places them at higher risk for mental health and other neuro-developmental disorders.

For instance, as the EPA reports, "the median blood lead level for children living in families with incomes below poverty level is higher than for children living in families at or above poverty levels." Over their lifetime, these individuals are therefore placed at a significant disadvantage with regard to their physical and mental health, as well as their social and economic status. In fact, economic analyses of lead-exposed children who develop cognitive deficits estimate that for every one IQ point that is lost, the person forgoes or is not able to earn about $9,600 in earnings.

Environmental Practices

Therefore, discriminatory environmental practices have contributed to a disproportionate burden of mental health and neuro-developmental disorders being experienced by lower-income children and their families. Unfortunately, the evidence suggests that this impact can last a lifetime as it compromises various aspects of the person's functioning, including his or her mental health. Globally, some countries such as Sweden and Norway have made a commitment to decreasing and eliminating the use of toxic chemicals and being more proactive and protective of the environment.

In other large nations such as China and Latin America, progress has been variable partly due to political barriers as well as concerns around hindering economic development. Within the United States, this latter has also been an issue that continues to be hotly debated in political circles. While some progress has been made with addressing some of the environmental concerns, there has been resistance to reducing and or eliminating the older power plants that are well known to contribute to the majority of toxic chemicals such as mercury that can potentially impair the central nervous system of the unborn child, when ingested by the mother through consuming foods such as fish and other seafood. Concerns also remain that this is one of the chemicals that could be implicated in the increase in autism spectrum disorders.

However, several court cases that have been initiated by the business community have challenged the ability of the Clean Air Act of 1970, which was amended and expanded in 1990 and sought to regulate toxic pollutants from power plants, vehicles, and other sources in order to improve the air quality. In June 2015, the U.S. Supreme Court struck down regulations that were meant to reduce the levels of mercury and other toxic emissions.

Initiatives such as the Clean Power Plan proposed by President Obama in August 2015, which aimed to reduce toxic emissions and encourage the growth of a green economy, also drew extensive criticism from the same players and again laid the groundwork for a legal challenge. Unfortunately, while those who oppose such environmental legislation tend to be well organized and well funded, this has not always been the case with parents and other advocates of those who are negatively affected. Therefore, while there has been progress in reducing some of the barriers to healthy childhood outcomes, discriminatory environmental practices have continued to place an undue burden, especially on lower-income families who are most at risk of having children who are vulnerable to developing neuro-developmental disorders.

TREATING CO-OCCURRING DISORDERS

Who Provides Treatment and Where?

In terms of treatment, there has clearly been substantial progress made with regard to addressing substance use disorders and other mental health disorders. But full integration with in the mental health network has not yet occurred. Partly due to a better understanding of mental illness, as well as a documented high rate of mental illness of approximately one in two persons, which has been identified among persons in substance use treatment, applicants who apply to a treatment program for substance use disorders are screened/assessed for the presence of mental health disorders. Unfortunately, although this occurs as part of the screening/intake admission procedures, many substance use programs still might not have licensed mental health professionals on-site who can diagnose and treat persons with mental health concerns. The same is also true for some mental health programs. Thus, behavioral health care services may still be fragmented for some clients, as they would need to be referred to either external substance use or mental health providers.

Medical Staff

A majority of programs across the nation do have physicians and registered nurses. However, their backgrounds do not necessarily include specific expertise with diagnosing and treating mental health disorders. In fact, some communities in the United States still do not have sufficient numbers of qualified psychiatrists. As a result, physicians in other specialties may be more likely to assess and prescribe medications for persons with mental illness.

Due to the paucity of qualified psychiatrists internationally, WHO has recommended that this strategy be used to provide some kind of mental health treatment to underserved populations. Although controversial, to address this need in some states within the United States, psychologists have been provided with prescribing privileges to supplement other professionals such as physicians' assistants and registered nurse practitioners with specialties in psychiatry. While it is certainly preferable that persons with mental health disorders receive some kind of treatment as compared with none, one wonders whether optimal treatment outcomes can be obtained when we use these stopgap measures.

Nonmedical Staff

While it is often not recognized, qualified social workers—individuals with a minimum of a master's degree in social work, who have completed testing and supervision requirements as stipulated by the Council on Social Work Education—are often licensed to provide both diagnosis and psychotherapy. Many qualified social workers also hold advanced licensure in providing mental health services as independent professionals. Data from a national study reported by the National Association of Social Workers indicated that qualified social workers are the largest group of professionals providing mental health services across the United States, when those individuals who have graduated from accredited bachelor of social work programs are also taken into account.

Among the social workers employed in behavioral health clinics, close to 80% reported that their practice area was mental health. Additionally, social workers who provided services to adolescents identified 75% as having mental health problems and 44% as having substance abuse issues. Staff vacancies in organizations, especially within public and nonprofit organizations that serve children and families, mean that sufficient qualified clinicians may not be available to provide adequate services. More recently, the service provider network has been expanding to include additional professionals such as licensed mental health counselors, licensed marriage and family therapists, and licensed chemical dependency counselors. This has increased accessibility to mental health care in some communities. However, issues such as high staff turnover, large caseloads, and staff who are experiencing burnout also affect the quality of services to vulnerable persons who are dealing with mental health and other co-occurring disorders. Thus, lack of attention to factors that affect the available workforce can translate into less than optimal or even discriminatory care for persons with mental health disorders.

Treatment Locations

The current mental health treatment network can be characterized by its diversity. One way to organize it is to look at the levels of care. These levels depend on the severity of the person's illness. For example, some individuals are described as having SPMI or SMI. Conditions such as schizophrenia, bipolar disorder, and major depression can thus be preventing them from being able to fully participate in their daily lives, especially as they may be prone to episodes in which the symptoms escalate, and they can decompensate. A person with a known diagnosis can also have a baseline of being stable. However, an event such as a loss of a loved one can trigger an episode of decompensation. A primary goal of treatment is therefore to keep the person with mental illness stable and prevent escalation of the symptoms and rehospitalization.

State Psychiatric Hospitals

At the highest level, a person with mental illness is hospitalized in an institution or state hospital, which bears similarities to the asylum. Often, the individual is there for an indeterminate period of time; however, they are closely monitored and regularly evaluated by the psychiatrist. An individualized treatment plan is developed with the input of the person and his or her family. This details the goals and objectives that he or she is expected to accomplish, as well as the supports that would be provided by service providers such as the psychiatrist, case managers, and recreational therapists.

An important part of this plan is usually the supervision of medication management. Additionally, the individual engages in milieu therapy, where he or she participates in an array of socialization, recreation, and other therapeutic activities. Once the person is deemed to have stabilized and no longer needs this intensive array of services, he or she can be discharged back to the community. This is regarded as one of the more expensive levels of psychiatric treatment and is usually used as a last resort when there are concerns that the person with mental illness is not stable enough to maintain his or her safety or that of others in the community.

Regular Hospitals

A second level of care involves hospitalization but for a much shorter period of time. This occurs through either voluntary or involuntary commitment. In the first instance, the person arrives at the hospital's emergency room in a crisis, that is, she is not stable, and there is a concern that she will hurt herself or someone else. In this instance, the physician, after evaluation, makes a determination whether the person is stable enough to be discharged. Conversely, the person may need to be more closely observed for a longer period of time. In this case, the physician can implement a 72-hour observation period using the involuntary commitment statutes that are available in most states. A patient can thus be monitored in an extended observation bed (EOB), or temporary holding ward, which is available within comprehensive psychiatric emergency programs (CPEP). Therefore, the person is not fully admitted to the hospital, but is receiving all of the necessary treatment to prevent further decompensation.

If the individual is assessed as stable by the end of this time frame, he or she is discharged back into the community. In the event the individual is deemed to still be a danger to himself or herself and others, he or she can now be admitted into the hospital for a short-term stay. This can last anywhere from a day or two through a few weeks. Generally, hospitalizations that go beyond a few weeks are transferred to the state psychiatric hospitals such as Creedmoor or Bronx State Psychiatric in New York State.

Adult Homes and Shelters

There are also a number of adult homes and shelters, many of which are private, that make up part of the mental health treatment system. Persons with mental illness can have difficulty maintaining their daily tasks and taking care of themselves on their own. Given that, a network of homes provides a supportive living environment in which persons with mental illness can receive assistance to take their medications, to maintain their hygiene and personal care, and to manage their personal finances and living expenses. These adult homes and shelters have come under scrutiny for abuses including insanitary conditions, poor supervision, and economic abuse of the mentally ill. Based on the Olmstead Decision, the focus is on relocating persons into their individual apartments where they can be fully integrated into all aspects of living in the community.

Transitional and Private Housing

For those persons who have the wherewithal to live on their own in private apartments, incidental assistance may still be needed. They can be assigned intensive case managers (ICMs) who maintain contact with them at least on a monthly basis. The ICMs are responsible for ensuring that the person is appropriately engaging in the activities of daily living that can prevent hospitalization and keep him or her stable in the community. Thus, the ICM will check on events such as whether the person is keeping his or her various appointments, complying with medications, paying rent, or attending his or her group and/or individual therapy sessions. Individuals can also live in supportive housing that is less restrictive than the adult homes, where they can access ICM services.

Assisted Outpatient Treatment

Assisted outpatient treatment (AOT) refers to court-ordered outpatient treatment that can last from six months or more. If a person with serious mental illness is not complying with his or her medications, and there is a risk that the person can be a public safety, a court order can be sought by an interested party such as a spouse, to mandate the person into treatment. AOT is also called Kendra's Law, based on the legislation authorizing mandatory mental health treatment that went into effect in New York State in 1999 and was renewed in 2005. Sadly, Kendra Webdale was pushed under an oncoming train, by a person with serious and persistent mental illness. An evaluation study reported on the New York State OMH's website indicates that AOT was successful in reducing hospitalizations and incarceration, and in facilitating medication compliance.

Health Homes

A recent addition to the treatment environment is the health home. Authorized by the Affordable Care Act, health homes are expected to act as a central coordinating point for patients who have chronic, complex, medical, and behavioral care needs. States such as New York and Rhode Island have embraced this model and are working to refine its implementation. This includes how to best engage patients who are assigned to care managers and assure continuous communication among all service providers, while adhering to confidentiality and privacy. Health homes are expected to prevent the gaps in care that are common for persons with behavioral care needs. Potentially, this can help to improve mental and physical functioning, while decreasing or preventing hospitalization, and yielding cost savings, especially in the treatment of persons with serious and persistent mental illness.

Individual Providers

Lastly, while many persons receive their mental health care in a clinic, there are others who go to private individual providers. It is difficult to determine what percentage of persons this is, since data on this are not readily available. However, it appears that mental health clinics have high numbers of persons who may depend on public health insurance. It would make sense that those who could afford to would see private physicians and/or therapists, since it might be more convenient and afford them greater privacy.

Psychotherapy

It should also be clarified that not everyone needs to be medicated for a mental health disorder. Some individuals can successfully participate in therapy for a defined time. Others may need to continue on an ongoing basis. Given that there are several evidence-based models of psychotherapy such as cognitive behavioral therapy and dialectical behavioral therapy, an individual can be engaged using a specific model that has demonstrated positive outcomes.

MENTAL ILLNESS AND PTSD—THE VETERAN CONNECTION

What Is Stress?

One of the major contributors to mental illness is stress. But what is stress? It can be regarded as a mental (cognitive, emotional) and physical response to the environment in which we live. We do not all respond to the same stressor or stimuli in exactly the same manner, since our individual psychological differences contribute to how we perceive and react to various situations. Stress can be positive as well as negative. For instance, an individual may experience what is sometimes termed good stress when he is faced with the challenge of a new job. This can actually function as a catalyst and help promote new learning and adaptation in order for the person to do well.

Good stress can thus play a role in the individual's feelings of job satisfaction. If, however, the person has difficulty adapting and/or perceives the environment negatively, he may begin to experience higher levels of stress that can then become a barrier to optimal functioning. Instead of waking up and wanting to get to work, the person may become anxious and even fearful and may want to avoid the situation entirely. In chronic stressful situations, a person can eventually develop other medical and mental health conditions such as cardiovascular disease and depression that are related to how they perceive and react to their environment.

The Stress Response

While there are several frameworks that drive how we look at stress from a clinical perspective, the work of the classical theorist and endocrinologist, Hans Selye (1907–1982), has been extensively used. According to Selye, our bodies use specific biological mechanisms to respond to stress. He organizes these mechanisms into a three-part process that he calls the General Adaptation Syndrome.

Thus, once we perceive a stressor, we go into the alarm stage, or fight or flight, where we make a cognitive assessment of how harmful the stressor is. At the same time, the body begins to marshal the forces it may need such as releasing the stress hormones—adrenaline and cortisol. Based on our assessment, we proceed into the resistance stage in which we actively try to deal with the stressor. As part of this, the body continues to maintain elevated hormone levels, which trigger, in turn, higher heart and pulse rates, as well as quicker, shallower breathing.

Lastly, in the exhaustion stage, the body is still attempting to resolve the threat presented by the stressor. The shorter the time to resolution, the better; the longer it takes, the greater the likelihood that the body becomes overwhelmed and its resources are depleted. High stress situations that place an individual in this biological state for extended periods of time thus have both a mental and physiological impact on the individual.

Unfortunately, many people in the general population may not be familiar with theories or the research related to stress. Thus, the belief continues to exist that those individuals who are more vulnerable to stress are weak. If this individual happens to be an enlisted military person, he or she could find himself or herself in an isolated position, as the person may be hesitant to share how he or she is feeling with the platoon members or even the superiors. For example, some veterans report going to great extents to try to mask how they were feeling as they did not want to be perceived as unreliable or letting their peers down. Specifically, since service members are highly dependent on one another particularly when they are in a combat zone, individuals believed that it would significantly affect how other members of their platoon viewed and treated them. Thus, many were less inclined to come forward to seek support for stressful situations, as they knew that military culture emphasized strength and self-reliance. Others also believed they would be ridiculed if they showed weakness by seeking help.

Trauma

For the majority of us in the civilian population, the stressors that we encounter can be managed sufficiently so that they do not become detrimental to our bio-psycho-social functioning in the short and long terms. However, incidents such as an automobile accident, rape, a violent encounter on the street, a natural disaster, or war can be so much outside of our usual sphere of functioning that we experience what is called trauma. Trauma can be described as an incident that is so deeply disturbing that it activates our stress responses in an atypical manner.

Therefore, theoretically, if we apply Selye's framework, we should be able to move from the alarm, to the resistance stage, and hopefully resolve the issue/stressor at some point during the exhaustion stage. If this occurs, the body can return to a state of homeostasis. However, if we experience an event that is so unusual and disturbing, we might be unable to make sense of what occurred. Thus, it can be more difficult to work with or to find a resolution for such a stressor. Many individuals experience numbness and shock immediately after a disturbing traumatic event. Some schools of thought such as the psychodynamic perspective see this as possibly being one way that the unconscious mind is trying to help protect the person. Others may not experience the major stress reactions until a significant time has passed. This can be weeks, months, or even years. For another subset of persons, the reactions may be immediate and continue over a protracted period.

While stress responses can decrease over time, for some persons, they can become disruptive and interrupt how they live, work, and overall function for the rest of the life span. This impaired functioning is particularly true for some individuals such as veterans. In fact, our veterans are one of the main groups who have been affected by severe stressful situations. As a result, they have a higher likelihood than many other persons in the general population of developing a particular mental health condition—PTSD.

Across several studies, military/combat exposure has been found second, only to interpersonal violence (physical and sexual assault), in having the highest probability of contributing to PTSD. Unfortunately, while both male and female veterans report higher levels of sexual assault than civilians, women are still more likely to experience interpersonal violence than men. Therefore, female veterans are at a higher risk than men of developing

PTSD due to both interpersonal violence and combat exposure. Data from the National Stressful Events Survey (October, 2013) found that close to 13% of women had lifetime PTSD as diagnosed by the DSM-V criteria, as compared with about 6% of men. Women's PTSD was, however, associated with more than one precipitating event.

Responding to Veterans

Since the advent of World War I, it became evident that persons who faced military/combat exposure situations appeared to develop specific symptoms. It was not until during World War II, however, that the need was recognized for formal diagnostic criteria for what was then called several other names such as shell shock, combat fatigue, and battle stress. The Veterans Administration (VA) was the first entity to systematically create a conceptual framework and standardize the symptoms for PTSD. According to published reports, by the time the APA had published its own manual, the DSM-I in 1952, they were labeling the symptoms of PTSD under the umbrella of the gross stress reaction. The term "PTSD" did not come into common usage until during the Vietnam War and was included in the APA's third diagnostic manual. While this helped to create a framework for examining PTSD on a wider scale, it did not immediately lead to improvements in diagnosing or treating persons with this condition.

Individuals who faced combat situations were still routinely ignored, and the belief was that they were exaggerating or making up their symptoms. As large numbers of Vietnam veterans returned, the public did not necessarily embrace the service they had provided. Thus, lack of a social and political will and deficits in resources led to the absence of mental health care for veterans. Despite complaints of symptoms among those who served, they were often ignored by the VA as well as the regular mental health treatment system.

Undoubtedly, this lack of much needed care for veterans was in fact discriminatory, especially when it is compared with that received by those who sustained physical injuries. This situation contributed to many veterans engaging in destructive behaviors, post-service, as they sought to cope with the symptoms of PTSD as well as other mental health conditions. This includes high rates of substance use, family violence, unemployment, and homelessness. Sadly, while those with physical injuries were considered to be entitled to receive health care services, those with hidden mental health conditions such as PTSD were not eligible.

Advocacy as well as increased incidences of social dislocation and disruptive behavior from veterans led to more attention being paid to PTSD.

Despite greater acknowledgment that it was a legitimate mental health condition that could have serious outcomes, a concerted campaign was still carried out to minimize the number of veterans who would be officially diagnosed and thus be eligible for ongoing veterans' benefits. Thus, veterans have also been discriminated against with regard to their eligibility to be deemed disabled, and thus be able to collect financial benefits, which many have desperately needed. In fact, policies were only put in place during the administration of President Obama, which mandated that the VA should thoroughly assess, treat, and provide all service-related benefits to veterans who were affected by PTSD.

Suicide

One of the major problems that has emerged for veterans is the risk of engaging in an attempted or completed suicide. Some studies support PTSD as one of the major contributory factors to suicide, especially among Vietnam veterans. Other data reported by the VA indicate that since 2000, the rate of suicide among veterans has ranged from 18 to 22 persons daily, or roughly one person every 65 minutes. Male veterans were three times more likely to commit suicide than female veterans. Females, however, were twice as likely to engage in this act, as compared with women in the civilian population.

Additionally, veterans who had not been deployed to Iran or Afghanistan were found to have a rate of suicide that was close to 15% higher than those who faced active service. The VA has not been able to conclusively determine what accounts for this differential rate of suicide. However, since 2007, aggressive initiatives have been put into place to identify the risk factors for suicide among the veteran population and to make intensive outreach and effort to reduce and prevent suicide. The Joshua Omvig Suicide Prevention Act was signed into law on November 5, 2007, to target veterans in crisis and those at high risk for suicide. The Veterans Suicide Prevention Hotline Act of 2007 was also enacted to provide a 24-hour hotline.

Families of veterans who have committed suicide are deeply affected by what occurs. Some have reported that once such an act occurs, they have been shunned by other veterans' families or by the men and women with whom their loved one served. Since the act of suicide can sometimes be seen as one of weakness or even selfishness, family members also feel ashamed of what their loved one has done and are very sensitive to any indication that they are being avoided by others. In addition, family members report experiencing deep-seated feelings of guilt and often blame themselves for not having been able to prevent this outcome.

Despite any accomplishments veterans may have achieved, those who commit suicide become ineligible for awards such as the Purple Heart. Families question whether their actions, which might represent helplessness and hopelessness, should prevent them from earning recognition that they had already earned. Thus, official policies can be regarded as discriminatory with regard to that issue.

Unfortunately, for a long time, there has been no official policy of reaching out to the family to provide support after a tragedy like suicide has occurred. While this policy remains nonexistent, families themselves have formed support groups and have started an extensive peer support network to assist one another in their time of need. Addressing such resource gaps to help families move on and deal with ongoing emotional stress and their own trauma is still needed.

PTSD Indicators

As part of addressing the historical concerns with the poor treatment of veterans, the VA is engaging in education and awareness campaigns using public service announcements, videos, peer educators, and peer counselors, as well as informational handouts and materials. For example, on its website, the VA alerts veterans and their families to the four types of symptoms they should look out for that can point to PTSD—reliving the event; avoiding people, places, and things associated with the event; experiencing arousal or strong feelings; and negative thoughts or beliefs.

The first involves reliving the situation over and over. For example, the person may have nightmares and flashbacks. In the latter, the person feels that he or she is still going through or is trapped in the incident.

The second type of symptom to look for is avoidance. With this, the individual may begin to avoid people, places, and things that reminds him or her of the traumatic event. For instance, a veteran once shared with this writer how difficult it was for him to commute to and from his appointments. Although he lived in a large city and the underground subway system was very reliable, he could not bring himself to use it, as the sound of the train arriving and departing reminded him of ammunition being fired during his tour of duty in Vietnam. He reported how the few times he had tried to use the subway he would become fearful and begin to sweat. He would also feel his heart racing, and his breathing would become labored.

The physiological responses reported by this veteran would continue for a period of time after he left the environment and would contribute to difficulty sleeping. He indicated that it took him days before he got back to some sense of normalcy. The responses described by this person are typical of the third type of symptom of PTSD that is called hyperarousal.

Lastly, an individual can undergo negative changes in how he or she views the world. Thus, combat veterans especially may experience a great deal of guilt and shame regarding the actions that they were compelled to take during their tour of duty. When this involves the loss of life, it could be even more difficult for the person to move forward and sustain more balanced beliefs and feelings.

Family members and friends should thus observe the individual to determine whether there are changes in his or her functioning. These can include bouts of anger, nightmares, and uncontrollable impulses. In fact, the veteran should be encouraged to discuss any signs that suggest that there are differences from what the person's normal is with their health care provider.

Suicide Indicators

Similarly to being aware of the indicators of PTSD, family members and friends should also become familiar with the indicators of suicide. This can help to recognize whether they need to encourage a loved one to seek emergency mental health treatment. Additionally, being better informed about what could be going on can also assist the family in decreasing the stigma that is associated with mental illness. The U.S. Army's Department of Behavioral Health indicates that the four S's process can be used as a suicide prevention guide. This refers to screening the individual about how he or she is feeling. It should include directly asking whether the person is feeling to hurt himself or herself; spotting the inconsistencies in the person's behavior such as giving away his or her possessions; securing the person by obtaining any needed care such as calling emergency services; and supporting the person's ongoing treatment.

Familiarity with this tool can thus be invaluable as part of a suicide prevention plan. Family members should also be aware that conditions such as PTSD, TBI, other mental health disorders that have already been diagnosed, or physical injuries such as loss of a limb can also place the veteran at an elevated risk of suicide.

Issues Contributing to Ongoing Discrimination

How veterans are perceived by some individuals can contribute to ongoing discrimination against them. Specifically, they can be regarded as individuals who chose combat as a way to resolve concerns versus using a more conciliatory approach. This can lead them to being treated in an indifferent or even hostile manner by some segments of the civilian population. Veterans can also be discriminated against by others as they can be experiencing an episode of mental illness and may be reacting to particular symptoms. Thus, they can be seen as somewhat strange by persons who are not familiar with and do not understand what is going on with them. Veterans can also engender fear if persons are familiar with their status as trained professionals and believe that they have ongoing access to their service weapons. High-profile cases involving veterans who have committed public acts of aggression and violence have also made many persons somewhat more cautious of interacting with veterans who may present as impaired.

One of the factors affecting veterans has been the absence of sufficient qualified mental health professionals to provide timely and effective services. Media reports about extensive backlogs of persons applying for services have acted as a catalyst to help bring needed changes to the system. Thus, as part of the national movement to improve veterans' services, the VA has been actively recruiting and/or attempting to train mental health professionals. An overall shortage of these providers in several communities, however, means that vacancies may continue to exist for several key positions for some time to come. This is also affected by the perception that treating veterans can be a difficult prospect; thus, newer graduates especially may be concerned as to whether they have the requisite knowledge, skills, values, and attitudes to work with the veteran population.

Data collected from the Veterans Suicide Prevention Hotline highlight that the majority of callers to the 24-hour hotline were males, who were between the ages of 50 and 59. About one-fifth of the callers to the hotline call more than once per month. A corresponding decrease was observed in the number of veterans who reattempted a suicide event. Although the number of women veterans who commit suicide is less than men, women are often socialized as caregivers and might be less willing to reach out to the hotline for help, especially since they also face higher levels of shame, guilt, and stigma that are associated with mental illness as well as the field of employment that they have chosen. Thus, while the number of female veterans who are receiving services is reportedly growing, maximal outreach is still needed to ensure that these women can feel supported and engaged, and to identify their needs prior to the onset of a crisis.

It should also be remembered that additional to PTSD, veterans may also be experiencing other mental health conditions including substance use disorders that can exacerbate their symptoms. The VA report indicated that there was a high prevalence of attempted suicides that were related to overdose or intentional poisoning. Female substance users often face more difficulty accessing and remaining in treatment due to their caregiving functions, as well as discrimination and stigma related to their use of substances. While interventions are needed to prevent the onset of substance use disorders in veterans as a group, for female veterans especially, what arrangements are being made to assist them with child or dependent care and other supports that would be required to help optimize their treatment?

Thus, despite the gains being made in addressing veterans' issues, there are still pockets of discrimination that exist, which are related to how veterans as well as mental illness are viewed. Public service announcement campaigns have tried to directly target the veterans who are at risk for suicide and mental health treatment to link them with services. Education is still needed for the civilian population at large to ensure a better understanding of what mental illness is. Further, the public needs to be more aware of how concerned community members can best help support veterans who are experiencing symptoms of mental illness.

Addressing the following questions can thus help to decrease discrimination and further the cause of veterans. How should a neighbor or other community member respond if they believe a veteran is decompensating? Is it better for a concerned citizen to contact a VA health care center, if they realize a veteran is in need of mental health services, or should they just call 9-1-1? Does law enforcement have responders who are sensitive to the issues they might be facing? How can civilians who have never served reach out to veterans in their communities to assist them with the post-deployment reintegration process?

CHAPTER 8

Mental Illness and the Criminal Justice System

WHO ARE THE CRIMINALLY INSANE?

The criminally insane can be defined as persons with a diagnosis of any mental health disorder who have been convicted of one or more acts that are against the law of a particular jurisdiction. For a long time, the general connotation of who the criminally insane are has focused on persons who commit serious crimes such as rape, homicide, or that involving severe bodily injury. Increasingly, however, this has been expanded to incorporate primarily persons who commit crimes such as drug possession, use, and sales, as well as property crimes like theft and burglary.

HISTORICAL TREATMENT OF THE CRIMINALLY INSANE

Issues related to what to do with persons with mental illness who commit crimes appear to have bedeviled society since time immemorial. However, records suggest that efforts have been made to ensure that persons with mental illness are not discriminated against from a legal perspective. For example, early cultures such as the Mesopotamians and Romans tried to ensure that persons who did not have the cognitive ability to recognize that they had committed a crime were not unfairly punished. Within the modern era, by 1724, a legal precedent was set in the British courts where an acquittal of a person with mental illness was based on whether the person was functioning like a wild beast or a babe and was therefore unable to demonstrate the cognition and responsibility expected of an adult individual.

Another early piece of legislation that tried to deal with mental illness and crimes was the 1800 Criminal Lunatics Act, which was passed by the British after an attempt on the life of the king. Records indicate that it focused on persons who had committed felonies, for instance murder and treason, and imbued the crown as well as certain legal individuals such as the JP and the lord chancellor, to provide for the safe custody and confinement of persons with mental illness.

An additional law—the 1840 Insane Prisoners Act—addressed persons who had committed misdemeanors. Once an inquiry established that the person was mentally ill, he or she could be ordered to be confined in a lunatic asylum. By 1843, an assassination attempt on the British prime minister that resulted in the death of his secretary triggered an extensive social and legal examination about culpability related to insanity.

This resulted in the M'Naughten or McNaughton Rules that have been applied in multiple jurisdictions within the United States and around the world, since approximately 1851. Specifically, these rules identify a set of questions that should be used by the court as a guide when faced with a defendant who potentially has mental illness, to help determine whether the person was able to distinguish right from wrong at the time the crime was committed. Based on these, a person could be found to be guilty of a crime, but not culpable due to insanity. In other words, the person was non compos mentis, that is, not in his right mind and therefore not guilty due to insanity.

There continues to be a great deal of controversy regarding the application of the McNaughton Rules. For example, some individuals question why they should be used to support medical conditions that could be stabilized with appropriate treatment. And some jurisdictions have tried to clarify their application. The majority of places continue to require at least two formal psychiatric or psychological evaluations of competence as part of a determination of insanity. However, while this is not seen as a black-and-white issue, the legal processes that have been put in place have served to provide a check and balance to decrease discrimination for persons with mental health disorders who must face the courts for serious issues.

Several high-profile cases have demonstrated the use of this process. For example, the trial for the defendant in the Aurora, Colorado, incident highlighted this. Specifically, the defendant, in July 2012, entered a movie theater during a scheduled midnight screening of a new movie, *The Dark Knight Rises*. As per news reports, armed with multiple weapons, the defendant opened fire that left 12 individuals deceased and 70 severely injured. Both court-appointed psychiatrists for the prosecution indicated that he had the presence to know (or had a guilty mind) that the act he was engaged in (the guilty act) was wrong at the time. However, both also agreed that the significant factor behind this heinous act was the fact that he was affected by delusional thinking related to his diagnosis of mental illness.

In this case, the jury concurred in that it found the defendant guilty of multiple counts of murder and attempted murder at the conclusion of his trial in July 2015. However, in the sentencing phase, they elected not to use the death penalty for the defendant, but recommended life imprisonment without parole. Apparently, some members' belief that the mental health status of the defendant was critical to his conduct played a role in their deliberations. Thus, the jury could not unanimously agree that the defendant deserved the death penalty. Due process had clearly worked, and the defendant had been afforded the full protection offered by the court to plead his case of insanity. But are all defendants with mental illness who become involved in the criminal justice system receiving the necessary legal representation and due process to ensure equity in their cases? A closer examination of the criminally insane and some of their presenting issues can help to clarify this.

CURRENT ESTIMATES OF THE CRIMINALLY INSANE

Over the past decade, the United States has become known as the country with one of the highest incarceration rates in the world. According to the Bureau of Justice Statistics (2015), roughly 1 out of every 110 adults are behind bars, the highest number of any developed nation in the world. As reported in the Sourcebook of Criminal Justice Statistics (2013), from 2010 through 2012, the rate of persons in U.S. jails ranged from 242 through 237 per 100,000 individuals in the civilian population, while the rate for those in prison ranged from 500 through 480 per 100,000 persons respectively in the civilian population.

When compared with the actual rates of crime across a variety of places around the globe, the rate of incarceration within the United States is much higher and has actually increased even when crime rates are down. As a result, advocates for sentencing reform point to this as evidence of discrimination with regard to who is the most likely to be incarcerated. Since persons with mental illness who become involved with the criminal justice system are more likely to commit certain types of crimes such as assault or are likely to have a co-occurring substance use disorder, are they facing discriminatory legal practices at a higher rate than offenders without mental illness?

Among individuals who are incarcerated for drug crimes, 18% had engaged in the sale and/or manufacturing of a drug, with the remaining 82%

being convicted of drug possession. But what is drug possession? An individual usually gets this charge if he or she is found to be carrying a certain amount of a substance that the person knows is illegal. For instance, if a person is searched and heroin or cocaine is found on his or her person, the individual can be charged with drug possession. The amount of the substance that the person has makes a difference depending on where he or she is arrested, since each state sets its own measurements for what constitutes simple possession, that is, the individual has the drug because he or she is using it. If the person has a larger quantity of a drug, he or she can be charged with having the intent to sell or distribute it.

Additionally, if a drug is not found on an individual's person, but is in his or her belonging such as in a vehicle, the person can still be charged with constructive possession of the drug. Exceptions to the fourth amendment right to unnecessary search and seizures that have been authorized by the Supreme Court have played a major role with regard to these cases. Some civil rights advocates question as discriminatory, how aggressive application of the exceptions has been applied primarily to a narrow section of the populace.

Given the large numbers of persons incarcerated for drug possession, the data suggest that the majority of persons with a history of drug crimes may in fact be affected by a substance use disorder, as the drugs were in their possession. Even for those persons who were charged with the intent to distribute, how accurate was this assessment? Data from a study conducted by the Bureau of Justice in 2006 indicated that approximately 75% of state prisoners and local jail inmates had substance use disorders. About 35% of these also reported using drugs at the time they committed their offense.

PROBLEM-SOLVING COURT MODEL

In jurisdictions like New York State and California, however, the drug court or problem-solving court model as it is also called has been embraced. As of August 1, 2014, New York State has 146 functioning problem-solving courts. These are developed with specific themes in mind so that the resources can best be harnessed to address specific issues. Thus, there are several drug treatment courts, domestic violence courts, human trafficking courts, mental health courts, sex offender courts, veterans courts, and the like distributed throughout the state. Offenders are steered toward a court based on their presenting issues.

In New York State, for example, there are seven mental health courts that serve defendants whose mental illness has played a major role in their criminal offence. In California, 40 mental health courts, including 11 that serve juvenile offenders, address crimes that are related to the person's mental illness. A team-based approach is used to offer psychological services. In addition, intensive supervision/court monitoring and collaboration among service providers are encouraged to help the defendant address his or her needs and attain stability. In the event the individual fails to follow through with necessary appointments, treatment, and so on, the person can face sanctions up to incarceration for a few days or weeks, or his or her full sentence. Thus, the court still retains its right to implement a judicial outcome at any point that it deems it necessary.

Similarly as in California and other jurisdictions, these problem-solving courts have demonstrated decreased recidivism and reoffending for persons who are enrolled for services. What seems somewhat controversial is that although behavioral courts were set up since the late 1980s in several jurisdictions, and they have demonstrated effectiveness, they have often not served some of the individuals who could benefit the most from their structure. For example, part of the eligibility criteria might be that the person has to be a first-time offender. Thus, even in a progressive state like New York, access to mental health treatment may not come in time to prevent the offending behavior, as the persons who are served have already engaged in a detrimental act.

Another issue is that the number of defendants who require problem-solving services may actually overwhelm the system. Thus, only a percentage can obtain the team-based approach offered by the Mental Health Court. Sometimes, also, alternative sentencing initiatives have been rejected by the respective district attorneys in favor of a tough-on-crime stance of increased conviction rates and harsher charges and penalties. While many offenders could have been redirected to treatment earlier, possibly even prior to the onset or escalation of an additional co-occurring disorder, this issue is not assessed in all jurisdictions; or if assessed, it is overlooked in favor of a more punitive approach to addressing crime.

When one considers the large numbers of individuals within the penal system with mental health disorders, the need for early assessment and redirection becomes even more critical. In fact, according to the Bureau of Justice (2006), more than half of incarcerated persons have mental health problems. Within the federal and state prisons, 45% and 56% of persons had mental illness respectively, while within the local jails, 64% of individuals have a mental health problem. In Pennsylvania, for example, reports indicate that approximately one in three incarcerated individuals has mental illness (*The Sacramento Bee*, August 2, 2015).

In New York State, the Independent Budget Office (2014) reported that approximately 40% of inmates (or about 4,400 individuals) suffer from a mental health disorder, on any given day. These same individuals are over-represented in about two-thirds of the violent incidents that occur as per the NYS Correctional Department (2013). As a result, inmates with mental illness are often placed in isolation at higher rates than those without mental health issues. This demonstrates a lack of understanding of the characteristics of several mental health disorders, and this can actually have fatal results as defendants who are placed in isolation have a higher rate of attempting or committing suicide.

TRAINING OF CORRECTIONAL PERSONNEL

One of the major controversial concerns is what type of training is required by correctional officers and individuals who are responsible for supervising the incarcerated population. Specifically, how should correctional officers respond to individuals with mental illness? If a person is diagnosed with a particular mental health condition, to what degree does supervising officers need to know what is going on with that individual? Also, given the variety and presentation of mental health disorders, what is the best way to train correctional officers so that they can interact with persons in a manner that would elicit more cooperative responses?

Unfortunately, poorly trained officers and volatile offenders with mental illness can set the stage for a great deal of conflict. As a result, the use of excessive force to subdue inmates with mental health disorders has become a major concern, and this has come to light in several jurisdictions. Additionally, there has been an increase in the number of women entering the prison system. Some of these have been casualties of the drug war and have been incarcerated for crimes such as transporting drugs or being mules. Women in the general population, however, tend to experience higher rates of mental illness than men. Within the penal system, this pattern remains the same. According to the Bureau of Justice (2006), 61% of women in federal prisons, 73% in state prisons, and 75% in local jails have mental health disorders, as compared with 44%, 55%, and 63% of males. The failure of correctional officers and those responsible for supervising these women to exhibit ethical conduct has resulted in documented sexual and thus psychological victimization.

It should also be noted that male prisoners have experienced sexual and psychological assault at the hands of other inmates as well as correctional personnel in violation of their constitutional rights. This has been a particular concern for those males who identify as gay, bisexual, transgender, and queer. These men, and also women, are likely to be humiliated and to experience physical violence related to their sexual orientation, which is clearly discriminatory.

CIVIL RIGHTS OF INSTITUTIONALIZED PEOPLES ACT (CRIPA) OF 1980

Large-scale abuses within the penal system drew the attention of advocates including the DOJ. The latter is entrusted with ensuring protections for the institutionalized population under the Civil Rights of Institutionalized Peoples Act of 1980. According to the act, any person who is in the care of a state institution, including a jail, prison, nursing home, mental health facility, or institution for persons with intellectual challenges, has a right to be safe and free from oppression. In the event that the Office of the Attorney General identifies abuses within the system, it is authorized to intervene on behalf of the institutionalized population to protect their rights.

Given the complaints of advocates that there were major abuse within the penal system, legal action was undertaken in several states to ensure the rights of incarcerated persons. For instance, California became one of the first states where an investigation was undertaken to ascertain complaints about abuses within the criminal justice system as a whole, as well as that targeting persons with mental illness. Thus, since about 1996, the DOJ has been conducting civil investigations within the California prison system. The DOJ found "a pattern of constitutionally deficient mental health care for prisoners, including inadequate suicide prevention practices; . . . that conditions under which prisoners with mental illness were housed exacerbated the risk of suicide;" and that excessive force was used against prisoners with mental illness. As of August 5, 2015, the DOJ enacted court-enforceable compliance agreements within the Los Angeles County Jails in California to address the abuses that were substantiated.

In addition to California, the DOJ is investigating more than 30 other jurisdictions for a range of abuses including Westchester County Jail in New York and Jackson Detention Center in Mississippi. It also has ongoing voluntary and mandatory agreements with a number of jurisdictions. Undoubtedly, this initiative has contributed to reducing abusive and discriminatory treatment of vulnerable prisoners with mental health issues, as well as to overhauling the system that existed in some states that allowed this abuse to proliferate.

APPROACHES TO PUBLIC SAFETY

What has been happening within the current infrastructure suggests that society as a whole still needs to take a closer look at how we deal with issues such as law enforcement, public safety, punishment versus rehabilitation, and prevention. The data from multiple sources highlight that there is a significant skew in the system related to how policing is done and how individuals are sentenced. Some researchers point to the incarceration rates of minorities, who are primarily African American and Latino, for drug-involved crimes, which have reached as high as 80% in some jurisdictions. Since similar rates of drug involvement are found among majority individuals within the United States, some question the reasons why their rates of incarceration differ so significantly and whether discriminatory racial profiling is being used.

It might be more meaningful, however, to focus on whether incarceration should be the legitimate response for substance users. Prominent advocacy entities such as the American Civil Liberties Union indicate that the War on Drugs that was initiated in 1969, under the administration of President Nixon, has been a failure and has resulted in a great deal of devastation to poorer communities because of the unequal toll that it has had on family, social, economic, and political life. In fact, increasingly, legislators have been called on to recognize the inherent discriminatory approach that has been entrenched within the criminal justice system and how it treats persons with substance use and other mental health disorders.

Mandatory sentencing laws have contributed to discrimination. For example, the "Rockefeller Drug Laws" passed in New York State in 1973, authorized minimum sentences of 15 years to life for drug-involved defendants. The Anti-Drug Abuse Acts passed by Congress in 1986 and 1988 included the stipulation that 1 gram of crack should receive the same sentence as 100 grams of powdered cocaine. It did not help that crack was being used primarily by lower-income, minority persons, as compared with cocaine being associated with more affluent, non-minorities. The "Three Strikes and You're Out," law passed in California in 1994, authorized a minimum of 25 years to life for second and third drug-involved offences, which were often regarded as falling under the serious or violent category. Little or no attention was paid to the mental health status of the defendant, as the need for treatment was subjugated by the goal of punishment.

Attempts have been made to address some of the legal and racial disparities with the Fair Sentencing Act of 2010. This reduced the ratio of cocaine to crack from18 grams to 1 gram, among other reforms. Unfortunately, once an individual with mental illness is incarcerated, he or she is now facing the stigma of mental illness or of having a substance use disorder, as well as that of having been in jail or prison. The scars from incarceration can thus last a lifetime, especially as it is now harder for the person to establish a stable lifestyle. A well-known author and researcher on criminal justice issues, Michelle Alexander, indicates that there are no prohibitions regarding legally discriminating against ex-offenders in several areas such as employment, housing, and participating in the political process. Many states remove the right to vote, and prevent formerly incarcerated persons from obtaining transitional benefits such as food stamps.

Since it can already be more stressful for the person with mental illness to seek resources and or to advocate for himself or herself, the individual might find himself or herself in a situation where he or she is living on the margins of society and is now even more vulnerable to the impact of depression, anxiety, and other clinical disorders, as well as substance use and poor overall physical health. Thus, individuals with mental illness and a background of incarceration tend to be at a higher risk of recidivism and might find themselves in and out of the revolving door of prison or jail. Punitive and discriminatory criminal justice policies thus play a major role in facilitating this inequitable situation.

SCARCE RESOURCES

Some of the ongoing controversies involve how scarce resources should be used to address criminal justice concerns especially for persons with mental illness, and responding to this question is closely intertwined with one's perspective on how public safety should be approached.

LEGAL REPRESENTATION

The first controversy relates to legal representation for persons who are arrested and indigent. Sadly, this applies to many of the persons with mental illness who become involved with the criminal justice system. One of the rights afforded to any person in the United States who is arrested for a crime that has a potential sentence of jail or prison time is that the individual is entitled to legal representation. As a result, all jurisdictions have some type of Indigent Defense Services, which consist of public defenders or attorneys who are hired by the state. Due to the widespread involvement of persons with mental illness with the criminal justice system, these defense attorneys are often called on to represent the indigent mentally ill in court. Newspaper reports and articles discuss how overworked and overwhelmed public attorneys carry caseloads of clients that are so high that it is very difficult for them to adequately represent the concerns of those who have committed crimes.

In addition, attorneys who may not be very familiar with mental illness and some of its presenting concerns may be assigned to represent a defendant. Since mental illness is episodic for many individuals, this aspect of the functioning of the indigent client with mental illness might be totally ignored or may never be identified as the person goes through the courts. Thus, someone who may benefit more from being mandated to treatment may be sentenced to go to jail, without any interventions. While there, stressful circumstances can exacerbate his or her situation, so that the individual starts acting out as he or she decompensates. This is likely to lead to the person going back in front of the judge to plead guilty to a crime such as assault that the person committed while in jail. Thus, his or her sentence becomes extended, and the individual still may not get the benefit of the mental health treatment that he or she requires.

Another concern is that the person may be placed in solitary confinement as a form of punishment and/or controlling his or her behavior. However, his or her already fragile mental state now places the individual at a higher risk of suicide. As indicated earlier, persons who are placed in solitary confinement are at a much higher risk of suicide that the remaining prison population. Persons with mental illness are also more likely to remain incarcerated for longer periods. The New York City Independent Budget Office (May 2015) found that inmates with mental illness spent on average 77 days more in jail than persons without mental health disorders.

In states like New York, California, and New Mexico that have introduced the problem-solving courts, there is a greater likelihood that the person with mental illness may be identified. However, as indicated, the assessment of many professionals who are familiar with the system is that the majority of persons with mental illness who can benefit never come into contact with the mental health courts. Since scarce resources play a role in the restricted criteria that is used to steer persons through this type of legal intervention, what might be a better way to determine who needs this type of intervention and how can it be best funded?

Another issue is that the problem-solving courts are set up, in some jurisdictions, with a focus on a specific issue like mental health or substance use. This may actually create an artificial barrier as there is a high likelihood of the person having a co-occurring disorder. However, social attitudes regarding substance use have at times been more stigmatizing than that related to mental illness. Thus, the substance user is often viewed pejoratively as a person who is engaged in an illegal act, as well as an individual who can control his or her substance use if the person makes a greater effort. From a policy position, we may be playing into these underlying memes by maintaining separate Drug Courts and Mental Health

Courts. As we move forward in refining these models, it may thus be more helpful to approach it from the Behavioral Health Court perspective, as tested in California. Integration can best yield benefits in simplifying assessment, coordination, and monitoring of all needed services, using a one-stop shop.

REHABILITATION VERSUS PUNISHMENT

The second controversy has to do with rehabilitation versus punishment and at its heart lies a central question. What do we want the penal system to look like? Should we continue to lock people up and throw away the keys, especially when the data show it has not enhanced public safety? Rather, it has led to overcrowded prisons and jails and escalating costs of incarceration.

According to the DOJ (2006), for instance, it costs approximately $65,000, annually, of taxpayers' money to maintain an individual within the federal prison system. Costs vary in the state jails and prisons, with the DOJ reporting a range from $21,000 to $43,000, per inmate, per year. States with higher costs of living, such as New York and California, can see higher costs, per person, for incarceration. In New York State, for instance, the cost per inmate, per year, was close to $168,000 in 2012 (Independent Budget Office, 2014).

We know that persons with mental illness are more likely to be rearrested and to cycle through the system multiple times. What is the underlying value society places on rehabilitation? Is it to reintroduce these individuals to their communities so that they can lead productive lives after they have paid their debt to society? Or is the system meant to simply punish the person while he is incarcerated and continue to place roadblocks in his or her way to stability, long after the person leaves the jail or prison? How should we continue to finance the growing costs of prisons and jails? Should we be expanding these institutions rather than seeking more creative ways to have individuals comply with social mores and avoid the extensive personal and social costs faced by incarcerated persons? Further, what needs to happen when a person is incarcerated? What is the best way to spend taxpayers' money so that the risk of recidivism is minimized?

Prison-based initiatives that were implemented in the 1970s and 1980s focused heavily on education and vocational training for individuals who were sometimes illiterate. The data indicate that those persons who received education including high school diplomas and college degrees were at a lower rate of reoffending. Punitive legislative policies during the

1990s removed access to Pell grants, which prisoners were allowed to use to seek a college education. And any person who had a felony was deemed ineligible to apply for student loans or to receive financial aid.

While some states tried to bypass these restrictions, the sum total was that access to educational programs was significantly decreased for incarcerated persons. Post-incarceration also, the individual was not able to receive assistance to facilitate the development of economic self-sufficiency. For persons with mental illness who have already experienced multiple barriers and interruptions in stabilizing, such legislative policies have clearly been discriminatory.

While the administration of President Obama has signaled a willingness to consider federal funds to test the implementation of creative strategies that would provide supports for educational programs, there still continues to be a great deal of disagreement regarding this. In making a decision, however, it might be necessary to consider what is the greater public good—to support a person in prison for much of his life or to help provide him or her with a pathway to self-reliance. The mental health gains that can be obtained from helping a person to stabilize also need to be examined.

The research shows a relationship between better education and better health and an enhanced quality of life. Can helping a person with mental illness move from less educated to more educated and better able to make positive decisions also make an impact on their mental health? Factors such as medication adherence and medical follow-up, effective communication with the health care provider, and preventive medical care can all make a difference in helping an individual to stabilize from mental illness. Evidence suggests that the returns on any cost outlay to help persons with histories of incarceration and mental illness would be regained.

POST-INCARCERATION RESOURCES

The third controversy has to do with post-incarceration resources. While there are several programs in some states that are focusing on re-entry, one of the major deficits with nearly all of these lies with housing. As we know, it is critical to all of us to have a place to call our own where we can safely leave our belongings, and go to sleep, or simply relax and regenerate when we need to. For persons with mental illness who pass through the criminal justice system, this becomes more of a distant reality.

High rates of homelessness are found among persons with mental illness. In fact, it is not quite clear, which comes first, the chicken or the egg. Thus, are persons homeless first and develop poor mental health, or is the mental illness one of the primary contributory factors to the homelessness? Both perspectives are most likely correct for some segment of the population with SMI.

The NYC Department of Homeless Services (December, 2005) reported on the comparative causes of hospitalization among non-homeless and homeless adults in New York City. They found that among non-homeless persons, 5% were hospitalized for mental illness, 3% for substance use, and 2% for alcoholism. Among homeless persons, however, 14% were hospitalized for mental illness, 31% for substance use, and 24% for alcoholism. Reported illnesses were also more severe for the homeless adults who spent a longer time being hospitalized than their counterparts. The mortality rate of homeless adults was also found to be higher than those in the non-homeless population. It should additionally be noted that while several federal and local initiatives have addressed chronic homelessness among veterans, they still comprise a significant part of the homeless population.

Since persons with mental illness including a co-occurring substance use disorder can be at a higher risk of engaging in a violent crime such as assault, they are also likely to end up with a criminal justice record, including felonies. In several states that provide subsidized housing including in government-managed sites, the rules for eligibility may stipulate that no felons need apply. In some instances, other family members can also face eviction when a family member with mental illness ends up with a felony conviction and may have to go through an extensive appeals process that they are not guaranteed to win. In many ways, this is clearly discriminatory.

Some may point to the other persons who live in public housing and indicate that they have a right to feel safe and to live in an environment that does not unduly expose them to persons with mental illness who have criminal justice backgrounds. Others highlight that what the family actually needs is assistance addressing the concern and that evicting the family or individual with mental illness makes the problem worse. Left untreated, the substance use and other mental health disorder/s are more likely to become worse and eventually lead to higher costs of medical care. They can additionally contribute to increased incidents related to homeless persons with mental illness menacing or even attacking passersby.

Rather than just ignoring the problems or using solely a punitive approach, treatment and other needed services are therefore a more effective intervention to ensure the safety of all parties—the person with mental illness, their families, and the community-at-large. Initiatives led by the U.S. Department of Housing and Urban Development (HUD), in conjunction with local governments, have been attempting to address this, especially in larger cities such as New York and Los Angeles, where 20% of the homeless population can be found (HUD, November 21, 2013).

Voluntary and Involuntary Commitment

Another controversy regarding persons with mental illness relates to involuntary commitment. This refers to the act of admitting a person with mental illness into a hospital for psychiatric reasons without his or her consent. Dual concerns underlie this practice—concern for the safety of the individual, as well as the safety of the public. Historically, fear and lack of understanding about mental illness have acted as catalysts for involuntarily confining persons to the asylums. As previously indicated, English legislation from the 1850s created a system where the person had to be seen by a physician and an assessment had to be documented as to the reason/s the person needed to be admitted. Eventually, no one was to be confined in a facility for persons with insanity without this assessment. In addition, court assessments or inquiriendos were used as part of the commitment process, especially for the chancery lunatics. One of the problems with the early attempts at involuntary commitment in the United States was that there was no clear-cut process or coordination for doing this across the states. Thus, persons might be adjudged as insane in one state and be ordered to be transported miles away to an institution in another state. Expenses to complete this transfer were also not forthcoming including providing basic safeguards for the person with the mental illness and their monitor/s. For instance, by the late 1800s, officials in various states such as Alaska were trying to seek guidance from their representatives and the DOJ. They reported that their obligations were unclear with regard to accepting responsibility for those involuntarily committed. Further, there was no mechanism in place for them to obtain the finances that were required to transport persons with mental illness across the country to the locations of the insane asylums. In one case, the person was mandated to be transported from Alaska to California for commitment.

2-PC or Two Physicians Certify

Over the years, however, better infrastructure has been put into place to deal with involuntary commitment in a more appropriate manner that takes into account the rights of persons with mental illness. Specifically, if there is a psychiatric emergency, that is, a person is acting in a manner that presents a danger to himself or herself or to others, the person may need to be temporarily hospitalized for psychiatric care. Ideally, the person might be able to recognize his or her need for treatment and to consent for admission into a hospital. However, if the person refuses or does not have the level of volition that is needed to act in his or her best interests, the individual can still be involuntarily committed.

An interested person such as a parent, spouse, or a professional who is treating the person in an outpatient setting can contact emergency services to have the person transported to the emergency room. Once there, the person needs to be evaluated by a physician to determine whether his or her present condition necessitates inpatient care. In many instances, the mechanism that is often called the 2-PC or two physicians certify procedure is used. This refers to two independent physicians evaluating the person. If they can substantiate that the person presents a risk and there is a need for inpatient treatment, they can recommend hospitalization, even if the person objects.

Many general hospitals now have CPEP rooms that are staffed with psychiatrists, registered nurses, and other licensed personnel. In some cases, the person can be observed and/or treated for 72 hours in this dedicated area, under the supervision of the physician. For individuals who need treatment beyond this time frame, they can choose to voluntarily consent for admission and ongoing psychiatric care. If they cannot or would not consent, the two-physicians-certify procedure can be used.

In all instances, the physician is required to clearly document the person's initial and ongoing conditions. State laws are in place that specify the duration for which a person can be involuntarily committed. If the psychiatrist's evaluation is that the person's inpatient hospital stay needs to go beyond the stipulated time frame, the physician must follow the legal procedure of applying for a court order, unless the patient voluntarily consents. It should be noted that any patient who objects to his or her commitment can also request a court hearing.

Generally, states are bound by the U.S. Supreme Court Decision, *Addington v. Texas* (1979). This case was based on the Fourteenth Amendment to the constitution that no person could be deprived of life, liberty, or property without due process of law. Thus, in order to involuntarily deprive a person with mental illness of his or her liberty, the court still needs to have proof of clear and convincing evidence that the individual needs to be hospitalized against his or her will.

In some states, designated judges routinely visit the psychiatric hospitals and hold hearings that can be generated by the hospital or the patient. Additionally, hospitals are required to promptly notify patient advocate bodies such as the Mental Hygiene Legal Services in New York State, if a person is involuntarily admitted. These advocates are often present at patient hearings to ensure that the rights of the person with mental illness are not violated.

Involuntary commitment can be mandated through the court when a person is facing certain charges or a particular issue has been adjudicated. For example, we earlier looked at some of the issues involved in the Aurora, Colorado incident. If an individual is charged with a crime and there are questions as to his or her mental competency, a judge can issue an order of examination, as was done in the defendant's case. This mandates inpatient hospitalization for a specified brief period of time so that the person can be psychiatrically evaluated. In some instances, the judge may extend the time frame in order to assess whether the person will stabilize sufficiently to face trial. In these instances, when a mandated person is hospitalized in a regular hospital setting, it is usually the norm for law enforcement personnel to be assigned to guard the person.

There is a long historical precedent of persons who are mentally ill being charged with crimes. If the person is adjudicated as "non compos mentis," or not of sound mind, he or she may be found not guilty due to this reason. However, the person can still be involuntarily committed, and this is usually in secure detention. Increasingly, states are opening secure detention centers where persons who are involuntarily committed for serious crimes such as those related to sexual offending are hospitalized.

As we noted from the DOJ data, about one in two individuals in jail or prison is experiencing mental health issues. In fact, at the time that they are remanded to the prison, a significant subset of individuals may already be experiencing mental health concerns. Thus, many persons decompensate while being incarcerated due to the additional stressful conditions and not knowing how to adequately cope with them. These individuals may need to be transferred to a psychiatric ward in a regular hospital setting. Because of their incarceration status and the fact that law enforcement will continue to supervise them during their hospital stay, this group of persons are also considered to be involuntarily committed.

There continues to be concerns about involuntary commitment. For instance, it appears that both the medical and judicial communities tend to err on the side of involuntary commitment rather than risk a potential harmful public or personal outcome. Undoubtedly, some of the major public incidents that have occurred have influenced the actions of physicians, law enforcement, and others entrusted with the public's safety. Thus, what is the appropriate balance between the rights of the person with mental illness to have freedom in the community versus the welfare of others? Further, despite the current focus on evidence-based models of evaluation and risk assessment, to what degree can a physician or anyone else predict the eventual behavior of any person? And how much more difficult might this prediction be if the person has mental illness?

Therefore, while it may appear to be discriminatory in some respects, involuntary commitment actually serves the benefit of protecting the person, sometimes from his or her own impulses. Until we can find more targeted ways to evaluate persons who are experiencing mental health conditions across the spectra, there seems to be little choice but to continue to use involuntary commitment as a tool to help persons get the help they need, while minimizing the risk to the public.

MANDATORY MEDICATION MANAGEMENT

Voluntary

Medication management refers to the process in which a particular medication regimen is prescribed for a person, and is monitored by the physician and is adjusted as needed on an ongoing basis. It has emerged as a controversial issue partly due to its capacity to be invasive. Today, one of the basic rights of patients is to be allowed to give prior consent for medication management. However, patient consent has not always been considered to be necessary. Historical annals of physicians such as Benjamin Rush document that when persons with mental illness were unwilling to ingest calomel, the physician would spread it thinly on a slice of buttered bread to mask its presence. With the advent of newer medications, medicating persons with mental illness became even more widespread and was ripe for abuses. But under what circumstances, if any, should we medicate persons against their will?

We could recall that the introduction of the earlier psychiatric medications such as Thorazine and Prolixin played a major role in deinstitutionalization. As their efficacy became apparent, there was a greater push toward administering them to patients with or without their consent. However, persons with mental illness still needed to grapple with the side effects that these psychotropic medications could cause. In some cases, these contributed to a great deal of discomfort, and unless previously informed, patients were not prepared to deal with these side effects. Thus, as a basic right, every person, to the best of the individual's ability, should be engaged around the goals of a specific medication and the potential benefits and problems that can arise. To do any less would be to disregard the right of the individual to have basic autonomy over his or her person.

An example of how lack of proper information and planning regarding medication management was detrimental to persons with mental illness could be seen in the poor outcomes of deinstitutionalization. While there was a rush to medicate individuals with SPMI and discharge them back to their communities, not enough was done to thoroughly educate them or their families and advocates about medications, or to help put into place a support system in their communities. We should also consider that many persons with mental illness may stop taking their prescribed medications, sometimes due to their desire to feel "normal." This may be perceived as being nondependent on medication. In some instances, it may simply be that persons forgot or that they do not have the necessary structure, by themselves, to continue the medication management process.

At other times, persons with mental illness may engage in the abusive use of alcohol and other drugs that compromise the efficacy of the medication and can exacerbate their symptoms. Without the necessary supports, including ongoing education and reinforcement of the benefits of medication management, it would only be a matter of time before the person decompensates. Thus, medication education including an understanding of the side effects and any contraindications is important for all interested parties to understand to help promote autonomy and collaboration with the patient.

Involuntary

Unfortunately, if a person begins to act in a manner where he or she is an imminent danger to himself or herself or others, the issue of one's individual rights versus that of the public comes into play. Thus, states allow the provision of emergency medication if a patient is experiencing a psychiatric emergency. However, once the emergency passes, if ongoing medication is medically indicated and the person refuses, a psychiatrist usually has to seek involuntary or mandatory medication management using certain procedures. These may differ from state to state. Usually, they involve a court hearing or hearing from another duly constituted committee that could be made up of professionals in the field and advocates for persons with mental illness.

Even in cases where persons are already involuntarily committed, or is an offender facing a criminal charge, states still require a hearing if the person refuses medication. For example, since 1986, New York State has recognized the right of persons with mental illness to have due process if they did not wish to be medicated against their will. The NYS Court of Appeals ruled, in the *Rivers v. Katz case*, that neither mental illness nor institutionalization removed a person's fundamental right to participate in his or her treatment decisions.

Family members and loved ones often grapple with this right. Some complain that they are the ones who have to directly deal with the individual when he or she is decompensating and question what are the rights of other family members. Is it discriminatory for them to want to override the wishes of the person with mental illness to refuse medication in order to ensure he or she remains stable? While their concerns are legitimate, it is important for us to think about whether we want to go back to the days of forcing persons to have medical procedures and to ingest medication against their will. Are we as a society responsible for ensuring the protections of the most vulnerable among us especially when they might be the least able to advocate for themselves? Therefore, while persons may need to be medicated, this still cannot be done without using the due process procedure as stipulated by the court.

Persons with mental illness who are in the criminal justice system are also protected. In the Supreme Court Decision, *Sell v. U.S.* (2003), the court ruled that both the Fifth and Fourteenth Amendment clauses of due process protect the liberty of individuals to refuse psychotropic medications. Thus, if the state wants to proceed with the prosecution of a person, it cannot mandate involuntary medication management simply to meet the state's need to prosecute. Instead, the decision spells out four specific criteria that must be met, which are often referred to as the Sell test. This includes that the treating psychiatrist must clarify what is the proposed treatment plan for the person with mental illness, with back-up recommendations if the initial plan of care does not prove to be effective.

State and Supreme Court decisions have therefore gone a long way in protecting persons from being discriminated against with regard to involuntary medication management. Even for incarcerated persons, legislation spells out the procedures that must be followed once an offender is in the custody of the attorney general, based on the Sell decision. Although there are still instances when the intent and letter of the law may not be thoroughly applied, their existence have gone a long way to afford persons with mental illness a better opportunity to have a voice about their medical care, regardless of their legal status.

CHAPTER 9

Preventing Discrimination against the Mentally Ill

We have reviewed many ways in which persons with mental illness have been discriminated against over time. As we looked at what has occurred from a historical perspective, we can see that one of the earliest ways we defined mental illness, as bad or evil, has had a significant impact on how we treated the persons with mental illness. Up to today, religious interpretations still exist for mental illness and continue to play a role in how persons are treated in some communities. As we moved toward a more scientific basis of determining what it was, during the Enlightenment, a greater focus was placed on what causes mental illness, and we moved closer to understanding that issues such as stress could contribute to making an individual more vulnerable to mental illness.

Even before a scientific approach to understanding mental illness had evolved, society was being called upon to deal with persons who developed this condition. Whether it was an adult or a child, as persons with serious mental health disorders demonstrated behaviors that were difficult to manage, families, friends, and neighbors struggled to meet their needs in an informal manner. As this safety net became overwhelmed, or unable to meet these needs, more formal responses were required. How these were shaped, however, was reflective of the thinking of the time, including what resources if any should be provided for the indigent, and overall, how should persons with mental illness be treated.

Religious institutions were one of the first formal entities to offer both financial and practical assistance. As this expanded to local, city, and state governments, political decisions were made as to how best to use scarce resources. Diverse advocates played a major role in developing a formal system of care for persons with mental illness. As they observed abusive and sometimes blatantly discriminatory practices that negatively affected where and how persons with mental illness could live, work, receive medical care, be educated, could participate in the political process, and could even raise families, these advocates challenged the status quo. Letter writing, preaching, campaigning, protesting, and others—multiple strategies—were used over time to highlight physical, psychological, medical, and socioeconomic abuses and/or the absence of adequate resources.

This advocacy was instrumental in creating support for improving the conditions of persons with mental illness. While it took a great deal of time and effort, crucial legislation was passed that has helped to make lasting changes for persons with mental illness.

But these gains have not been universal. While mental illness is now better understood and the incidence and prevalence of it has been increasing in many places around the globe, there are glaring discrepancies with regard to how mental illness is being viewed and treated in high-income versus low-income countries. Critical resources are still lacking in some low-income countries to help identify who may be affected. Further, issues such as shame and stigma still prevent individuals and communities from acknowledging the presence of mental illness and/or seeking needed care. Complicating this is the nature of mental illness itself. Since it can be episodic, some still believe that the person has control over the decompensation process and that it is some lack or deficit in the individual that drives the onset of the mental health episode. Or it may be misconstrued as a person being eccentric or not being able to fit in, with no thought being given to whether something else is occurring with the individual.

As a result, there are still many places in which even SMI goes untreated or persons are still dealt with in an abusive manner. In places where there has been conflict, natural disasters, and ongoing terrorism, the need for mental health care may not be sufficiently addressed. Among segments of the population who live in rural areas or in places that are still difficult to access with the usual forms of transportation, this need can be even more outstanding.

As part of its global education campaign, the WHO has been seeking to assist especially lower-income countries to identify the scope of mental illness within their society. It is also helping to educate and train physicians and other health care professionals about mental illness and to provide strategies that can be used to immediately intervene with persons who need mental health care.

Is Discrimination Preventable?

Since the majority of gains in addressing mental health issues has been made in the high-income countries, those are also the most likely to have decreased discrimination toward this group. However, given the nature of discrimination, and the fact that attitudes and values that can contribute to it can be unconscious and be expressed in subtle as well as overt ways, is discrimination preventable?

Many sociologists, psychologists, philosophers, and the like would disagree that we can ever fully eradicate discrimination as a whole or discrimination that directly targets persons with mental illness. As we have previously discussed, there are many occasions on which these two aspects can interact. However, it may be possible to put checks and balances in place across our society, so that we can more readily identify whether a discriminatory practice or approach is being used. This can give us the opportunity to make corrections as often as is needed to ensure that we provide as much protection as possible so that persons with mental illness can live full lives and enjoy all constitutional rights and duly assigned privileges.

What Are the Ways to Prevent Discrimination?

Focusing on Prevention

Given the nature of mental illness, and that some types have a genetic component, eradicating it may not be a reality. However, from a prevention perspective, it is possible that we can reduce the incidence and prevalence of some kinds of mental illness, such as PTSD, that are associated with human conditions that can be avoided—war, terrorism, traumatic brain injuries, toxic exposure, and the like. In some instances, however, social attitudes have militated against policies that can more effectively address and prevent the onset of some types of behavioral issues.

For instance, as previously discussed, researchers have been able to identify that there is a relationship between early lead exposure and the development of multiple problems in children. This includes deficits in learning ADHD, autism spectrum disorders, and conduct disorders. Poorer children continue to be disproportionately affected by the presence of this toxin within their environments. However, universally, preventive measures have not always been aggressively applied to help avoid the onset of these conditions that can create lifelong distress. How we allot scarce resources has played a role in continuing this problem. Given that the risks of lead and other toxins in the environment are better understood, communities need to become more informed and to come together to advocate for and identify ways to eliminate these risks sooner rather than later. For example, this might involve using sweat equity to correct plumbing and painting concerns within dwellings, with technical support to ensure it is appropriately done. It might also mean communities taking a stand from within regarding the placement of certain types of factories and businesses that pollute the environment, unless proper environmentally sensitive safeguards are put into place.

Poverty and inadequate and/or unsafe living conditions are also associated with higher risks for poorer mental health, less access to appropriate treatment, and increased criminal justice involvement. In many places in the United States, spending for incarceration has increased while educational spending has decreased. Data from some states such as Texas and Los Angeles have found that the zip codes of a majority of individuals in prison from those areas in which educational funding has decreased coincide with the zip codes for the schools that are failing or have actually failed. From a prevention perspective, better schools and enhanced educational opportunities can therefore reduce mental health disorders including substance use, additionally to facilitating more pro-social outcomes.

Changing Societal Attitudes

Perhaps one of the main ways to prevent discrimination against persons with mental illness is to change societal attitudes. This includes beliefs such as mental illness being punishment or a curse, or that it is caused by moral weakness. It is still not unusual to hear people who are experiencing mental illness being encouraged to address it by seeking out their religious leaders. Thus, how can we best help individuals in the society-at-large understand that mental illness is not the fault of any person?

One potential way might be to ensure that mental health becomes an integral component of overall health care. Thus, every time we come in contact with a health care provider, the focus should be not only on the presenting medical issue or issues, but also on how is the person's emotional wellness. While some medical providers have begun to use screens such as for depression or anxiety, this is still the exception rather than the rule. Normalizing an assessment of one's mental health status and making this an ongoing health care component might help to remove some of the shame and guilt that persons can experience when they need to approach a mental health care provider.

Since stigma is still a real issue for persons experiencing mental illness, it may be that terms such as "mental health" or "psychiatric health" have become associated with negatives and are not the most helpful to use. As we know, language or how we discuss salient issues can make a difference with how persons receive specific messages. Thus, it may be necessary to find additional ways to discuss and to couch mental health issues that are not seen as negative or punitive. Culture plays a major role here especially since meanings can differ from one country to another and from one social context to another.

Sometimes, it can also be confusing translating certain mental health terms from one language to another, and this can create an additional problem for local mental health providers. Diverse focus groups can probably be used to brainstorm as well as to test the interpretation of the language we use to describe and discuss mental health issues. Since public service announcements should be one of the media measures that are used to help inform people about mental illness, ensuring that how we speak about mental illness conveys facts as well as empathy can thus make a difference to reach a wider audience.

Education needs to be one of the methods used to expand the conversation about mental illness. When we begin teaching children about basic physical health issues, it may also be the right time to include information regarding mental health as an integral component of health or wellness. There are multiple ways to integrate this into a curriculum, and of course, it would need to be age appropriate. However, it might actually be one of the main ways to cultivate a new generation who recognize and embrace mental health as central to who they are. And, just as cancer and other diseases may affect some persons through no fault of their own, so too can poor mental health do the same.

Besides providing targeted education on mental health as early as possible, more needs to be done to educate the community. Many of the higher-income countries such as the United States, Canada, and the United Kingdom are already in the process of doing this. Systematic coordinated efforts are in effect to align and to refine their existing health care systems to include a focus on mental health. In the United States, for example, the Substance Abuse and Mental Health Services Administration has taken the lead in publishing a National Behavioral Health Quality Framework. This aims to ensure better care, healthy people/communities, and affordable evidence-based care, as it relates to behavioral health. Multiple promotional events are also being conducted to make the public more aware of behavioral health issues and to encourage greater focus on overall mental and emotional wellness.

In lower-income countries around the globe, WHO has taken the initiative to interact with governmental and nongovernmental organizations (NGOs) regarding identifying any available mental health resources, related gaps, and how to address mental health care as an integral part of their social growth. A comparative assessment of mental health resources globally found that high-income countries had on average 91 hospital beds for psychiatric patients per 100,000 persons in the population. In low-income countries, however, there were less than two beds for psychiatric patients per 100,000 persons in the population. With regard to psychiatrists also, higher-income countries had on average one psychiatrist to 10,000 persons. In some lower-income countries, none were available (WHO, 2015).

While technical and financial assistance is being provided in some situations to help move lower-income countries forward in addressing behavioral health care for the population-at-large, it is apparent that resources are critically needed, including qualified mental health practitioners. It should be remembered that stigmatizing attitudes toward mental illness and persons with these disorders can also affect the professionals who enter these fields. Thus, they too can experience adverse and discriminatory consequences of treating persons with mental illness. How then can the brightest and the best be attracted to careers within the behavioral health care field? Or for those who emigrate to study, how can they be encouraged to return to their home countries where the need might be greatest?

Incentives may thus be temporarily needed to encourage individuals to pursue careers in the behavioral health care field to help address these glaring disparities. In the absence of this, WHO's current policy on empowering general medical practitioners to intervene with individuals with behavioral health disorders is sorely needed.

Ensuring Access to Quality Medical and Psychiatric Health Care

Given that the data on mental illness suggest that it has been increasing, it is imperative that barriers to access are addressed and that quality care be provided. As part of ensuring quality care and maximizing outcomes for all involved, there is a need to use intervention methods that are evidence based. Within the United States, there are several demonstration projects and other initiatives that have yielded positive outcomes including cost savings. The National Institute of Justice has supported the perspective that treatment decreases recidivism and the associated cost of re-offending. Its data found savings that ranged from $6,000 to $12,000, related to alternative courts including those addressing defendants with substance use disorders and mental health concerns.

Data published by the San Francisco Collaborative Courts Fact Sheet/Statistics (April, 2013), for instance, have reported that persons with SMI who were under the legal supervision of the Behavioral Health Court were 26% less likely to be charged with a new offence after receiving treatment, as compared with their peers who had not obtained treatment. With regard to new violent crimes, the finding was even more significant as they were 55% less likely to be charged with a new violent act. The San Francisco Court system has in fact calculated that the Behavioral Health Court saves at least $10,000 per defendant in the first year, as compared with the prior year when the person was not stable. For offenders in the Behavioral Health Court, every 90 cents that was spent on treatment reduced the cost of incarceration and its attendant issues by at least $1.

For offenders who were under the supervision of a Drug Court, there was a saving of approximately $14,000 per participant within a two-year period. The Drug Court intervention was found to save at least $1.46 for every dollar that was spent for services to the offender.

As part of preventing discrimination, it is thus important that communities learn about what is working and implement evidence-based models that have the best chance of success. For example, in New York City, a new initiative was rolled out (NYC-SAFE) to target the serious mentally ill who, "left untreated, are at risk of committing violence against themselves or others" (City of New York Press Office, August 6, 2015). As a comprehensive community-based initiative, part of its goal is to both prevent and intervene when needed with persons with SMI, by actively integrating criminal justice, health, and homeless services. Interventions like this that bring together evidence-based practices such as forensic assertive community treatment teams of specially trained police officers and clinicians can go a long way to break the cycle of offending, incarceration, increased mental and physical health problems, and overall poor outcomes.

Another gap in the system that needs to be addressed is connecting individuals with mental illness with the comprehensive care that is needed post-incarceration. Re-entry initiatives differ by state, and many are not adequately funded to meet the severe needs of the serious mentally ill. Wraparound services are thus necessary to reduce recidivism and to allow the person the best opportunity for stabilization. Perhaps the intent of the Brad H. Settlement could be revisited and more systematically applied. The Brad H. Settlement referred to a class action lawsuit that was brought against New York City, in 1999, by advocates for previously incarcerated persons with mental illness (*Brad H., et al. v. The City of New York, et al.*).

As of April 4, 2003, it became mandatory for New York City to ensure that any person with mental illness who entered the jails had to be provided with adequate discharge planning at their time of exit. As part of this, the person needed to be provided with a supply of at least seven days of medication, if this was being prescribed. He or she also needed to be linked with services in the community, including a mental health provider, health insurance, and a housing referral. While a recent evaluation of the implementation of the settlement continued to identify gaps in the provision of services, there was an improvement in completing the discharges as required.

The basic structure of this settlement can be used as a framework to target persons with mental illness who enter the criminal justice system and to develop the continuum of care that is clearly needed beyond the prison or jail walls. In fact, jail should probably not be the main line of intervention for persons with mental illness. However, for those who do commit crimes and need to be incarcerated to preserve public safety, triaging of their needs should begin to occur, in a reasonable time frame that allows their needs and the associated resources to be harnessed, before they are discharged back into the community.

Follow-up will also need to be a crucial part of this process, and an infrastructure already exists with the ICMs and health homes care managers. The missing link in many cases is that the various resources have not been pulled together in a way to shrink the gaps that allow vulnerable individuals to repeatedly fall through the cracks. The AOT model can serve as a guide here, since it has documented evidence of being effective. Thus, ideally, once it has been established that poor mental health was implicated as part of a person's offending behavior, at re-entry, the community-based supports should be able to facilitate ongoing medication management, drug treatment, transitional or regular employment, or other needed resources to decrease the risk of the individual re-engaging with the criminal justice system.

Additionally, ongoing pharmaceutical research is still needed into medications that can effectively obtain stabilizing outcomes, while minimizing the side effects. Since the uncomfortable effects of medication continue to be one of the reasons why individuals avoid it, addressing this can make a world of difference. While a great deal of progress has been made in this arena, including with timed release and more efficient dosage schedules, medication still remains one of the most effective interventions for a variety of psychiatric disorders. Perhaps this can be more closely aligned with new data that are emerging regarding genetics and epigenetics, so that medications can better target or even interrupt some of the biological mechanisms that contribute to psychiatric distress over a lifetime.

In conclusion, to be an equitable and humane society, we need to include both the greatest and the least among us. We know that money, power, education, upbringing, and so many other factors, by themselves, do not protect any individual from mental illness. While we have come a very long way from the days that we sent persons with mental illness out to sea in a ship of fools, we still have not fully turned the corner on discriminatory beliefs and practices that directly affect persons with mental illness. Therefore, as mothers and fathers, brothers and sisters, employees and employers, students and teachers—regardless of our station in life—advocating for those persons with mental illness who may not always be able to adequately do so for themselves is an ongoing responsibility.

PART III

Resources

Sources for Further Information

Websites

American Civil Liberties Union (ACLU), https://www.aclu.org/

American Psychiatric Association. Psychiatric News Alert. http://alert.psychnews.org/

American Psychological Association. Health and Emotional Wellness, http://www.apa.org/helpcenter/wellness/index.aspx

Association for Mental Health and Wellness. Awareness Campaigns, http://www.mhaw.org/advocacy/campaigns/

Coalition of Institutionalized Aged and Disabled (CIAD). CIAD TV: Videos about housing and residents' rights, http://www.ciadny.org/index.htm

Healthy Place: America's Mental Health Channel: Mental health videos, http://www.healthyplace.com/

Institute of Psychiatry, Psychology, and Neuroscience. Mental Healthcare: Discrimination and Stigma, http://www.mentalhealthcare.org.uk/discrimination_and_stigma

Mental Health Foundation, Stigma and Discrimination, http://www.mentalhealth.org.uk/help-information/mental-health-a-z/S/stigma-discrimination/

National Alliance on Mental Illness (NAMI), http://www.nami.org/

Substance Abuse and Mental Health Services Administration (SAMHSA). Behavioral Health Treatment Services Locator: Peer support (mental health), https://findtreatment.samhsa.gov/locator/link-focPeer

U.S. Department of Health and Human Services, Mental Health.gov. Let's talk about it, http://www.mentalhealth.gov/basics/recovery/index.html

U.S. Department of Justice Civil Rights Division. Information and technical assistance on the Americans with Disabilities Act: Video, http://www.ada.gov/videogallery.htm#olm

WebMD: Mental Health Center, http://www.webmd.com/mental-health/default.htm
Womenshealth.gov. Americans with Disabilities Act and Mental Illness, http://
womenshealth.gov/mental-health/your-rights/americans-disability-act.html

Books and Journals

Advances in Mental Health: Promotion, Prevention and Early Intervention, Vol.13,
Iss. 2, 2015. 1838-7357 (Print). 1837-4905 (Online). http://www.tandfonline
.com/toc/ramh20/
Aging and Mental Health, Vol.19, Iss. 12, 2015. 1360-7863 (Print), 1364-6915
(Online). http://www.tandfonline.com/toc/camh20/
Cahalan, Susannah. *Brain on Fire: My Month of Madness*. (2012). New York:
Free Press, A Division of Simon & Shuster.
Grandin, Temple, and Richard Panek. *The Autistic Brain: Thinking across the Spec-
trum*. (2014). New York: Houghton, Mifflin, Harcourt Publishing Company.
Hornbacher, Marya. *Madness: A Bipolar Life*. (2008). New York: Houghton, Mif-
flin, Harcourt Publishing Company.
Journal of Behavioral Health Services and Research, Vol. 11414. Iss. 1094–
3412. http://www.springer.com/public+health/journal/11414
Journal of Gay and Lesbian Mental Health, Vol.19, Iss. 3, 2015. 1935-9705 (Print).
1935-9713 (Online). http://www.tandfonline.com/toc/wglm20/. This entire volume
of six articles is dedicated to discrimination and mental health.
Journal of Mental Health, Vol. 24, Iss. 6, 2015. 0963-8237(Print). 1360-0567(Online).
http://informahealthcare.com/journal/jmh
Robison, John E. *My Life with Asperger's*. (2008). New York: Three Rivers Press.
Social Work in Mental Health, Vol.13, Iss. 6,2015. 1533-2985 (Print). 1533-2993
(Online). http://www.tandfonline.com/toc/wsmh20/
Wurtzel, Elizabeth. *Prozac Nation*. (1995). New York: Riverhead Books.

Articles

Batty, D. People with mental illness face widespread discrimination. *The
Guardian*, April 28, 2004. http://www.theguardian.com/society/2004/apr/
28/equality.mentalhealth
Bower, K.M., R.J. Thorpe, and T.A. LaVeist. (2013). "Abstract. Perceived Racial
Discrimination and Mental Health in Low-income Urban-dwelling Whites."
*International Journal of Health Services : Planning, Administration, Evalua-
tion*, *43*(2), 267–280. http://www.ncbi.nlm.nih.gov/pubmed/23821905
Cable News Network (CNN). Free mental safe houses open in New York City, July 7,
2015. http://www.cnn.com/2015/05/21/health/mental-safe-house/index.html
Gee, G.C., A. Ryan, D.J. Laflamme, and J. Holt. (2006). "Abstract. Self-Reported
Discrimination and Mental Health Status among African Descendants, Mexican
Americans, and Other Latinos in the New Hampshire REACH 2010 Initiative:
The Added Dimension of Immigration." *American Journal of Public Health*,
96(10), 1821–1828. http://www.ncbi.nlm.nih.gov/pubmed/17008579

Massie, M. K. (2015). The stress of workplace discrimination: What can employers and employees do. http://career-advice.monster.com/in-the-office/Workplace-Issues/Stress-from-Workplace-Discrimination/article.aspx

Nemec, P. B., M. Swarbrick, and L. Legere. (June 2015). *Psychiatric Rehabilitation Journal, 389*(2), 203–206. http://www.researchgate.net/publication/2783 30764_Prejudice_and_discrimination_from_mental_health_service_providers

Noh, S., V. Kaspar, and K.A.S. Wickrama. (2007). "Abstract. Overt and Subtle Racial Discrimination and Mental Health: Preliminary Findings for Korean Immigrants." *American Journal of Public Health*, 97(7), 1269–1274. doi:10.2105/AJPH.2005.085316. http://www.ncbi.nlm.nih.gov/pubmed/17538066

Padela, A. I., and M. Heisler. (2010). "Abstract. The Association of Perceived Abuse and Discrimination after September 11, 2001, with Psychological Distress, Level of Happiness, and Health Status among Arab Americans." *American Journal of Public Health*, 100(2), 284–291. http://www.ncbi.nlm.nih.gov/pmc/articles/PMC2804633/

Spencer, M. S., and J. Chen. (2004). "Effect of Discrimination on Mental Health Service Utilization among Chinese Americans." *American Journal of Public Health*, 94(5), 809–814. http://www.ncbi.nlm.nih.gov/pmc/articles/PMC1448342/pdf/0940809.pdf

Szabo, L. Cost of not caring: Stigma set in stone. Mentally ill suffer in sick health system. *USA Today*, June 25, 2014. http://www.usatoday.com/story/news/nation/2014/06/25/stigma-of-mental-illness/9875351/

Wykes, T. (February 2013). "Letter from the UK—Is This the End of Mental Health Discrimination as We Know It?" *Asian Journal of Psychiatry, 6*(1), 91–92. http://www.sciencedirect.com/science/article/pii/S1876201813000154

DOCUMENT 1: ATTITUDES TOWARD MENTAL ILLNESS

The following report, "Attitudes toward Mental Illness: Results from the Behavioral Risk Factor Surveillance System," was issued by the Centers for Disease Control and Prevention (CDC), in conjunction with the Substance Abuse and Mental Health Services Administration (SAMHSA), in 2012. It analyzes data about both the perceived effectiveness of mental health treatment and whether or not people believe individuals are caring and sympathetic toward those with mental illness. Although more than 80% of those surveyed agreed that treatment for mental illness is effective, only 35–67% believed that people are caring and sympathetic. This report is important as it provides concrete evidence that negative attitudes toward people with mental illness still persist, which in turn can lead to discrimination and act as barriers to treatment access and an improved quality of life for these individuals. However, since the article provides data specific to each jurisdiction surveyed, the CDC, SAMHSA, and each individual locale can proactively use this information to develop interventions to target discriminatory attitudes across the United States. This excerpt includes some of the key findings, along with the report's recommendations for combating stigma against mental illness.

Key Findings in Surveyed States

This section briefly summarizes the main findings. Readers can refer to the sections that follow for supporting data in the primary document. An excerpt of Table 4 is included on page 180.

Overall Study Results

Across states surveyed, most adults (>80%) agreed (slightly or strongly) that treatment can help people living with mental illness lead normal lives.... Yet, fewer adults (35–67%) agreed that other people are caring and sympathetic to people living with mental illness. . . . While no regional differences were identified in the analysis, states differed in overall level of agreement with both statements after controlling for individual level differences.

Treatment Effectiveness

- The vast majority of adults (>80%) in the states surveyed agreed that treatment is effective. . .
- Adults who reported receiving mental health treatment were generally more likely to strongly agree that treatment is effective (such as in the states of Colorado, Hawaii, Kansas, New Hampshire, and Texas). . .
- The probability of adults receiving mental health treatment increased when states provided more funding for their state mental health agencies. . .
- Some population subgroups (e.g., non-Hispanic blacks, Hispanics, those with less than a high school education) in some states were more likely to strongly disagree that treatment is effective (for example in the states of Georgia, California, Massachusetts, and Washington). . .
- Higher per capita expenditure on state mental health agencies was associated with less disagreement with—Treatment can help people with mental illness lead normal lives. . .‖

People Are Generally Caring and Sympathetic to People with Mental Illness

In general, smaller percentages of people in the states surveyed agreed that people are generally caring and sympathetic to people with mental illness (range 35%–67%). . . than that treatment is effective. . .

- Adults with mental illness symptoms (i.e., serious psychological distress [SPD], frequent mental distress [FMD]) and those reporting that they are currently receiving treatment for a mental illness or an emotional problem more often strongly disagreed that people are generally caring and sympathetic to people with mental illness . . .

- Adults living with existing chronic conditions (e.g., arthritis, heart disease, asthma) were also more likely to strongly disagree that people are generally caring and sympathetic to those with mental illness than adults living without these conditions. . .
- In some states, population subgroups such as women, adults who were unable to work or were out of work, adults living in households earning <$20,000/year and adults with less than a high school education were more likely to strongly disagree that people are caring and sympathetic to people with mental illness, (for example in the states of Colorado, Kansas, Nebraska, Montana, and Wisconsin). . .
- Adults who lived in areas with fewer mental health professionals were more likely to disagree that—People are caring and sympathetic to people with mental illness. . .‖
- Higher values of donated media for the What a Difference a Friend Makes campaign were associated with less disagreement with—People are caring and sympathetic to people with mental illness,‖ in states with greater percentages of younger adults (ages 18–24). . .

Strategies for Combating Stigma

Attitudes toward mental illness collected through the BRFSS identify areas for further study and population groups for intervention to reduce negative attitudes toward mental illness and promote social inclusion of those with mental illness symptoms. The cumulative findings in this report offer federal and state decision makers and other key stakeholders' insights about the public's attitudes toward persons living with mental illness as well as the relative impact of anti-stigma efforts on public attitudes toward mental illness.

The current data indicate the following strategies be considered by mental illness stakeholders and the general public to improve attitudes and behaviors toward persons with mental illness and promote social inclusion.

- Continue to explore how to monitor attitudes toward mental illness and evaluate innovative anti-stigma interventions.
- Implement culturally competent stigma reduction initiatives at local, regional, and state-wide levels. Guidance on event planning, partnership development, outreach to schools and businesses, mental health resources, and marketing to the general public is provided in SAMHSA's Developing a Stigma Reduction Initiative. (See http://store. samhsa.gov/shin/content/SMA06–4176/SMA06–4176.pdf.)

Table 4 Level of Agreement* with the Statement, People Are Generally Caring and Sympathetic to People with Mental Illness, by State and Territory—2009 BRFSS.

State	Unweighted Sample Size	Disagree Strongly	Disagree Slightly	Neither Agree Nor Disagree	Agree Slightly	Agree Strongly
California	3,621	9.8%	25.3%	0.8%	43.6%	20.5%
Georgia	5,122	13.5%	23.5%	4.7%	33.7%	24.6%
Hawaii	6,010	8.5%	24.1%	2.5%	39.7%	25.2%
Kansas	8,414	9.2%	24.3%	6.1%	38.2%	22.2%
Massachusetts	4,535	10.0%	24.1%	4.3%	36.4%	25.1%
Michigan	2,736	10.9%	27.7%	1.4%	36.9%	23.0%
Mississippi	9,964	17.8%	25.2%	2.5%	29.0%	25.5%
Missouri	4,522	11.7%	28.5%	2.9%	35.3%	21.6%
Nebraska	4,745	7.6%	23.7%	2.2%	41.4%	25.1%
Nevada	3,420	12.2%	28.9%	2.3%	34.6%	22.0%
South Carolina	8,775	10.4%	26.4%	1.1%	37.2%	24.9%
Tennessee	2,100	7.7%	21.4%	7.1%	27.9%	35.9%
Utah	2,366	7.0%	26.2%	0.9%	42.7%	23.2%
Vermont	6,094	8.3%	25.5%	2.7%	38.9%	24.5%
Washington	6,853	16.9%	28.3%	2.3%	33.7%	18.9%
Wyoming	5,476	9.2%	26.5%	1.6%	39.3%	23.5%

*Adjusted for sex, age group, racial/ethnic group, education, and household income level. Estimates are weighted; sample size is unweighted.

- Implement evidence-based mental health literacy programs such as Mental Health First-Aid USA in states and local communities. (See http://www.mentalhealthfirstaid.org/cs/program_overview/.)
- Offer technical assistance to local media regarding how they can reduce stigma by avoiding sensationalism about mental illness and ensure balance in broadcasting by encouraging stories about recovery, accomplishment, and contributions by people with mental illness.
- Support people with mental health problems by helping to develop community resources and by referring them to available community resources.
- Don't label people by their illness. Instead of saying, "she's bipolar," say, "she has bipolar disorder."
- Learn how to offer reassurance, companionship, emotional strength, and acceptance to a friend, family member, neighbor, or others with mental health problems.

Source: Centers for Disease Control and Prevention, Substance Abuse and Mental Health Services Administration, National Association of County Behavioral Health & Developmental Disability Directors, National Institute of Mental Health, The Carter Center Mental Health Program. Attitudes toward Mental Illness: Results from the Behavioral Risk Factor Surveillance System. Atlanta (GA); Centers for Disease Control and Prevention; 2012. http://www.cdc.gov/hrqol/Mental_Health_Reports/pdf/BRFSS_Report_InsidePages.pdf

DOCUMENT 2: CHANCERY LUNATICS

This article provides a guide as to what occurred in the United Kingdom, from around the late 1100s, when persons with mental illness owned property (the chancery lunatics). Created by a centralized government organization that represents the UK National Archives, the guide gives an overview of the chancery lunatics, based on original documents that are deposited in the archives. It is important as it provides historical details on the process by which a person became a chancery lunatic as well as some of its pitfalls. The guide highlights that the well-being of the person with mental illness was not the primary focus. Instead, the removal of the individual's right to manage his or her property left open an avenue for persons with mental illness to become ready targets of discrimination and, in some instances such as that of women, to increase their levels of marginalization.

6. Property of lunatics and idiots—the role of Chancery

For most of the past the state has only become involved in assessing people's mental health when they owned a certain amount of property. Many of the relevant legal records relate to attempts to establish whether or not a person was of sound mind for the purposes of administering or disposing of their property. Pauper lunatics were dealt with locally.

The Crown took charge of the property of idiots and lunatics, as well as deciding on their care. They were the responsibility of the Lord Chancellor (although the Court of Wards took this over from 1540 to 1646), and were sometimes known as the 'Chancery lunatics'. The king was entitled to administer the lands of an idiot during his life, but of the lunatic only during periods of insanity. The lands or possessions were not generally retained in Crown hands, but granted out for the term of the lunacy or idiocy to 'committees' (that is, those to whose care the lunatic or their estate was committed—possibly the next of kin).

Although the Crown's interest was at first paramount, over time the priority appears to have become the proper administration of the lunatic's estate, an issue often of vital importance to the next of kin. The point of getting a person declared of unsound mind by a Chancery inquisition was to take away his or her power of independent legal action in the disposition of property: it had nothing to do with committal to an asylum, which was a separate medical procedure. In many cases the alleged lunatic was already in an asylum when the inquisition took place: the only requirement for committal to an asylum was for two doctors to issue a certificate.

6.1 Being Made a Chancery Lunatic

Lunatics and idiots were brought to the Chancellor's attention by people with a particular interest. These could include relatives, solicitors, or others, acting as the executors of a will, or trustees, where one of the beneficiaries was a supposed lunatic. The Lunacy Commissioners might also be involved, fearing that the money of an asylum inmate was being misappropriated. Creditors of the alleged lunatic might also alert the Chancellor, as they could claim payment from the Master in Lunacy once their debtor had been declared of unsound mind.

All petitioners had to support their request for a commission of inquiry with at least two sworn affidavits supporting their opinion of the state of mind of the supposed lunatic. These affidavits do not generally survive…

6.2 Commissions and Committees of Lunacy

The Lord Chancellor had to establish whether or not a person was of sound mind. He did this by ordering commissioners to hold an inquisition.

If the person was deemed not to be of sound mind, the Chancellor committed the custody of the lunatic and his estate to suitable people (called 'committees'). He then had to examine the accounts of the committees.

Commissions and inquisitions are in Latin until the interregnum, and between 1660 and 1733. For the interregnum and from 1733 they are in English.... There are few lunacy commissions for England in the twentieth century. The later records, however, include copies of inquisitions taken in Ireland, and in some British colonies. The latter are concerned with the mental health of the person, and with getting them transported back to Britain.

6.3 Disputed Inquisitions

Disputes ('traverses') on the validity of an inquisition are in the records of the common law ('plea') side of Chancery. Pleadings for Edward I–James I are well-listed, in C 43 and C 44; pleadings for Elizabeth I to Victoria are in C 206. There are remembrance rolls in C 221 and C 222, and writs in C 245.

6.4 The Clerk of the Custodies

Information on the estates and possessions of a lunatic was sent to the Clerk of the Custodies, who granted out the custody of the estates of lunatics and idiots, and the care of the people themselves, by the issue of letters patent to the committees. These were not generally enrolled on the patent rolls, but in a separate series of rolls, which unfortunately appear to have been destroyed in the later nineteenth century....

6.5 Committees' Accounts

Accounts were supposed to be submitted annually by the committee to the Chancery Master....

[...]

Source: The National Archives of Great Britain. Mental Health: Property of Lunatics and Idiots– The Role of Chancery. Kew, Richmond, Surrey: The UK Government. Contains public sector information licensed under the Open Government License v2.0. http://www.nationalarchives. gov.uk/records/research-guides/mental-health.htm

DOCUMENT 3: THE AMERICANS WITH DISABILITIES ACT (ADA)

Title I of the Americans with Disabilities Act (ADA) of 1990 was passed by the U.S. Congress to address discrimination against persons with disabilities including those with mental illness, after a great deal of

advocacy from persons with disabilities and their advocates. The ADA particularly focused on the right of persons with disabilities to work and specified that potential or current employers could not discriminate against a qualified candidate based on his or her disability. Amendment to the act in 2008 clarified and extended the definition of a disability. The ADA is of critical importance as it marked the first time that comprehensive civil rights legislation was passed to protect persons with disabilities from discrimination. It continues to be a major tool in helping to reduce and/ or eliminate discrimination against persons with disabilities, including mental illness. Below is Title I, which covers issues related to employment.

Subchapter I—Employment

Sec. 12111. Definitions
As used in this subchapter:

(1) Commission
   The term "Commission" means the Equal Employment Opportunity Commission established by section 2000e-4 of this title.
(2) Covered entity
   The term "covered entity" means an employer, employment agency, labor organization, or joint labor-management committee.
(3) Direct threat
   The term "direct threat" means a significant risk to the health or safety of others that cannot be eliminated by reasonable accommodation.
(4) Employee
   The term "employee" means an individual employed by an employer. With respect to employment in a foreign country, such term includes an individual who is a citizen of the United States.
(5) Employer
   (A) In general
      The term "employer" means a person engaged in an industry affecting commerce who has 15 or more employees for each working day in each of 20 or more calendar weeks in the current or preceding calendar year, and any agent of such person, except that, for two years following the effective date of this subchapter, an employer means a person engaged in an industry affecting commerce who has 25 or more employees for each working day in each of 20 or more calendar weeks in the current or preceding year, and any agent of such person.

      (B) Exceptions

          The term "employer" does not include

          (i)   the United States, a corporation wholly owned by the government of the United States, or an Indian tribe; or

          (ii) a bona fide private membership club (other than a labor organization) that is exempt from taxation under section 501(c) of title 26.

  (6) Illegal use of drugs

      (A) In general

          The term "illegal use of drugs" means the use of drugs, the possession or distribution of which is unlawful under the Controlled Substances Act [21 U.S.C. 801 et seq.]. Such term does not include the use of a drug taken under supervision by a licensed health care professional, or other uses authorized by the Controlled Substances Act or other provisions of Federal law.

      (B) Drugs

          The term "drug" means a controlled substance, as defined in schedules I through V of section 202 of the Controlled Substances Act [21 U.S.C. 812].

  (7) Person, etc.

      The terms "person", "labor organization", "employment agency", "commerce", and "industry affecting commerce", shall have the same meaning given such terms in section 2000e of this title.

  (8) Qualified individual

      The term "qualified individual" means an individual who, with or without reasonable accommodation, can perform the essential functions of the employment position that such individual holds or desires. For the purposes of this subchapter, consideration shall be given to the employer's judgment as to what functions of a job are essential, and if an employer has prepared a written description before advertising or interviewing applicants for the job, this description shall be considered evidence of the essential functions of the job.

  (9) Reasonable accommodation

      The term "reasonable accommodation" may include

      (A) making existing facilities used by employees readily accessible to and usable by individuals with disabilities; and

      (B) job restructuring, part-time or modified work schedules, reassignment to a vacant position, acquisition or modification of equipment or devices, appropriate adjustment or modifications of examinations, training materials or policies, the provision of qualified readers or interpreters, and other similar accommodations for individuals with disabilities.

(10) Undue hardship

    (A) In general

    The term "undue hardship" means an action requiring significant difficulty or expense, when considered in light of the factors set forth in subparagraph (B).

    (B) Factors to be considered

    In determining whether an accommodation would impose an undue hardship on a covered entity, factors to be considered include

        (i)   the nature and cost of the accommodation needed under this chapter;

        (ii) the overall financial resources of the facility or facilities involved in the provision of the reasonable accommodation; the number of persons employed at such facility; the effect on expenses and resources, or the impact otherwise of such accommodation upon the operation of the facility;

        (iii) the overall financial resources of the covered entity; the overall size of the business of a covered entity with respect to the number of its employees; the number, type, and location of its facilities; and

        (iv) the type of operation or operations of the covered entity, including the composition, structure, and functions of the workforce of such entity; the geographic separateness, administrative, or fiscal relationship of the facility or facilities in question to the covered entity.

Sec. 12112. Discrimination

(a) General rule

    No covered entity shall discriminate against a qualified individual on the basis of disability in regard to job application procedures, the hiring, advancement, or discharge of employees, employee compensation, job training, and other terms, conditions, and privileges of employment.

(b) Construction

    As used in subsection (a) of this section, the term "discriminate against a qualified individual on the basis of disability" includes

    (1)   limiting, segregating, or classifying a job applicant or employee in a way that adversely affects the opportunities or status of such applicant or employee because of the disability of such applicant or employee;

(2) participating in a contractual or other arrangement or relationship that has the effect of subjecting a covered entity's qualified applicant or employee with a disability to the discrimination prohibited by this subchapter (such relationship includes a relationship with an employment or referral agency, labor union, an organization providing fringe benefits to an employee of the covered entity, or an organization providing training and apprenticeship programs);

(3) utilizing standards, criteria, or methods of administration
   (A) that have the effect of discrimination on the basis of disability;
   (B) that perpetuates the discrimination of others who are subject to common administrative control;

(4) excluding or otherwise denying equal jobs or benefits to a qualified individual because of the known disability of an individual with whom the qualified individual is known to have a relationship or association;

(5)
   (A) not making reasonable accommodations to the known physical or mental limitations of an otherwise qualified individual with a disability who is an applicant or employee, unless such covered entity can demonstrate that the accommodation would impose an undue hardship on the operation of the business of such covered entity; or
   (B) denying employment opportunities to a job applicant or employee who is an otherwise qualified individual with a disability, if such denial is based on the need of such covered entity to make reasonable accommodation to the physical or mental impairments of the employee or applicant;

(6) using qualification standards, employment tests or other selection criteria that screen out or tend to screen out an individual with a disability or a class of individuals with disabilities unless the standard, test or other selection criteria, as used by the covered entity, is shown to be job-related for the position in question and is consistent with business necessity; and

(7) failing to select and administer tests concerning employment in the most effective manner to ensure that, when such test is administered to a job applicant or employee who has a disability that impairs sensory, manual, or speaking skills, such test results accurately reflect the skills, aptitude, or whatever other factor of such applicant or employee that such test purports to measure, rather than reflecting the impaired sensory,

manual, or speaking skills of such employee or applicant (except where such skills are the factors that the test purports to measure).

(c) Covered entities in foreign countries

    (1) In general

        It shall not be unlawful under this section for a covered entity to take any action that constitute discrimination under this section with respect to an employee in a workplace in a foreign country if compliance with this section would cause such covered entity to violate the law of the foreign country in which such workplace is located.

    (2) Control of corporation

        (A) Presumption

            If an employer controls a corporation whose place of incorporation is a foreign country, any practice that constitutes discrimination under this section and is engaged in by such corporation shall be presumed to be engaged in by such employer.

        (B) Exception

            This section shall not apply with respect to the foreign operations of an employer that is a foreign person not controlled by an American employer.

        (C) Determination

            For purposes of this paragraph, the determination of whether an employer controls a corporation shall be based on

            (i) the interrelation of operations;

            (ii) the common management;

            (iii) the centralized control of labor relations; and

            (iv) the common ownership or financial control of the employer and the corporation.

(d) Medical examinations and inquiries

    (1) In general

        The prohibition against discrimination as referred to in subsection (a) of this section shall include medical examinations and inquiries.

    (2) Preemployment

        (A) Prohibited examination or inquiry

            Except as provided in paragraph (3), a covered entity shall not conduct a medical examination or make inquiries of a job applicant as to whether such applicant is an individual with a disability or as to the nature or severity of such disability.

(B) Acceptable inquiry

A covered entity may make preemployment inquiries into the ability of an applicant to perform job-related functions.

(3) Employment entrance examination

A covered entity may require a medical examination after an offer of employment has been made to a job applicant and prior to the commencement of the employment duties of such applicant, and may condition an offer of employment on the results of such examination, if

(A) all entering employees are subjected to such an examination regardless of disability;

(B) information obtained regarding the medical condition or history of the applicant is collected and maintained on separate forms and in separate medical files and is treated as a confidential medical record, except that

(i) supervisors and managers may be informed regarding necessary restrictions on the work or duties of the employee and necessary accommodations;

(ii) first aid and safety personnel may be informed, when appropriate, if the disability might require emergency treatment; and

(iii) government officials investigating compliance with this chapter shall be provided relevant information on request; and

(C) the results of such examination are used only in accordance with this subchapter.

(4) Examination and inquiry

(A) Prohibited examinations and inquiries

A covered entity shall not require a medical examination and shall not make inquiries of an employee as to whether such employee is an individual with a disability or as to the nature or severity of the disability, unless such examination or inquiry is shown to be job-related and consistent with business necessity.

(B) Acceptable examinations and inquiries

A covered entity may conduct voluntary medical examinations, including voluntary medical histories, which are part of an employee health program available to employees at that work site. A covered entity may make inquiries into the ability of an employee to perform job-related functions.

(C) Requirement

Information obtained under subparagraph (B) regarding the medical condition or history of any employee are subject to the requirements of subparagraphs (B) and (C) of paragraph (3).

Sec. 12113. Defenses

(a) In general

It may be a defense to a charge of discrimination under this chapter that an alleged application of qualification standards, tests, or selection criteria that screen out or tend to screen out or otherwise deny a job or benefit to an individual with a disability has been shown to be job-related and consistent with business necessity, and such performance cannot be accomplished by reasonable accommodation, as required under this subchapter.

(b) Qualification standards

The term "qualification standards" may include a requirement that an individual shall not pose a direct threat to the health or safety of other individuals in the workplace.

(c) Qualification standards and tests related to uncorrected vision

Notwithstanding section 12102(4)(E)(ii), a covered entity shall not use qualification standards, employment tests, or other selection criteria based on an individual's uncorrected vision unless the standard, test, or other selection criteria, as used by the covered entity, is shown to be job-related for the position in question and consistent with business necessity.

(d) Religious entities

(1) In general

This subchapter shall not prohibit a religious corporation, association, educational institution, or society from giving preference in employment to individuals of a particular religion to perform work connected with the carrying on by such corporation, association, educational institution, or society of its activities.

(2) Religious tenets requirement

Under this subchapter, a religious organization may require that all applicants and employees conform to the religious tenets of such organization.

(e) List of infectious and communicable diseases

(1) In general

The Secretary of Health and Human Services, not later than 6 months after July 26, 1990, shall

(A) review all infectious and communicable diseases which may be transmitted through handling the food supply;

(B) publish a list of infectious and communicable diseases which are transmitted through handling the food supply;

(C) publish the methods by which such diseases are transmitted; and

(D) widely disseminate such information regarding the list of diseases and their modes of transmissibility to the general public.

Such list shall be updated annually.

(2) Applications

In any case in which an individual has an infectious or communicable disease that is transmitted to others through the handling of food, that is included on the list developed by the Secretary of Health and Human Services under paragraph (1), and which cannot be eliminated by reasonable accommodation, a covered entity may refuse to assign or continue to assign such individual to a job involving food handling.

(3) Construction

Nothing in this chapter shall be construed to preempt, modify, or amend any State, county, or local law, ordinance, or regulation applicable to food handling which is designed to protect the public health from individuals who pose a significant risk to the health or safety of others, which cannot be eliminated by reasonable accommodation, pursuant to the list of infectious or communicable diseases and the modes of transmissibility published by the Secretary of Health and Human Services.

Sec. 12114. Illegal use of drugs and alcohol

(a) Qualified individual with a disability

For purposes of this subchapter, qualified individual with a disability shall not include any employee or applicant who is currently engaging in the illegal use of drugs, when the covered entity acts on the basis of such use.

(b) Rules of construction

Nothing in subsection (a) of this section shall be construed to exclude as a qualified individual with a disability an individual who

(1) has successfully completed a supervised drug rehabilitation program and is no longer engaging in the illegal use of drugs, or has otherwise been rehabilitated successfully and is no longer engaging in such use;

(2) is participating in a supervised rehabilitation program and is no longer engaging in such use; or

(3) is erroneously regarded as engaging in such use, but is not engaging in such use; except that it shall not be a violation of this chapter for a covered entity to adopt or administer reasonable policies or procedures, including but not limited to drug testing, designed to ensure that an individual described in paragraph (1) or (2) is no longer engaging in the illegal use of drugs.

(c) Authority of covered entity

A covered entity

(1) may prohibit the illegal use of drugs and the use of alcohol at the workplace by all employees;

(2) may require that employees shall not be under the influence of alcohol or be engaging in the illegal use of drugs at the workplace;

(3) may require that employees behave in conformance with the requirements established under the Drug-Free Workplace Act of 1988 (41 U.S.C. 701 et seq.);

(4) may hold an employee who engages in the illegal use of drugs or who is an alcoholic to the same qualification standards for employment or job performance and behavior that such entity holds other employees, even if any unsatisfactory performance or behavior is related to the drug use or alcoholism of such employee; and

(5) may, with respect to Federal regulations regarding alcohol and the illegal use of drugs, require that

(A) employees comply with the standards established in such regulations of the Department of Defense, if the employees of the covered entity are employed in an industry subject to such regulations, including complying with regulations (if any) that apply to employment in sensitive positions in such an industry, in the case of employees of the covered entity who are employed in such positions (as defined in the regulations of the Department of Defense);

(B) employees comply with the standards established in such regulations of the Nuclear Regulatory Commission, if the employees of the covered entity are employed in an industry subject to such regulations, including complying with regulations (if any) that apply to employment in sensitive positions in such an industry, in the case of employees of the covered entity who are employed in such positions (as defined in the regulations of the Nuclear Regulatory Commission); and

(C) employees comply with the standards established in such regulations of the Department of Transportation, if the employees of the covered entity are employed in a transportation industry subject to such regulations, including complying with such regulations (if any) that apply to employment in sensitive positions in such an industry, in the case of employees of the covered entity who are employed in such positions (as defined in the regulations of the Department of Transportation).

(d) Drug testing

(1) In general

For purposes of this subchapter, a test to determine the illegal use of drugs shall not be considered a medical examination.

(2) Construction

Nothing in this subchapter shall be construed to encourage, prohibit, or authorize the conducting of drug testing for the illegal use of drugs by job applicants or employees or making employment decisions based on such test results.

(e) Transportation employees

Nothing in this subchapter shall be construed to encourage, prohibit, restrict, or authorize the otherwise lawful exercise by entities subject to the jurisdiction of the Department of Transportation of authority to

(1) test employees of such entities in, and applicants for, positions involving safety-sensitive duties for the illegal use of drugs and for on-duty impairment by alcohol; and

(2) remove such persons who test positive for illegal use of drugs and on-duty impairment by alcohol pursuant to paragraph (1) from safety-sensitive duties in implementing subsection (c) of this section.

Sec. 12115. Posting notices

Every employer, employment agency, labor organization, or joint labor-management committee covered under this subchapter shall post notices in an accessible format to applicants, employees, and members describing the applicable provisions of this chapter, in the manner prescribed by section 2000e-10 of this title.

Sec. 12116. Regulations

Not later than 1 year after July 26, 1990, the Commission shall issue regulations in an accessible format to carry out this subchapter in accordance with subchapter II of chapter 5 of title 5.

Sec. 12117. Enforcement

(a) Powers, remedies, and procedures

The powers, remedies, and procedures set forth in sections 2000e-4, 2000e-5, 2000e-6, 2000e-8, and 2000e-9 of this title shall be the powers, remedies, and procedures this subchapter provides to the Commission, to the Attorney General, or to any person alleging discrimination on the basis of disability in violation of any provision of this chapter, or regulations promulgated under section 12116 of this title, concerning employment.

(b) Coordination

The agencies with enforcement authority for actions which allege employment discrimination under this subchapter and under the Rehabilitation Act of 1973 [29 U.S.C. 701 et seq.] shall develop procedures to ensure that administrative complaints filed under this subchapter and under the Rehabilitation Act of 1973 are dealt with in a manner that avoids duplication of effort and prevents imposition of inconsistent or conflicting standards for the same requirements under this subchapter and the Rehabilitation Act of 1973. The Commission, the Attorney General, and the Office of Federal Contract Compliance Programs shall establish such coordinating mechanisms (similar to provisions contained in the joint regulations promulgated by the Commission and the Attorney General at part 42 of title 28 and part 1691 of title 29, Code of Federal Regulations, and the Memorandum of Understanding between the Commission and the Office of Federal Contract Compliance Programs dated January 16, 1981 (46 Fed. Reg. 7435, January 23, 1981)) in regulations implementing this subchapter and Rehabilitation Act of 1973 not later than 18 months after July 26, 1990.

Source: Americans with Disabilities Act of 1990, Pub. L. No. 101–336, § 1, 104 Stat. 328 (1990).

Document 4: The Mental Health
Reform Act (MHRA) of 2015

The Mental Health Reform Act (MHRA) of 2015 was introduced to the U.S. Senate on August 5, 2015, the first comprehensive attempt in more than 50 years to address psychiatric, psychological, and supportive services for persons with mental illness. Sponsored by Senators Chris Murphy (D-Conn.) and William Cassidy (R-LA), the bill integrates the feedback from a broad spectrum of organizations known for their advocacy for persons with mental illness. These include NAMI, Mental Health America (MHA), and the American Psychiatric Association (APA). A relatively similar bill, The Helping Families in Mental Health Crisis Act (HFMHC) of 2015, was also presented in the House by Representatives Tim Murphy (R-Penn.) and Bernice Johnson (D-Texas) in June 2015. The MHRA is important as it represents an official recognition of the ways in which discrimination against persons with mental illness has impacted their lives, that of their families, and the wider community, including with regard to indiscriminate incarceration. As the discussion in the book indicates, systematic, evidence-based intervention and prevention is needed. Proposed provisions of MHRA that address discriminatory mental health coverage limitations, strengthening behavioral health care, prevention outreach, as well as early childhood intervention and treatment can go a long way to fill the gaps and help to begin to mend a broken system. The sections included here deal with expansion and parity of mental health coverage.

Title VI: Medicare and Medicaid Reforms 601.

Enhanced Medicaid coverage relating to certain mental health services

(a)

Medicaid coverage of mental health services and primary care services furnished on the same day

(1)

In general

Section 1902(a) of the Social Security Act (42 U.S.C. 1396a(a)) is amended by inserting after paragraph (77) the following new paragraph:

(78) not prohibit payment under the plan for a mental health service or primary care service furnished to an individual at a community mental health center meeting the criteria specified in section 1913(c) of the Public Health Service Act or a Federally qualified health center (as defined in section 1861(aa)(4)) for which payment would otherwise be payable under the plan, with respect to such individual, if

such service were not a same-day qualifying service (as defined in subsection (ll)).

(2)

Same-day qualifying services defined

Section 1902 of the Social Security Act (42 U.S.C. 1396a) is amended by adding at the end the following new subsection:

(ll) Same-Day qualifying services defined

For purposes of subsection (a)(78), the term *same-day qualifying service* means—

(1) a primary care service furnished to an individual by a provider at a facility on the same day a mental health service is furnished to such individual by such provider (or another provider) at the facility; and

(2) a mental health service furnished to an individual by a provider at a facility on the same day a primary care service is furnished to such individual by such provider (or another provider) at the facility.

(b)

State option To provide medical assistance for certain inpatient psychiatric services to nonelderly adults

Section 1905 of the Social Security Act (42 U.S.C. 1396d) is amended—

(1)

in subsection (a)—

(A)

in paragraph (16)—

(i)

by striking effective and inserting (A) effective; and

(ii)

by inserting before the semicolon at the end the following: and (B) qualified inpatient psychiatric hospital services (as defined in subsection (h)(3)) for individuals over 21 years of age and under 65 years of age; and

(B)

in the subdivision (B) that follows paragraph (29), by inserting (other than services described in subparagraph (B) of paragraph (16) for individuals described in such subparagraph) after patient in an institution for mental diseases; and

(2)

in subsection (h), by adding at the end the following new paragraph:

(3) For purposes of subsection (a)(16)(B), the term *qualified inpatient psychiatric hospital services* means, with respect to individuals described in such subsection, services described in subparagraphs (A) and (B) of

paragraph (1) that are furnished in an acute care psychiatric unit in a State-operated psychiatric hospital or a psychiatric hospital (as defined section 1861(f)) if such unit or hospital, as applicable, has a facility-wide average (determined on an annual basis) length of stay of less than 20 days. [...]

Title IX: Mental Health Parity

901.

GAO study on preventing discriminatory coverage limitations for individuals with serious mental illness and substance use disorders

Not later than 1 year after the date of enactment of this Act, the Comptroller General of the United States, in consultation with the Assistant Secretary for Mental Health and Substance Use Disorders, the Secretary of Health and Human Services, the Secretary of Labor, and the Secretary of the Treasury, shall submit to Congress a report detailing the extent to which covered group health plans (or health insurance coverage offered in connection with such plans), including Medicaid managed care plans under section 1903 of the Social Security Act (42 U.S.C. 1396b), comply with the Paul Wellstone and Pete Domenici Mental Health Parity and Addiction Equity Act of 2008 (subtitle B of title V of division C of Public Law 110–343) (in this section referred to as the law), including—

(1) how nonquantitative treatment limitations, including medical necessity criteria, of covered group health plans comply with the law;
(2) how the responsible Federal departments and agencies ensure that plans comply with the law; and
(3) how proper enforcement, education, and coordination activities within responsible Federal departments and agencies can be used to ensure full compliance with the law, including educational activities directed to State insurance commissioners.

902.

Report on investigations regarding parity in mental health and substance use disorder benefits

(a)

In general

Not later than 1 year after the date of enactment of this Act, and annually thereafter, the Administrator of the Centers for Medicare & Medicaid Services, in collaboration with the Assistant Secretary of Labor of the

Employee Benefits Security Administration and the Secretary of the Treasury, and in consultation with the Assistant Secretary for Mental Health and Substance Use Disorders, shall submit to Congress a report—

(1)

identifying Federal investigations conducted or completed during the preceding 12-month period regarding compliance with parity in mental health and substance use disorder benefits, including benefits provided to persons with serious mental illness and substance use disorders, under the Paul Wellstone and Pete Domenici Mental Health Parity and Addiction Equity Act of 2008 (subtitle B of title V of division C of Public Law 110–343); and

(2)

summarizing the results of such investigations.

(b)

Contents

Subject to subsection (c), each report under subsection (a) shall include the following information:

(1) The number of investigations opened and closed during the covered reporting period.
(2) The benefit classification or classifications examined by each investigation.
(3) The subject matter or subject matters of each investigation, including quantitative and nonquantitative treatment limitations.
(4) A summary of the basis of the final decision rendered for each investigation.

(c)

Limitation

Individually identifiable information shall be excluded from reports under subsection (a) consistent with Federal privacy protections.

[…]

Source: Mental Health Reform Act of 2015, S. 1945, 114th Congress (2015). https://www.govtrack.us/congress/bills/114/s1945/text

DOCUMENT 5: WHAT A DIFFERENCE A FRIEND MAKES ANTI-STIGMA CAMPAIGN

The following text is from a brochure entitled "What a Difference a Friend Makes." It was published by the Substance Abuse and Mental Health Services Administration (SAMHSA) in 2007 as part of a national health marketing series called Campaign for Mental Health

Recovery. The brochure integrates data primarily from two sources—the proprietary HealthStyles Survey, which focuses on health orientation and practices, and which has collected data annually since 1995 from about 37,000 adults, and the National Survey on Drug Use and Health (NSDUH), which, since 1971, has gathered data on substance use and mental health issues from about 70,000 persons, aged 12 and older in the noninstitutionalized population. As the book indicates, tools are needed to both intervene with and prevent discrimination. This brochure is therefore important as it serves both purposes. It provides education about mental illness and negative attitudes that perpetuate stigma. Additionally, it offers concrete guidance as to how family and advocates of persons with mental illness, as well as adolescents can be supportive of and help persons recover.

What a Difference a Friend Makes

Social Acceptance Is Key to Mental Health Recovery

National mental health anti-stigma campaign encourages education and support from friends.

The opportunity for recovery from mental illness is more likely in a society of acceptance. Many Americans are misinformed about mental illness and respond negatively when confronted with a friend's mental illness. According to the 2006 HealthStyles Survey conducted by Porter Novelli, fewer than one-third of adults believe a person with mental illness can recover, and about 1 in 4 adults age 18–24 believes a person with mental illness can recover. To help improve awareness about recovery from mental illness, SAMHSA and the Ad Council have developed an anti-stigma campaign, targeted to men and women 18–24 years old, which focuses on friends as a key component of mental health recovery.

Facts Friends Need to Know About Friends with Mental Illnesses
- Mental illnesses (e.g., depression, anxiety, bipolar disorder, schizophrenia) are more widespread than most people realize. According to SAMHSA, in 2005 there were an estimated 24.6 million adults age 18 or older who experienced serious psychological distress (SPD), which is highly correlated with serious mental illness. Almost every family in America is affected by someone with a mental illness (SAMHSA, 2005).
- Among 18- to 25-year-olds, the prevalence of SPD is high (18.6% for 18–25 vs. 11.3% for all adults 18+), yet this age group shows the lowest rate of help-seeking behaviors (SAMHSA, 2005).

- Mental illness can happen to anybody regardless of race, ethnicity, gender, age, or background.
- Nearly 1 out of 5 persons 18–24 reports having a mental illness.
- Major depression and anxiety disorders are the most prevalent mental health problems experienced by young adults, who experience most serious mental illnesses at a higher rate than the general population.
- The incidence of eating disorders among 18- to 24-year-olds was more than twice as prevalent than among all ages.
- Mental illness is treatable. There are more treatments, strategies, and community support systems available than ever before, including medication, rehabilitation, psychotherapy, group therapy, self-help, or a combination of these.
- People with mental illness can and do recover. Studies show that most people with mental illnesses get better, and many recover completely.
- Mental health recovery is a journey of healing and transformation enabling a person with a mental health problem to live a meaningful life in a community of his or her choice while striving to achieve his or her full potential.
- Those with mental health conditions in this age group have a high potential to minimize future disability if social acceptance is broadened and they receive the right support.
- One of the main reasons why people don't seek help is because of the stigma associated with mental illness. Stigma is a big barrier to recovery.
- People with mental illnesses are good employees. Studies by the National Institute of Mental Health (NIMH) and the National Alliance to the Mentally Ill (NAMI) show that there are no differences in productivity when people with mental illness are compared with other employees.
- People with a mental illness need to be treated with respect, compassion, and empathy just as anyone with any other serious but treatable condition.
- Almost two-thirds of 18- to 24-year-olds know someone with depression or alcoholism and more than 40 percent of the 18- to 24-year-olds know others with a drug addiction.
- Young adults are more likely than the general population to know someone with a mental illness. Targeting young adults with public education programs is likely to have a broader impact on reducing stigma and discrimination.
- Two-thirds of Americans believe that treatment and support can help people with mental illnesses lead normal lives.

- Only 1 in 5 persons surveyed feels that persons with mental illness are dangerous to others.
- Everyone can do something to help a person with mental illness... like avoiding the use of "label words," showing kindness and respect, or helping to eliminate discrimination against housing, employment, or education.
- One of the most important factors in recovery is the understanding and acceptance of friends. Friends can make a difference by offering reassurance, companionship, and emotional strength.
- The emotional and psychological aspects of mental illness make supportive friends and family even more important to a person's recovery.
- Friends can express an interest and concern for people with a mental illness by asking questions, listening to ideas, and being responsive. Friends can help break down the stigma and encourage society to treat mental illness like any other healthcare condition.
- Friends can dismiss any preconceived notions about mental illness and embrace a more helpful way of relating to people.

Source: Substance Abuse and Mental Health Services Administration, National Mental Health Anti-Stigma Campaign, *What a Difference a Friend Makes (2007): Social Acceptance Is Key to Mental Health Recovery*. Rockville, MD: USDHHS. http://store.samhsa.gov/shin/content/SMA07-4257/SMA07-4257.pdf

GLOSSARY

Adult home—A supportive living facility for persons who are homeless and meet other criteria such as poor mental and/or physical health.

Almshouse—A facility that was funded by charity and provided support for the poor and/or infirm.

Anticonvulsant—A drug that is used to treat seizure disorders.

Assisted outpatient treatment (AOT)—A type of outpatient treatment for mental illness that is court-ordered for persons who are not compliant with their prescribed care and are at risk of being a danger to themselves or others.

Asylum—A large facility used to provide services to persons with mental illness including housing and medical care.

Behavioral disorder (or co-occurring disorder)—A mental health condition that involves both substance use and other mental illness.

Chemical restraint—The use of high dosages of medication that cause side effects such as excess sedation or sleep to control the behavior of a person.

Common law—The basic legal system in the United States, which is based on British law developed over time from judicial rulings.

Comorbidity—Having two or more medical conditions.

Comprehensive Psychiatric Emergency Program (CPEP)—A hospital-based program that provides psychiatric emergency services including outreach and crisis intervention, residential observation, and extended observation for up to 72 hours, for both voluntary and involuntary patients.

Confidentiality—The process mandated by law to protect a client's information such as his medical/mental health status.

Decompensation—The process during which the psychiatric functioning of an individual with a mental health disorder deteriorates; for example, a normally well-groomed person may stop taking care of his daily hygiene needs and appear unkempt.

Deinstitutionalization—The term used to describe a social movement that began in the 1960s. In order to reduce the patient population in the large psychiatric facilities, persons with mental illness were discharged into the community, regardless of their ability to successfully transition.

Delusion—A belief that is not true about a particular person, event, or object; however, the person continues to focus on it. This can be a symptom of some mental disorders.

Diagnosis—The label that is used to describe a particular medical condition that is identified after a patient's symptoms are carefully and thoroughly evaluated from a bio-psycho-social perspective.

Diagnostic and Statistical Manual of Mental Disorders (DSM-V)—The official classification system that is used to describe the symptoms of various types of mental disorders, which is used by clinicians to diagnose patients.

Discrimination—The act of treating an individual or group of people differently from how you would treat others in a way that places them at a disadvantage.

Electroconvulsive therapy (ECT)—The administering of an electric current or shock to one or more sides of the brain, as a treatment for severe depressive disorders. Currently, shocks are applied usually only on one side of the brain, with the aid of sedatives and muscle relaxants to minimize pain and discomfort.

Epigenetics—The study of changes that can occur in the genes due to environmental factors, without affecting the DNA sequence.

Hallucination—An experience that engages one or more of a person's five senses, such as seeing an image or hearing voices, that is usually not caused by stimuli in the person's environment. Some chemicals of addiction such as cocaine can also produce these sensory experiences. This can be a symptom of some mental disorders.

Health Homes (HH)—A model of patient care that focuses on patients who have chronic, complex, medical, and behavioral care needs, and uses an individual called a care manager, to help the patient coordinate all of his health care and prevent any gaps in services.

Indoor relief—Charity that was provided to poor persons who were thought to be unworthy, or undeserving; thus, they were required to enter an institution such as a poorhouse or orphanage if they wanted assistance.

Intensive case managers (ICM)—Trained social service workers who maintain frequent contact with persons diagnosed with chronic mental disorders to coordinate their care and monitor their compliance.

Involuntary commitment—The judicial process that is in place to mandate a person into a facility for mental health assessment and/or treatment, without their consent.

Lobotomy—A medical procedure that involved the severing of one or more nerves in the frontal lobe of the brain, which was regarded as a treatment for some types of mental illness.

Mandatory sentencing—The judicial process found in some states that does not allow judges the discretion to determine what a defendant's sentence should be. Instead, there is already a predetermined sentence that must be implemented. For example, the three-strikes guideline in the State of California, which mandated life imprisonment if a person was arrested for a third offence.

Mental competency—A person's ability to demonstrate that he or she is able to use adequate thinking and judgment, and that can be evaluated if required. Mental competency testing may be done for persons who are facing criminal charges to ensure they have the capacity to understand and face the charges.

Mental disorder—One of several different medical conditions such as schizophrenia or depression that are characterized by a cluster of symptoms that can lead to impaired functioning in one or more areas of an individual's daily life.

Mental health—A person's sense of whether or not he is experiencing well-being at any given point in time.

Mental illness—A medical condition that can involve changes in how a person thinks, feels, or acts, and can lead to impaired functioning in one or more areas of daily life.

Neurodevelopmental disorders—Disorders or medical conditions that can affect a child's brain and central nervous system and affect how he or she develops in terms of the ability to think (cognitions), process feelings (emotions), and act (behavioral functioning). According to the DSM-V, they can be categorized based on the primary domain in which symptoms fall—intellectual, communication, autism spectrum, attention deficit, specific learning, and motor disorder.

Neuroscience—The field of study that focuses on the brain and nervous system.

Outdoor relief—Charity that was provided to poor persons in their own home, as they were assessed as being worthy or deserving to receive cash or in-kind assistance such as food and clothing.

Physical restraint—The use of objects such as chains, ropes, manacles, handcuffs, or the strait jacket to prevent a person's ability to move freely.

Poorhouse—A facility that housed the poor where they were supported by charity.

Postpartum depression (or perinatal disorder)—A mental health condition that can occur within 2–3 months after a woman has given birth and can include symptoms such as sadness, crying, and feeling hopeless.

Prosocial—The capacity to act in a manner that demonstrates positive social attributes or attitudes.

Psychotherapy—The use of various methods of talk therapy to treat mental health disorders.

Psychotropic medication—Medications that are used to treat various symptoms of mental illness and that can cause changes in how the patient thinks, feels, and behaves. Also called psychiatric medications.

Self-exclusion agreements—A contract that is voluntarily agreed to by a person with a gambling disorder, in which he agrees that he would not be allowed to benefit from or receive any gambling winnings. The person can make this contract more restrictive, for example, by agreeing that he should not be permitted to enter the casino. He can also officially make this a legal document.

Serious and persistent mental illness (SPMI)—A chronic mental health condition in which the person experiences serious or severe discomfort, which contributes to significant impairments in how the person functions over time. For example, conditions such as schizophrenia and bipolar disorder usually are chronic (persist over time); once symptoms are present, they cause serious discomfort, and this can affect the person's usual functioning over the life span.

Stereotype—Viewing or labeling a group of people using a narrow, one-dimensional perspective.

Stigma—The shame and guilt that is experienced by a person because of how others view him or her.

Symptoms—The signs that suggest that an underlying medical condition might exist.

Tardive dyskinesia—One of the side effects that can occur from the long-term use of prescribed psychotropic medications such as Haldol, which involves restlessness, involuntary twitching, or rolling of the tongue.

Trauma—Exposure to a very disturbing incident or event that is outside of our usual experience that triggers long-term responses such as ongoing anxiety and fear.

Traumatic brain injury (TBI)—An injury to the brain that results in impairments to the person's functioning, which can range from mild to severe, and contribute to long-term problems of daily living.

Trepanning—A medical procedure in which piece/s of bone was removed from the skull, as a means of treating mental illness.

Voluntary commitment—The process that is in place to admit a person into a facility for mental health assessment and/or treatment, with his or her consent.

Workhouse—A jail or facility used to house the poor in which they were mandated to work.

TIMELINE

Mental illness has been among us from the dawn of civilization. As the prevalence and incidence increased, and persons developed more severe symptoms, the society-at-large had little choice but to respond in a meaningful way. But the development of adequate formal systems has not occurred easily, and barriers presented by discrimination continue to be encountered even today. While not exhaustive, this timeline attempts to capture some of the ways in which persons with mental illness have faced discrimination over time, as well as some of the interventions being used to address this.

Around 400 BCE   The Greek physician Hippocrates introduces a scientific focus that mental illness could be caused by imbalances in the body. This is later expanded by Galen (129–200 BCE) and sets the stage for mental illness to be viewed as both biological and emotional in nature.

Prior to the 1350s   Ancient and medieval cultures, such as the Egyptians, Greeks, and Romans, view mental illness as being cursed or punished by the gods, or inhabited by evil spirits. This superstitious thinking contributes to a higher likelihood that persons with mental illness were ridiculed, isolated, and treated in a discriminatory manner. In cultures that saw mental illness more as an unusual gift (Muslim Arabs), there was likely to be less discrimination.

1400s–1600s   The Renaissance helps to stimulate secular thinking about the causes of mental illness. The Reformation dislocates many primary, religious-based social safety nets for treating persons with mental illness, especially within British society.

The Catholic Inquisition focuses on heretics and deviants, and persons with mental illness become easy targets for discrimination. Many are identified as practicing witch-craft and suffer the death penalty.

1601   The British Poor Law is passed. It lays the foundation for how the deserving and undeserving poor would be treated for centuries in the United Kingdom and United States. This contributes to discriminatory treatment in housing indigent persons with mental illness in the workhouses or jails, poorhouses, and almshouses, and in how they should be treated. This also relates to the United States, as with the settlement of the Virginia Colony in 1607, British Common Law is transported to the Americas.

1700s   The Age of Enlightenment (1700/1800s) emphasizes the scientific causes of mental illness. Advocates such as the French physician Phillippe Pinel and the founder of the York Retreat, William Tuke, encourage and put into practice moral restraint-free treatment for persons with mental illness. The York Retreat comes to be regarded as a model facility for humane care of persons with mental illness.

The Madhouse Act of 1774 is passed to address abuses in the private and informal system of housing (the mad-houses) that care for persons with mental illness.

Early 1800s   British legislation authorizes the collection of taxes to con-struct new asylums, but this is resisted at the local level. Additional legislation mandates this process and estab-lishes an oversight system. Advocates such as Dorothea Dix bring the plight of persons with mental illness to the fore in the United States. Ms. Dix travels to prisons, alms-houses, and the like documenting the conditions she ob-serves and presenting this to the legislatures.

Late 1800s   Ms. Dix's campaign contributes to the passage of the Bill for the Benefit of the Indigent Insane by the U.S. Congress in 1854. President Franklin Pierce vetoes any appropria-tion of lands and funds for the construction of facilities for persons with mental illness.

Private and religious benefactors, and state and local au-thorities help to fund the construction of hospitals and asylums. By the late 1800s, asylums are widely available across the United Kingdom, United States, and Europe. But mental illness remains a source of ridicule and stigma, with overcrowding and poor treatment, especially in the large asylums.

In 1867, a Bill for the Protection of Personal Liberty is passed in Illinois. It indicates that all persons accused of insanity, including wives, have a right to a fair public hearing.

In 1875, a Bill to Approve the Postal Rights of Inmates of Insane Asylums is passed in Illinois. This makes it illegal to intercept or prevent persons with mental illness from writing to individuals of their choice. Elizabeth Parsons Ware Packard was a major advocate. Despite the 1867 Bill, she was involuntarily committed to the Jacksonville Insane Asylum by her spouse and denied the right to a hearing for three years. This underscored the additional discrimination that women faced, and many were at the risk of involuntary commitment.

The asylums are primarily custodial. Relatively few persons stabilize and are discharged.

Overt discrimination of persons with mental illness is sanctioned. The language of the U.S. Immigration Act of 1882 officially stipulates the exclusion of lunatics and idiots.

Early 1900s

Renewed efforts on how to treat persons with mental illness results in psychological, physical, and medical interventions. Sigmund Freud pioneers the field of psychoanalytic therapy, but this is not a good fit for many persons with serious mental illness.

The U.S. Supreme Court supports the discriminatory eugenics movement by upholding *Buck v. Bell* (1927), setting the stage for forcible sterilization of "defectives." Intrusive lobotomies and electroshock therapy (ECT) become standard physical interventions for persons with mental illness. Camphor and insulin are used to medically induce seizures and comas, to treat schizophrenia and depression.

The Hiawatha Insane Asylum is closed in 1935, after more than 30 years of incarcerating indigenous persons for defying the status quo.

1950s

The pharmaceutical companies introduce new antipsychotic medications—Thorazine, Haldol, and Prolixin—and market these to state governments as a cost-saving mechanism. Lithium is also found to be effective for bipolar disorder. State hospitals and universities collaborate to implement widespread medication trials, including testing high dosages on unsuspecting patients.

By 1955, nearly 600,000 are institutionalized including those in general hospital wards, poorhouses, orphanages, and reform schools. An advocacy movement grows to address abuse and protect the rights of persons with mental illness. The state hospitals start discharging more persons back into their communities who appear to be stable.

1960s   The Mental Retardation Facilities and Community Mental Health Centers (CMHC) Construction Act, or the Community Mental Health Act, is passed in 1963. It authorizes funds for construction and staffing of mental health centers within communities to provide ready rehabilitative services for persons who needed them. This was an attempt to decrease marginalization of those with mental illness and increase access to adequate care. Many historians regard it as the catalyst for or the beginning of the deinstitutionalization movement.

The Civil Rights Act (1964) is passed and bans discriminatory practices such as segregation in schools, the workplace, and public places. While it targets African Americans and women, it also addresses abuses toward persons with mental illness including protecting persons over age 40 against employment discrimination. This became the framework for the later Americans with Disabilities Act (1990).

1970s   In *Wyatt v. Stickney* (1971) in the state of Alabama, the court establishes a minimum level of care for persons who are involuntarily committed (the Wyatt Standards). It also determines that the person must be placed in the least restrictive environment. The decision is upheld by the Court of Appeals in 1974 and becomes the national standard. It places pressure on jurisdictions all over the country to address marginalization of persons with mental illness and helps to speed up deinstitutionalization.

In January 1972, Geraldo Riviera conducts the Willowbrook expose describing the pervasive abuses inside the Willowbrook State School in Staten Island, New York. A court case is settled with the Willowbrook Consent Decree in 1975. This mandates closure of the facility and relocation of clients, and helps to establish a system of community-based group homes, with active day treatment and other supports.

The Rehabilitation Act of 1973 is passed, with part of its intent to address discrimination based on disability including mental illness. It authorizes and expands services to persons with disabilities across states and also prohibits discrimination from any federally financed entity.

In 1974, *Tarasoff v. Regents of the University of California* establishes the duty to warn for mental health professionals. The Health Insurance Portability and Accountability Act (HIPAA) of 1996 also incorporates the reporting of serious and imminent threats by mental health professionals.

In *O'Connor v. Donaldson* (1975) in the state of Florida, the court rules that the client's right to liberty was violated as he was involuntarily confined for 15 years. Client had no treatment, was not a danger to himself or others, and was prevented from using his supports in the community to help him remain stable.

1980s

The Civil Rights of Institutionalized Peoples Act (CRIPA) of 1980 is passed to protect any person in the care of a state institution—a jail, prison, nursing home, mental health facility, or institution for persons with intellectual challenges. If abuses are identified, the Office of the Attorney General is authorized to intervene on behalf of the institutionalized population to protect their rights.

The National Mental Health Systems Act of 1980 is signed into law by President Carter to re-prioritize funding and community initiatives for persons with serious and persistent mental illness. It is repealed by President Reagan less than a year later. Lack of funding results in the closure of community mental health centers and creates more of a vacuum for persons with mental illness who are already deinstitutionalized.

In November 1981, Congressional Deinstitutionalization Hearings address widespread problems across states. It concludes that the process had not worked as intended. Rates of homelessness had increased, especially in large states such as New York and California. Admissions to public general hospitals, nursing homes, and prisons had also increased.

In *Rivers v. Katz* (1986), the New York State Court of Appeals rules that even if a person was mentally ill or institutionalized, he or she still has a right to participate in treatment decisions. The person has a right to a due process hearing if he or she does not wish to be medicated against his or her will.

1990s

Grass roots and mainstream support grows for improved protections for persons with disabilities. The disability movement adopts some of the disruptive practices of the Civil Rights Movement including demonstrating and occupying buildings. The Capitol Crawl takes place on March 13, 1990, when hundreds of multiple-abled persons climbed the steps of the Capitol building to protest delays in Congress's passing the Americans with Disabilities Act (ADA).

Congress enacts the Americans with Disabilities Act (1990) to address ongoing serious and pervasive isolation and segregation of individuals with disabilities, including mental illness. The act prohibits discrimination by public entities, similarly to the Rehabilitation Act of 1973, Section 504.

The Mental Health Parity Act of 1996 attempts to decrease discrimination with regard to insurance coverage. It requires that annual dollar limits for mental health benefits should be on par with the total lifetime benefits.

In 1996, the U.S. Department of Justice, based on CRIPA, begins to conduct civil investigations within the California prison system regarding complaints about abuse targeting persons with mental illness.

In June 1999, the Supreme Court upholds the Olmstead Decision (*Olmstead, Commissioner, Georgia Department of Human Resources, et al. v. L.C.*). In the original case, two women (L.C. and E.W.), diagnosed with intellectual challenges, schizophrenia and a personality disorder respectively, challenge the refusal of the state of Georgia to transition them from institutional care to a community-based, less restrictive setting. The Court rules that institutional segregation, which was not indicated, constituted discrimination as it violated the ADA. The request for assistance with a community placement was thus reasonable.

2000/2009   In *Sell v. US* (2003), the Supreme Court rules that both the Fifth and Fourteenth Amendment clauses of due process protect the liberty of individuals to refuse psychotropic medications. The state cannot medicate a person against his or her will, even if the state wants to stabilize the person to stand trial.

2006   The incarceration of persons with mental illness has been increasing since deinstitutionalization. This is affected by an increased incidence of substance use disorders and co-morbidity. The Bureau of Justice finds extensive evidence of mental illness within the U.S. prison system. Rates range from 45% within the federal prisons, to 56% within the state prisons, and 64% within the local jails. About 75% of state prisoners and local jail inmates also have substance use disorders. Approximately 35% of these also report using drugs at the time they committed their offense. Women in prison are also noted to have higher rates of mental illness than men.

2007 The Veterans Administration (VA) implements comprehensive suicide prevention as a response to high rates of suicide in the veteran population. Since 2000, the VA noted that the rate of suicide ranged from 18 to 22 veterans daily or roughly 1 every 65 minutes. Males are three times as likely to commit suicide than females. Female veterans were twice as likely to commit suicide as compared with women in the civilian population. The Joshua Omvig Suicide Prevention Act was signed into law to target veterans in crisis and those at high risk for suicide. The Veterans Suicide Prevention Hotline Act mandated a 24-hour hotline.

2008 The Mental Health Parity and Addiction Equity Act (MHPAEA) expands the 1996 act. It requires benefits for mental health and substance use disorder treatment to be no more restrictive than that for medical/surgical benefits. But it does not mandate that an insurer must offer mental health and substance use disorder treatment benefits. The act thus retains a coverage gap that can negatively affect persons needing behavioral health care.

In 2008, the Americans with Disabilities Act Amendments Act (ADAAA) broadens the definition of a disability and clarifies the intent of the act. This serves to address prior narrow court interpretations that had reinforced discrimination against persons with disabilities including mental illness.

2009 The White House launches the "Year of Community Living." This focuses on redoubling efforts to ensure adequate community-based housing and supports for persons with disabilities, including mental illness. The intent of this is to enforce the Olmstead Decision that persons should receive services in the most integrated settings, thus supporting the reduction/elimination of discrimination where persons with mental illness can live, work, and socialize.

2010–2015 The Patient Protection and Affordable Care Act (PPACA) was signed into law on March 23, 2010. This prohibits insurance companies from withholding coverage due to pre-existing conditions or arbitrarily capping needed care. It introduces an individual mandate with subsidies based on income thresholds and tax penalties for nonparticipation. The PPACA is beneficial for many persons with mental illness and other behavioral health disorders, as it assures coverage for those who go in and out of periods of employment, and lose coverage at the same time that they are in dire need of services. It thus helps to decrease discrimination in health coverage for persons with behavioral health disorders, who are often high users of services.

The Mental Health Parity and Addiction Equity Act (MH-PAEA) officially goes into effect in July 2010. This is also part of the PPACA.

2013
On May 27, 2013, the World Health Organization adopts the Comprehensive Mental Health Action Plan for 2013–2020. This addresses leadership, responsiveness, prevention, evidence-based interventions, and data management. Universal indicators and outcome targets are also identified. This integrated public health approach is a tangible step to create an infrastructure that would better serve the needs of persons with mental illness, and decrease stigma and marginalization globally.

2014
Ongoing enforcement of the Olmstead Decision results in an investigation and the first settlement with a state, Rhode Island. The state agreed to address segregation in sheltered workshops and day programs, which are seen as discriminatory under the ADA.

2015
As of May 2015, the New York City Independent Budget Office finds that inmates with mental disorders spend on average 77 days more in jail than persons without mental illness.

June–July 2015
The enforcement of the Olmstead Act continues to address discrimination with regard to community integration. The U.S. DOJ—Civil Rights Division initiated investigations of Georgia and West Virginia and determines that there are discriminatory violations. The DOJ also filed Statements of Interests in existing cases across several states including Indiana, Alabama, and Pennsylvania with the intent to monitor for potential violations.

As of August 5, 2015, the DOJ enacts court-enforceable compliance agreements with the Los Angeles Correctional System. This is a result of extensive evidence of deficient mental health care within the California Prison System, including inadequate suicide watch, housing conditions that exacerbate the risk of suicide, and excessive force against prisoners with mental illness. The DOJ is also investigating more than 30 other jurisdictions including Westchester County Jail in New York and Jackson Detention Center in Mississippi. Thus, progress is being made in some settings to decrease/eliminate discrimination against persons with mental illness within the penal system.

August 2015

A jury in the Aurora, Colorado, shooting incident rejects the defendant's plea of insanity. But it cannot unanimously decide on the death penalty. Testimony on the defendant's diagnosed schizophrenia contributes to his sentence of life without the chance of parole. Heated public debates ensue regarding appropriate punishment of persons with mental illness who commit crimes.

November 2015

Ongoing public incidents, allegations from students with mental health issues about being discriminated against on college and university campuses, and advocacy contribute to political responses. On August 4, 2015, the Mental Health Reform Act of 2015 is introduced in the U.S. Senate. It aims to increase the availability of, access to, and support for mental health services for individuals and families. On November 4, 2015, an amended bill—Helping Families in Mental Health Crisis Act of 2015, is forwarded to the U.S. House of Representatives and the Senate for consideration. If signed into law, this bill has the potential to implement significant changes across the mental health system in the United States.

Index

Activities of daily living, 4–5, 80, 130–31. *See also* Living skills, daily; Tasks, daily

ADA Amendments Act of 2008 (ADAAA), 84–85, 213. *See also* Disability

Addiction, defined, 86, 117; alcohol, drug/s, 201; chemicals of, 113, 116, 204; cocaine, 111, 115; field, 86; and mental illness, 58, 114, 204; nicotine, 112, 116; opioid/s or opiate(s), 86, 116; specialists, 87; statistics, 14, 200; and Supreme Court, 86; treatment protection, 96; and veterans, 117. *See also* Alcohol; Cocaine; Consolidation of 822 or Outpatient Chemical Dependency Programs; Diagnoses; Drug use disorders; Gambling disorders; System of care

Adolescents and children: with autism, 98; benefits and rights, 84, 92; child abuse and neglect reporting, 95 (*see also* Disclosures); child and dependent care supports, 73, 140 (*see also* Veterans); custodial care, 98; custody hearings, 96 (*see also* Disclosures); disorder types, 123; early advocacy group, 83; housing, orphanages and workhouses, 37, 161; indentured and enslaved, 32, 51, 97 (*see also* Indentured servants and slaves); in media, 101; prevention, 165; reform schools, 79, 97; schooling barriers, 97; service gaps, 128; special needs, 99; statistics on, 14–15, 124–25, 128; sterilization of, 68 (*see also Buck v. Bell*); toxins effects, 125–27, 163; vulnerability to mental illness, 14. *See also* Early intervention services; Women and mental health

Adult Homes, 130–31. *See also* Shelters

Advocacy activities, 54–55, 83, 156, 162. *See also* Advocates of mental health reform; Dix, Dorothea; Dwight, Louis

Advocacy organizations for mental health, 14, 77, 83, 104, 156. *See also* World Wars I and II

Advocates of mental health reform: Bancroft, Jesse, 64, 70, 94 (*see also* Design of hospitals; New

ABOUT THE AUTHOR

Monica A. Joseph, PhD, is an adjunct lecturer at Columbia School of Social Work, New York, and an assistant professor in the Behavioral Sciences and Human Services Department at Kingsborough Community College of the City University of New York, Brooklyn, New York. Dr. Joseph has a wealth of policy, managerial, and clinical experience providing services to persons with mental illness and other disabilities, within residential and outpatient treatment settings. As a qualified surveyor for the Commission on the Accreditation of Rehabilitation Facilities, Dr. Joseph conducts international accreditation surveys that focus on ensuring quality behavioral health care including for persons with co-occurring disorders.